THE OPPORTUNIST

*The political life of Oswald Pirow, 1915–1959*

*By the same author*

*Voices in the desert – Margaret and William Ballanger: A biography* (Benedic Books, 1997)

*Voorloper – Die lewe van Schalk Pienaar* (Tafelberg, 2001)

*Prophet without honour – F.S. Malan: Afrikaner, South African and Cape liberal* (Protea Book House, 2011)

*Iron in the soul: The leaders of the official parliamentary opposition in South Africa, 1910–1993* (Protea Book House, 2017)

# THE OPPORTUNIST

*The political life of Oswald Pirow, 1915–1959*

F.A. MOUTON

PROTEA BOOK HOUSE
PRETORIA
2020

*The opportunist: The political life of Oswald Pirow, 1915–1959*
F.A. Mouton

First edition, first impression in 2020 by Protea Book House
PO Box 35110, Menlo Park, 0102
1067 Burnett Street, Hatfield, Pretoria
8 Minni Street, Clydesdale, Pretoria
info@proteaboekhuis.co.za
www.proteaboekhuis.com

Editor: Danél Hanekom
Proofreader: Carmen Hansen-Kruger
Cover design: Hanli Deysel
Cover image: At van Wyk
Typography: 10.5 pt on 12.75 Times New Roman by Ada Radford
Printed by **novus** *print*, a division of Novus Holdings

ISBN: 978-1-4853-1169-0 (printed book)

# Contents

# Preface

Oswald Pirow believed in nothing, nothing but his own ambition. His burning ambition to become prime minister was the underlying motive for every political action by him and he had a ruthless ability to adjust his sails to prevailing political winds. He hitched his ambitions to the political momentum of influential persons such as Tielman Roos and J.B.M. Hertzog in the National Party with his considerable charm, sycophantic flattery and unquestioning loyalty. As a Roos acolyte in the 1920s, he was an uncompromising republican, while as a Hertzog loyalist in the 1930s, he was a trustworthy ally of Britain. He rejected republicanism and national socialism and was a friend and defender of the Jewish community. After September 1939, with the collapse of the Hertzog government and with Nazi Germany seemingly winning World War II, he overnight became a radical republican, a national socialist and an anti-Semite.

Pirow's career was one of calculated opportunism. For him political parties and people such as Roos and Hertzog were mere vehicles for his desire to secure power, but he was willing to take risks to satisfy his political ambitions. This was evident in September 1940. With his parliamentary career at a dead end, he gambled on a military victory by Nazi Germany with the founding of the national socialist New Order for South Africa movement. It was a gamble that went for broke on a German victory. The defeat of Germany in 1945, combined with the loathing of D.F. Malan, J.G. Strijdom and H.F. Verwoerd – the leadership of the NP – for his opportunism, meant the end of his political career. His attempts to make a political comeback were to no avail and he remained trapped in the political wilderness. In 1958, the National Party brought him in from the cold by appointing him as the lead prosecutor in what became known as the Treason Trial. Desperate to secure the conviction of a large group of anti-apartheid leaders on the charge of treason, the apartheid state turned to Pirow, who in his heyday was an outstanding trial court advocate. Pirow in turn was desperate to break out of his isolation and, starved for respect and recognition, accepted the appointment although he was in poor health. He died in 1959 while the trial was in progress.

I became acquainted with Pirow in the mid-1980s while researching my master's degree in history on the Durban beerhall riots of June 1929. As the newly appointed Minister of Justice, he was determined to exploit the unrest to advance his career. In November 1929, he ordered a massive police raid on the city to crush the black boycott of municipal-controlled beerhalls. The police, personally observed by Pirow, used excessive force on non-resisting black workers. With ruthless state oppression, the boycott movement eventually petered out, while Pirow had established a reputation as a defender of white supremacy. His cynical abuse of power combined with his founding of the New Order made him in my eyes a figure beyond the pale. On the completion of my master's degree and a published article on Pirow's role in the police raid on Durban, I lost all interest in him and viewed him as an unattractive figure who deserved his historical oblivion.

Tilman Dedering, a colleague and friend at the University of South Africa (Unisa) rekindled my interest in him. As part of Tilman's research on airpower in South Africa in the 1930s, he needed biographical information on Pirow, who as the Minister of Defence as well as the Minister of Railways and Harbours, played a pioneering role in the development of civilian and military aeronautical strategies. This biography originated out of my attempts to assist him as I increasingly found Pirow an intriguing personality. He was ambitious, highly intelligent, cynical, charismatic, competent, energetic, a brilliant orator and an outstanding government minister. He was the founder of South African Airways, reviver and moderniser of the bankrupt railway system, and as the Minister of Defence, the rebuilder of the neglected Union Defence Force. In October 1938, the London *Sunday Times* expressed its admiration in the following terms: "Pirow is a remarkable man … as an administrator, he probably has no superior in the British Empire."[1] By August 1939, he was seen as the most brilliant star in the South African political constellation and the odds-on favourite to succeed Hertzog as prime minister.

The political life of Pirow is the story of a gifted person who through opportunism wrecked a promising career. His political career is much more than that of a politician without any principles. His public life, spanning from 1915 to 1959, was a period of great political ferment. It covers the rise of Afrikaner nationalism, the desire to create a South African identity by reconciling Afrikaners and English speakers, the impact of World War II on South Africa, the founding of the apartheid state, and black resistance to white minority domination. The political career of Pirow is very much part of the history of South Africa in the first half of the twentieth century.

The combination of a lack of personal papers and Pirow's determined effort to hoodwink historians, made it a considerable challenge to produce this biography. His private papers in the Archive for Contemporary Affairs at the University of the Free State in Bloemfontein, consists of only a handful of letters and a larger number of mainly undated newspaper clippings. The reason for the absence of personal letters is simple – Pirow was determined to leave no paper trail. In 1936, M.E. Antrobus, acting British High Commissioner in South Africa, noticed that Pirow was so secretive that he avoided putting his thoughts in writing and went out of his way not to write letters.[2] In addition, his recollections (published in the New Order's newssheet, *Die Nuwe Orde,* between 1945 and 1946; revised and recycled in his biography of Hertzog, *James Barry Munnik Hertzog,* in 1957) was written to boost his image and reputation. To do so he distorted historical events from what it was to what it should have been. This meant that they had to be used with circumspection.

1 G.H. Calpin, *There are no South Africans* (London, 1941), pp. 260, 264.

2 National Archives (hereafter NA), Kew, DO 35/186B/11, M.E. Antrobus – Sir Harry Batterbee, 22 May 1936.

Fortunately, I could make extensive use of the papers of his contemporaries such as D.F. Malan, J.G. Strijdom, C.R. Swart, A.L. Geyer, H.F. Verwoerd, J.B.M. Hertzog, J.H. Hofmeyer, C.F. Stallard and Jan Smuts, and the archive of the United Party, as well as the documents of the Ossewabrandwag. The archive of the Nederlandsch Zuid-Afrikaansche Vereeniging in Amsterdam provided important information on Pirow's student years in Europe. I have also consulted the records of the British Foreign and Dominion Office, as well as a file compiled by British intelligence on Pirow in the National Archives, Kew, London. Without file KV 2/908 it would have been impossible to reconstruct Pirow's relationship with Sir Oswald Mosley, a leading British fascist. Since the British authorities viewed Mosley as a threat to state security, his mail was intercepted. Pirow and Mosley's correspondence was copied and placed in the file British intelligence had kept on Pirow as a fascist sympathiser since the early 1940s. Historians have reason to be grateful for the vigilance of the British authorities as Mosley and Pirow failed to retain their correspondence. I have also made extensive use of contemporary newspaper reports that covered political meetings and parliamentary debates between the 1910s and 1940s in blow-by-blow detail. Hansard, the published debates of the House of Assembly, was another invaluable source. Despite its image as a dry-as-dust recording of speeches, it does convey the drama and cut-and-thrust of parliamentary clashes, as well as the changing nature of Pirow's politics.

In the course of my research and writing on Pirow I owe much to Luna Bergh, Surya Chetty, Frik Nöthling, John Lambert, Milton Shain and especially Lindie Koorts, Ian van der Waag, Evert Kleynhans and Victor Correira, Johan van Niekerk, Heinrich Schulze and Tilman Dedering who provided archival documents and information, as well as encouragement and advice. I am grateful to the staff of the many archives and libraries I visited for the assistance they have offered. I am particularly indebted to G.W. Prinsloo, archivist at the Department of Defence Documentation Centre, Anette Kellner and Evert Kleynhans of the North-West University Archive, Celeste Reynolds of the Special Collections at the University of Stellenbosch, Ernéne Verster of the Archive for Contemporary Affairs, Erika le Roux of the Western Cape Provincial Archives, Cape Town,

Henry Liebenberg of the microfilm section of the Unisa library, Ami Ryke of the United Party archives at Unisa, as well as Megan Dunmall, Lesley Whitelaw and Barnaby Bryan, archivists at the Honourable Society of the Middle Temple. A special word of thanks to Danél Hanekom, my highly regarded editor and friend, for saving me from too many long sentences and the odd historical error. This research was sponsored by Unisa and the National Research Foundation and is gratefully acknowledged. Finally, I would like to express my gratitude to my parents Hendrik and Annie, my mother-in-law Vinkie Williams, my wife Aline and our children, Albert, John and Tegan for their love and support. This book is dedicated to them.

F.A. Mouton
Pretoria

# 1
# The outsider, 1890–1924

Oswald Pirow was born on 14 August 1890 in Aberdeen in the Cape Colony, part of the vast British Empire. His mother, Henny Jasmine Marine Tomby, and his father, Carl Bernhard Ferdinand, a medical doctor, were German born and had immigrated to South Africa in 1888. He had two siblings: Hans, who would become the state's mining engineer, and Sylvia who married the well-known architect Gerard Moerdyk, designer of the Voortrekker Monument. She would become a leading Afrikaner cultural leader and newspaper columnist. When Pirow was three years old, his parents settled in Potchefstroom in the Transvaal where they became naturalised citizens of the South African Republic.

Very little is known about his parents and his early years. According to C.P. Bresler, who grew up in Potchefstroom, Dr. Pirow was a "kindly quiet person" and Mrs Pirow was "a small dynamic person who was fired with a consuming ambition for the future of her children".[3] It was in Potchefstroom during the South African War of 1899–1902 that Pirow witnessed the British conquest of the Transvaal, and its scorched-earth tactics.[4] In *Mlungu Mungoma*, his novel in the 1950s, he placed his father with the Boer commandos besieging Mafeking in 1899,[5] but it is uncertain whether this was

3 C.P. Bresler, *Tilt the sack* (Pretoria, 1965), pp. 152–153.

4 O. Pirow, *James Barry Munnik Hertzog* (London, 1957), p. 231.

5 O. Pirow, *Mlungo Mungoma (Die blanke waarsêer)* (Johannesburg, 1949), p. 55.

really the case. In his recollections, Pirow would claim that the war left him with a strong anti-British streak and a strong identification with Afrikaner nationalism.[6]

In 1905, because of the lack of educational facilities in Potchefstroom, Pirow's father sent him and Hans to study at Itzehoe Gymnasium in Holstein, Germany. While at the Gymnasium, he attempted to join the German Imperial navy, but his application was rejected as his father had renounced his German citizenship.[7] It is uncertain whether his desire to join Germany's navy was an attempt to show his schoolmates that he was a fully fledged German or a case of being swept along by the excitement of Germany's attempt to challenge British naval supremacy. Whatever the reason, his years in Germany did not dampen his identification with the Afrikaner cause and his desire to return to South Africa. On the completion of his secondary schooling, he was determined to study law at the University of Leiden in the Netherlands, but the Dutch refused to acknowledge his German qualifications. Despite the intervention of the Nederlandsch Zuid-Afrikaansche Vereeniging (NZAV) in Amsterdam on the prompting of Pirow's father and the deputy Dutch consul in Potchefstroom, the Dutch educational authorities refused to budge. On 15 October 1910 an unhappy Pirow registered at Middle Temple in London to study law. From his correspondence with Dr N. Mansveldt of the NZAV, he complained that the Dutch played into the hands of the British who wanted to control all aspects of life in South Africa. It was obvious that he feared that his studies in London would weaken his aspiration to be seen as an Afrikaner. He admitted to Mansveldt that after his years in Germany he found it difficult to write in Afrikaans.[8]

Pirow, despite his initial resentment, flourished at Middle Temple. One of his fellow students was the Cape Afrikaner H.A. Fagan who would become a leading advocate, playwright and politician. He served with Pirow in the Hertzog government between 1933 and 1939, and left parliament in 1943 to become a judge, and eventu-

6 *Die Nuwe Orde*, 3 January 1946.

7 *Rand Daily Mail*, 3 July 1934.

8 Zuid-Afrikahuis, Stichting Zuid-Afrikahuis Nederland, Amsterdam, NZAV 1, File 1494, Pirow – Mansveldt, 26 November and 20 December 1910.

ally the Chief Justice. Fagan fondly remembered Pirow as a good friend with whom he shared holidays, and that he was a brilliant and dedicated student. They also shared the view that Afrikaans, and not Dutch, had to be the officially recognised language of the Afrikaner. In 1912 they played a leading role in establishing the Afrikaanse Taal Vereniging (Afrikaans Language Society) in London. One of the society's members was Louis Leipoldt who would become a leading Afrikaner poet.[9]

While in London, Pirow distinguished himself as a sportsman. He was an outstanding swimmer and javelin thrower. He won the 50-feet event in a swimming competition in London and was the British javelin champion in 1913 (his friend Hans van Rensburg claimed that he held the British record for this event)[10] and represented England in an athletics meeting.[11] But it was as a law student that he distinguished himself. In his final examination he was placed first and awarded a certificate of honour. On 4 June 1913, he was called as a barrister to the Bar.[12] Pirow would claim that his sojourn in London did not eradicate his anti-British sentiment, but that it gave him a better understanding of the complexity of British attitudes and behaviour.[13]

In 1914 Pirow returned to South Africa after a lengthy tour of Europe. In his absence, the country had transformed dramatically. He had left the Transvaal in 1905 as a British crown colony and returned to a self-governing and unified South Africa governed by Afrikaners. In 1910 the four colonies of the Cape, Natal, Free State and Transvaal had merged to form the Union of South Africa with General Louis Botha, hero of the South African War, as the prime minister. With his South African Party (SAP) he set out to reconcile Afrikaners and English speakers as an integral part of the British Empire.

Many Afrikaners could not come to terms with the suffering of the South African War and felt marginalised in the new state. Sub-

---

9 Q. Fagan, *Henry Allan Fagan 1889–1963* (Cape Town, 1975), pp. 34–36.

10 H. van Rensburg, *Their paths crossed mine: Memoirs of the Commandant-General of the Ossewa-Brandwag* (Johannesburg, 1956), p. 50.

11 *Rand Daily Mail*, 3 July 1930.

12 Details of Pirow's enrolment provided by Megan Dunmall, assistant archivist, Honourable Society of the Middle Temple, 22 August 2016.

13 *Die Nuwe Orde*, 3 January 1946.

sequently a growing number of Afrikaners looked to General J.B.M. Hertzog, a bitterender in the South African War and a fighter for the principle of "South Africa first" in which South Africans had to put the interests of the country before those of the British Empire to champion their cause. His criticism of some English speakers as foreign fortune seekers, which created the impression that no English speaker could ever be recognised as a South African, led to Botha dismissing him from the cabinet. In January 1914, Hertzog formed the National Party (NP) to campaign for Afrikaner interests. The policies of the new party resulted in a more exclusive Afrikaner identity with Afrikaans as a symbol of its nationality.

Very little information is available on Pirow's first year back in South Africa. What is known is that he had settled in Braamfontein, Johannesburg – a predominately English-speaking city – as an article clerk at a law firm. In his later years he claimed that he associated himself with Afrikaner nationalism and the NP. Yet, with the outbreak of World War I in August 1914, and with the call for volunteers to invade the German colony of South West Africa (Namibia), he joined the Active Citizen Force (ACF) of the newly established Union Defence Force (UDF) and made the rank of an officer. As part of the British Empire, South Africa was automatically at war with Germany, but had the right to determine its active participation, if any, in the conflict. Botha had no hesitation in accepting the British request to invade German South West Africa. The NP, representing a growing number of Afrikaners, vehemently opposed this decision, and more than 11 000 Afrikaners resorted to an armed rebellion. Although the government suppressed the uprising with relatively little bloodshed, it deeply divided Afrikaners, thousands of whom deserted the SAP to join the NP. Especially the execution of Jopie Fourie, who had joined the uprising without resigning his commission as an officer of the ACF, alienated many Afrikaners.

Pirow's status as a former officer in the ACF became a potential source of embarrassment for him when he becamc a parliamentarian. Why, if he was an NP supporter, did he join the military? He covered his tracks with an elaborate story. In an interview with *Die Brandwag* magazine, published on 18 December 1953, he claimed that while in Johannesburg in August 1914, he gave a lecture at an Afrikaner Christian society on Louis Leipoldt's nationalist poem

*Oom Gert vertel*. The poem tells the harrowing tale of the public execution of young Cape Afrikaners in a rural town for treason after they had joined an invading republican Boer commando. This led to the other young Afrikaners in the district promptly joining the closest Boer commando. After the lecture, a young Afrikaner approached him with the request that the two of them should join the rebels. Pirow pointed out that as individuals they could achieve nothing, and that his joining the ACF as a commissioned officer in the Potchefstroom Ruiters, was part of a plot to support the uprising. The death on 15 September 1914 of General Koos de la Rey, who on his way to Potchefstroom was accidently shot by the police in pursuit of a violent foster gang, foiled this plan. According to Pirow, the old Boer war hero intended to hoist the old South African Republican flag at the local military base, which was under the command of General J.C.G. Kemp, and to march with these UDF units to Pretoria.[14] Andries Raath in his contribution to *Die Afrikanerrebellie 1914–1915* supports this claim by describing that Captain Oswald Pirow, and two other captains, Willem Bouwer and Hendrik de la Rey, the general's son, would have raised the republican flag on De la Rey's arrival.[15] In his *Die Brandwag* interview, Pirow furthermore claimed that he and other officers attended the memorial service for De la Rey at Lichtenburg on 20 September and that they wanted to arrest Botha and Smuts, but that General C. Beyers, commander general of the ACF, on hearing of the plan, forbade it.

According to Pirow, his pro-rebel sentiment led to his dismissal from the UDF. Piet Meiring in his biographical sketch of Pirow in *Tien politieke leiers* claims that he was arrested as a rebel, and that it cost him his commission in the UDF.[16] In a parliamentary debate on 12 June 1939 Pirow claimed that he had voluntarily left the UDF as he refused to participate in the suppression of the rebellion.[17] His military record in the Department of Defence Documentation Centre does not substantiate his pro-rebel claims. He was indeed attached

14 Pirow, *James Barry Munnik Hertzog*, p. 70.

15 D.J. Langer and A.W.G. Raath (eds), *Die Afrikanerrebellie 1914–1915* (Pretoria, 2014), p. 90.

16 P. Meiring, *Tien politieke leiers: Manne na aan ons premiers* (Cape Town, 1973), p. 75.

17 Debatte van die Volksraad, 12 June 1939, Col. 6820.

to the Potchefstroom Ruiters (11th Mounted Rifles) as a lieutenant between 24 October and 20 December 1914.[18] He joined the unit a month after the death of De la Rey – and a week before the first rebellion shot was fired in the Transvaal – and left his unit after the rebellion was crushed in the Transvaal. However, 20 December was also the day on which Fourie was executed. Why he left the UDF on that date cannot be determined, but what is certain is that he was not a member of the NP when he volunteered his military services, and by bolstering his Afrikaner nationalist credentials he distorted his role in the UDF by blatant lies.

In his *Die Brandwag* interview, Pirow claimed that his pro-rebel stance made it impossible for him to stay on at the Johannesburg law firm, and in 1915 he transferred to the Pretoria Bar to practise as an advocate. The early years of young, unknown and inexperienced advocates at the Bar can be challenging ones of economic hardship because law firms prefer to use the legal expertise of more experienced advocates. Pirow had the additional challenges of having no support structure from friends or family in Pretoria. A bigger handicap was that while British and German soldiers were facing one another, with a high casualty rate in Europe, English-speaking law firms in Pretoria viewed him as a German.

Pirow's personality – he could be cynical, blunt, brash and forceful, almost to the point of brutality[19] – also alienated some in the legal fraternity. On the other hand, his withdrawn and private personality made him a puzzling figure to many. He could for example be brutally honest about his own flaws. According to C.P. Bresler, a fellow advocate at the Pretoria Bar, nobody really knew him.[20] Leslie Blackwell, who practised at the Johannesburg Bar, described Pirow as "a curious fellow, very difficult to understand".[21] Hjalmar Reitz, a prominent attorney and eventually a member of the Pretoria Bar, who had a fine sense of humour, was irked by his inability to laugh

18 Correspondence with G.W. Prinsloo, archivist at the Department of Defence Documentation Centre, 20 December 2016.

19 L. Egeland, *Bridges of understanding: A personal record in teaching, law, politics and diplomacy* (Cape Town, 1977), p. 103.

20 P. Bresler, *Lineage of conflict. A South African miscellany* (Cape Town, 1952), p. 151.

21 L. Blackwell, *Farewell to parliament. More reminiscences of bench, bar, parliament and travel* (Pietermaritzburg, 1946), p. 74.

at himself. For him Pirow was a most capable man with a keen brain whom one could fear, but that it was not possible to have any affection for him.[22] Pirow struggled to fit into a group, and the Bar was an exclusive male club. Therefore, the odds were stacked against him, but he overcame them with his talent, and by becoming the protégé and close friend of Tielman Roos. He described Roos in his recollections as the best friend he ever had.

Roos was the product of an established and well-known Cape Afrikaner family who settled in Pretoria with the South African War ending in 1902. He became a fervent supporter of Hertzog's "South Africa first" policy, was a founding member of the NP and leader of the party in the province. Roos was a charismatic and popular politician, known as the "Lion of the North". He also established himself as the most outstanding and sought-after advocate at the Pretoria Bar.[23]

Roos and Pirow's friendship seemed odd to many as Roos was amiable, easy-going, witty and kind, generous to those in need. He had the quality of being loveable, while he was seen as lazy and avoided physical activity at all cost. Pirow on the other hand was short-tempered, snide, without any sense of humour, and self-centred. He certainly did not have the quality of being loveable. He was also hard-working, ruthlessly efficient, and an avid sportsman and hunter.[24] Pirow, who could use charm as a weapon to get what he wanted, set out to secure Roos's friendship.

In 1936 M.E. Antrobus, a member of the British High Commissioner's staff in South Africa, explained Pirow's use of charm in the following terms: "he [Pirow] is charming when he is getting something he wants but viperish and entirely outspoken when he isn't."[25] A hallmark of Pirow's charm throughout his career was his ability to flatter the people he needed, and to ingratiate himself. Roos, despite his jovial and successful image, was sensitive to criticism with

22 H. Reitz, *The conversion of a South African nationalist* (Cape Town, 1946), pp. 90, 128–130.

23 J. Brits, *Tielman Roos – political prophet or opportunist?* (Pretoria, 1987), pp. 3, 17–20, 26–32.

24 L. Blackwell, *African Occasions: Reminiscences of thirty years of bar, bench, and politics in South Africa* (London, 1938), p. 156.

25 NA Kew, Avia 2/1879, File 29827/Part IV, M.E. Antrobus – C.G.K. Syers, 25 March 1936.

a strong desire for acknowledgement and praise.[26] Pirow was more than willing to provide praise and support. He would even collect fees from attorneys on Roos's behalf. In exchange, Roos was a valuable friend to him. Roos, according to Bresler, would go to almost any lengths to assist a friend. He in fact valued friendship so highly that he was blind to the self-interest of some of those close to him.[27] Harry Morris, a hard-bitten advocate specialising in criminal cases, shared this opinion:

> His friendship paid dividends. He was a nepotist of the first order. He promoted his friends but did nothing for himself.[28]

Pirow and Roos became so close that they shared advocate chambers while he was Roos's junior counsel in numerous high-profile and lucrative court appearances. According to Bresler, they were an odd, but very efficient, combination in the courts:

> They supplemented each other's qualities perfectly: the one's urbanity and the other's ruthlessness, the one's diplomacy and the other's normal scorn and sometimes baleful lack of it, the one's silky forbearance and the other's acid impatience formed a formidable front of political rapier and sabre with very little defensiveness about it anywhere.[29]

Roos's support, combined with Pirow's own ability, drive and energy, meant that he had a meteoric rise at the Pretoria Bar, appearing in headline-grabbing civil and criminal cases.[30] He quickly developed a reputation that he treated court proceedings as if he was in a boxing ring. (Pirow was an enthusiastic amateur boxer who trained under Herman Striedl, a former German professional boxer who felt that Pirow was good enough to turn professional.)[31] Leslie Blackwell described Pirow's truculence as "calculated indiscretions", as he could

26 J.P. Brits, "Tielman Roos se rol in die Suid-Afrikaanse politiek, 1907–1935" (D.Phil, Unisa, 1977), pp. 170, 478.
27 Bresler, *Lineage of conflict*, p. 149.
28 H.H. Morris, *The first forty years: Memoirs of H.H. Morris K.C.* (Cape Town, 1948), p. 55.
29 Bresler, *Lineage of conflict*, p. 151.
30 "Oswald Pirow", *South African Law Journal*, (47), 1930, pp. 357–359; "The Minister of Justice", *The South African Law Times*, Vol. 1, No. 1, January 1932, p. 5.
31 *Die Burger*, 21 October 1959.

also be wise, diplomatic and conciliatory when it was needed.[32] His strength as an advocate was that he did not see himself as a jurist, an expert on the law, but as a passionate advocate for his client. His approach in court was that a judge was just another human being, and that you first had to win his sympathy, and only then you had to provide him with a legal argument for his judgment in your favour.[33] His court successes meant a significant income and the ability to buy a farm near Graskop in the eastern Transvaal. He loved his farm and surrounding natural beauty and lyrically referred to the cliffs, valleys, vegetation, fresh mountain air, fog and coldness of the area that he described as Icelandic. Infatuated by the environment, he called his farm "Valhalla", the home of the gods.

Pirow owed his political career to Roos. Same as at the Pretoria Bar, they were inseparable, addressing political meetings from the same platform. Pirow's powers as an orator, combined with his combative personality, made him an effective politician and a protector of Roos with his extreme sensitivity to criticism from within his party. In turn, Roos reciprocated by turning Pirow into a high-profiled figure. Pirow also boosted his political ambitions by financially supporting *Ons Vaderland*, the struggling official mouthpiece of the NP in the Transvaal, making it possible for them to carry on publishing.[34] It was a shrewd investment as the newspaper, later renamed *Die Vaderland*, would be a vocal supporter. On the eve of the 1915 general election, the NP had considerable support in the rural parts of the Transvaal. Roos contested the winnable seat of Lichtenburg.

Pirow – who had just joined the Bar – could not financially afford to be elected to parliament as it was difficult to maintain a decent standard of living on a parliamentary salary, but he was determined to establish his credentials as a fighter for the cause of the Afrikaner. These credentials, combined with some electoral experience, would secure him a winnable seat in the future when he had established himself at the Bar. This led to him contesting Parktown, the most

32 Blackwell, *African Occasions*, p. 615.

33 Potchefstroom, North West University archive, Ossewa-Brandwag archive (hereafter NWU OB archive), Interview with D.W.R. Hertzog, Tape, 202, 12 August 1977.

34 D. Richard, *Moedswillig die uwe: Perspersoonlikhede in die noorde* (Johannesburg, 1985), p. 23.

hostile seat for any NP candidate in the country as it was an electoral fortress for the pro-imperial Unionist Party. It was the home of Johannesburg's mining magnate aristocracy. Furthermore, Pirow had to face a strong Unionist candidate in the form of Richard Feetham, a prominent advocate at the Johannesburg Bar and a former member of Alfred Milner's kindergarten, the group of brilliant young men who assisted Milner in the administration of the Transvaal and Free State after the defeat of the Boer republics in the South African War. A Labour Party candidate, A.B. Barlow, also contested the seat, but as this party was deeply divided on whether to support the war, he was not a serious threat to the Unionists. Pirow took the cause of Afrikaner nationalism with gusto to the English-speaking voters of Parktown who regarded themselves as British and not as South Africans.

Pirow's campaign was the proverbial red rag for the Unionists. Especially his claim that their party originated in a small band of foreign adventurers and that it was a deliberate and ridiculous lie to claim that the NP was anti-British and disloyal to the Empire. The editor of *The Star*, a leading Johannesburg daily newspaper, was outraged and condemned him as a buffoon on 15 October. For the jingoist voters of Parktown, his Afrikaner nationalism was aggravated by his German surname. When confronted about this at a public meeting, Pirow answered that like the British royal family he too had a German background, but unlike them he was not willing to change his surname just because of the war. The subsequent uproar was enough to satisfy even the combative Pirow.[35]

Pirow would later describe the 1915 election as the most vicious one he had ever participated in. Since all his public meetings were disrupted by the Unionists, he arranged a group of working-class Afrikaners from Vrededorp, armed with clubs, to protect him.[36] Pirow was having fun, but it did him no favours at the polling booth. On election day Feetham romped home by 2001 votes to Pirow's 299 and Barlow's 192. Countrywide the NP, fully supported by the Dutch Reformed Church (DRC) and the Afrikaner elite, and outraged by the jingoism of English speakers, did reasonably well by winning 26 seats to the 54 of the SAP and the 40 of the Unionists. The NP had

35 *Die Burger*, 21 October 1959.

36 J. Smith, "Oswald Pirow", p. 30.

attracted the majority of Afrikaner votes and the SAP, although the largest party, had lost its overall majority and became dependent on the Unionists to govern.

After showing his mettle in Parktown, Pirow was nominated in the 1917 provincial election as the NP candidate for the Vrededorp constituency in Johannesburg. The Transvaal Provincial Council, responsible for local affairs such as roads and schools, met in Pretoria for a few weeks a year, making it possible for Pirow to focus on his legal practice. Vrededorp was a poor working-class area of mainly newly urbanised Afrikaners and was a winnable seat for the NP. The party had expected to win the seat in the 1915 general election but failed to do so by 60 votes. By 1917, a growing number of Afrikaners was deserting the SAP because of its military support for Britain. On 20 June 1917, Pirow was elected by defeating Major Hunt by a majority of 250 votes, securing 1092 votes to the SAP's 842. His victory made him the NP's sole public representative in Johannesburg. Although he seldom spoke in the Council,[37] he was a dedicated representative for Vrededorp. He claimed that he became such a familiar figure in the constituency that he could afford to leave his gold watch lying about.[38]

Vrededorp had a lasting impact on Pirow as the grinding poverty of its inhabitants, and their decency, made him determined to address the poor-white problem. Pirow did not contest Vrededorp in the provincial election of 1920 as he had his eye on a parliamentary seat. It could not be Vrededorp as T.C. Visser, the failed NP candidate in 1915, was already the parliamentary candidate for that area.

Established at the Bar with a flourishing legal practice, and with the foundation laid for a political career, Pirow married Elsa Piel in 1919. According to the British High Commissioner, she was a South African-born German, the daughter of a wealthy owner of cold storage works and a ham and sausage factory in Johannesburg (who was interned during World War I) and a very attractive lady.[39] Four children – two daughters and two sons – were born from this marriage. By then Pirow was a well-known figure in the Transvaal NP, and

37 M. Nathan, *Not heaven itself: An autobiography* (Durban, 1944), p. 125.

38 Bresler, *Lineage of conflict*, p. 150.

39 NA Kew, Avia 2/1879 File 29827/Part II, Dispatch from the High Commissioner, 15 August 1933.

Roos used his name in his conflict with Hertzog on the republican issue. Roos was determined to secede South Africa from the British Empire and to establish a republic. Hertzog was lukewarm about such a step as he felt that sovereign freedom could be achieved within the Empire. For him republicanism was not practical politics as the English-speaking community would never accept it and would undermine his attempts to bring about reconciliation. Roos was disappointed, making it clear to Hertzog that he and his supporters – specifically naming Pirow – viewed republicanism as a practical plank of their political platform.

In the parliamentary election of March 1920, Pirow contested Soutpansberg, a vast rural constituency in the northern Transvaal with a sparse white population of whom the overwhelming majority were poor and badly educated Afrikaners. It was one of the NP's target seats as the party had won the provincial constituency in 1917. Soutpansberg's poor infrastructure, bad roads and lack of bridges meant that Pirow had to travel on horseback to reach voters. He occasionally had to swim across rivers, while at night lions were a threat. The biggest daytime threat was snakes and he suffered minor but painful injuries when his horse, frightened by a large mamba, threw him into a thorn bush.[40] Pirow's opponent was the sitting MP, Colonel Hendrik Mentz, a local prosperous farmer and lawyer, and a member of the Smuts government as the Minister of Lands. He had been the constituency's representative since the Transvaal Colony's parliament and was a tough and shrewd political campaigner with a reputation as a thrice-wounded hero of the South African War. On election day he hung on to his seat by 988 votes to Pirow's 725. A disappointed Pirow felt that the only reason Mentz had won was because he had abused his status as Minister of Lands for electoral purposes, as he had created the perception amongst poor voters that they could secure government land if they supported the SAP.[41]

Countrywide the NP returned to parliament as the largest party with 46 seats compared to the SAP's 41, Unionists 25, Labour 21 and three independents. The Smuts government remained in power with the support of the Unionists. In November 1920, the Union-

40 Smith, "Oswald Pirow", p. 30.

41 House of Assembly Debates, 6 August 1924, Col. 221–225.

ists merged with the SAP. Seeking a mandate for the strengthened SAP, an election was held on 8 February 1921. Pirow again opposed Mentz. He was determined to avenge his defeat and hammered on the fact that the SAP had embraced the imperialist values of the Unionists, and that South Africa had the right to secede from the Empire after the approval of a public vote. Pirow once more failed to secure the seat, although he succeeded in reducing Mentz's majority by 164 votes, garnering 833 votes to the minister's 997. The SAP won the election, mainly at the cost of the predominantly English-speaking Labour Party, with an increased majority – 79 seats to the 45 of the NP. The dramatic growth of the NP had been halted, but the political mould would be shattered by the armed revolt of white miners on the Witwatersrand in 1922.

By 1921, South Africa was trapped in a worldwide financial slump and the gold-mining industry, the backbone of the South African economy, was operating at a loss. The mine owners, desperate to cut costs, were determined to abolish the industrial colour bar and to replace white labour with lesser-paid black workers. For the white miners, toiling in harsh conditions in which large numbers of them were killed by silicosis, the move to replace them with cheaper black labour was the final straw and they threatened industrial action.

Smuts attempted to prevent a strike and on 4 November 1921 met with trade union representatives to convince them of the necessity to use black labour more effectively. The miners rejected it outright as it meant abolishing the industrial colour bar. They made it clear that they would bring the mines to a standstill if this should be considered.[42] On 10 January 1922, the miners downed their tools. They were bent on conflict, a fight to the end with the mining capitalists.[43] The mine owners were just as confrontational, refusing to recognise or negotiate with trade unions as they were determined to reorganise the mining industry, even if it should lead to a strike.

By March, the strike escalated into an insurrection under the banner, "Workers of the world, fight and unite for a white South Africa". Jeremy Krikler in his *The Rand Revolt: The 1922 insurrection and racial killing in South Africa* argues that the slogan reflects the rac-

42 A.G. Oberholster, *Die mynwerkerstaking 1922* (Pretoria, 1982), pp. 78–79.

43 W.K. Hancock, Smuts: *The fields of force 1919–1950* (Cambridge, 1968), p. 72.

ism of the white miners, but that it was also a cry for their rights as citizens as they feared that they would descend to the level of the exploited black workers who had no rights. Their insurrection was the desire to create a system which would protect them against the despotism of capitalism as they wanted to limit the right of the state to act as a protector and enforcer for the mine owners. That the state had acted swiftly and coercively against the white labour movement in 1913 and 1914 fanned the flame of workers' radicalism. According to the miners, the Smuts government was serving the interests of its capitalist masters. As armed commandos of miners secured control of the Witwatersrand, the government had no choice but to proclaim martial law. Smuts mobilised the full military might of the state with artillery and bombardments from the air by South Africa's fledgling air force to crush the insurrection. In the end, the uprising cost the lives of 43 soldiers, 29 policemen and 81 civilians.

Roos, accompanied by Pirow, had met regularly with the miners in support of their efforts. When violence erupted, Pirow urged Roos to act as a mediator to prevent further bloodshed,[44] but this was vetoed by Mentz in his capacity as the Minister of Defence. Their involvement focused police interest on them. In a report Major A.E. Trigger claimed that they had colluded with extremist strikers as they had a close relationship with the Council of Action that led to the revolt. The report pointed out that Pirow, in contrast to Roos, was against violence by the miners.

Whether Roos and Pirow encouraged the extremism of the miners is a moot point, but it would lead to accusations by Smuts and Mentz that for opportunist reasons they had fanned the flames and encouraged bloodshed in an attempt to embarrass and undermine the government. Even in the NP there was some concern about Roos's behaviour. After the crushing of the Witwatersrand Revolt, Pirow and Roos defended some of the arrested miners free of charge.

In the short-term Pirow's involvement in the Rand uprising did not do him any harm, but in the long-term it would contribute to the perception of him as an opportunist. Another long-term consequence was that Pirow, on observing the air force planes bombing the miners into submission, became a lifelong convert to the effect of air power

44 Pirow, *James Barry Munnik Hertzog*, p. 92.

to suppress any possible revolt by the black majority. He became obsessed with flying and qualified as a pilot in 1928. He had a reputation as being reckless, surviving a crash landing on his second solo flight.[45] Being a pilot in the late 1920's was an exceptional feat and it raised his public profile. South Africans were duly impressed when he piloted a plane from Durban over the Drakensberg Mountains to Pretoria.[46]

The Witwatersrand Revolt was a severe blow to the reputation of Jan Smuts, creating a perception of an incompetent government resorting to unnecessary and excessive violence, while strengthening the NP and the Labour Party which were both outspoken in their criticism. The crushing of the uprising drove these two parties into an electoral alliance with the so-called Pact of 1923. After the 1921 election setback, the NP had toned down its republicanism to win English-speaking support. As part of the Pact the nationalists agreed not to campaign for secession from the Empire.

By 1924, with the country in the grip of an economic slump and a severe drought, the government was faltering, and Smuts felt obliged to call an early election. During the election campaign, the Pact hammered on the SAP's maladministration of national finances while advocating stricter racial segregation and the abolishment of the Cape franchise. The 1853 constitution of the Cape Colony accepted a franchise with educational and age qualifications that placed no bar on colour and advocated the principle of equal rights for all "civilised" (Westernised and educated) men. At the National Convention of 1908–1910, the Transvaal, Orange Free State and Natal were opposed to the Cape franchise. This impasse led to a compromise in which the Cape franchise was accepted for that province and entrenched in the constitution. The franchise could only be altered by a two-thirds-majority vote of both Houses of Parliament sitting together. Membership of parliament was restricted to white men while the Cape Provincial Council would be open to men of all races.

For Hertzog the Cape franchise was a threat to white political supremacy as black people across South Africa would hope that the vote would be extended to them. His solution was to exchange land

45 Smith, "Oswald Pirow", p. 38.
46 *Rand Daily Mail*, 3 July 1930.

for votes – to own land in tribal areas, the so-called reserves, black people had to sacrifice their claims to common citizenship. In exchange for the removal from the common voters' roll, the reserves – designated areas based on ethnicity – would be doubled in size, and here they could govern themselves. Most white people could identify with this policy. Pirow, like Hertzog, loathed the Cape franchise, but unlike the prime minister, he had no sense of paternalistic responsibility to the black majority. His stance was simply that South Africa belonged to the white man and that mere force was required to maintain this supremacy.

Pirow once more opposed Mentz in Soutpansberg and it was another bad-tempered contest. Mentz claimed that Hertzog's policy of expanding the black reserves meant that land would be taken from white farmers, and that young Afrikaners would be forced to move to the cities for work. Pirow accused Mentz of exploiting his status as a government minister to secure government land by underhand means in the constituency. What ultimately swung the election in Pirow's favour was that the voters of Soutpansberg were determined to punish the Smuts government for its poor economic record. He was elected to parliament by a majority of 226 votes, securing 1153 votes to the 927 of Mentz. Countrywide the Pact secured a comfortable victory with a majority of 27 seats in which four cabinet ministers, including Smuts, were defeated. Mentz would never forgive Pirow for his election tactics. When the SAP and NP merged to form the United Party in 1934, he refused to be in the same party as Pirow. He would be the first of many battered, bitter and vindictive opponents Pirow left in his political wake.

# 2

# The backbencher, 1924–1929

In the Westminster system newly elected parliamentarians of governing parties are humble backbenchers and under strict party control. It is expected of them to praise and support the government, keeping any doubts or criticism to themselves, while harassing the opposing party. Only after years of loyal and disciplined service could Pirow expect to be promoted to the senior front benches, parliamentary committees, and possibly gain a seat in the cabinet. With the backing of Roos, the second most powerful man in the government as the Minister of Justice, he was not an ordinary backbencher. His loyalty was not to the NP or Hertzog, but to Roos who he was confident would become the prime minister and had promised him a position in his government.[47] The only rule for a backbencher he applied with relish was that of bashing the SAP. The official opposition was determined to oppose any measures proposed by the NP in the hope of splitting its alliance with the Labour Party, and to bring about an early general election.

In this volatile atmosphere in the House of Assembly, Pirow's loquaciousness and abrasiveness, or impulsiveness as the *Cape Times* (23 July 1925) termed it, made an immediate impact. According to Ben Schoeman, who had witnessed many parliamentarians in his 31-

47 O. Pirow. "Drie manne uit die dae van samesmelting: Hertzog, Smuts en Tielman Roos", *Die Huisgenoot*, 5 December 1952, p. 8.

year parliamentary career, Pirow was the best speaker and debater he had ever encountered in the House of Assembly.[48] His unbridled aggression made him a feared debater. This was evident in his maiden speech on 6 August 1924. The tradition for a newly elected parliamentarian is to deliver a non-controversial maiden speech in which he would thank his predecessor for what he has done for the constituency. Pirow had no time for such niceties and launched a scathing attack on Mentz for allegedly using government land in Soutpansberg for his own financial gain. He accused him of being "hopelessly unreliable" and "thoroughly untruthful" in dealing with a question in a previous parliamentary session on how he had secured a government farm.[49]

Pirow also did not hesitate to cross swords with Colonel Deneys Reitz, a former cabinet minister and a swashbuckling parliamentarian with a reputation as feared debater with the ability to get under the skin of the NP MPs. During a debate on the Zululand Railway Construction Bill, he sneeringly accused Reitz of converting the debate on railways into one on the poor-white question, and that he was casting serious imputations upon a large section of people in the northern Transvaal. An indignant Reitz responded that Pirow was putting words into his mouth, but his attack on the Bill was deflated. In the press gallery the representative of *Die Burger* expressed his admiration for Pirow, especially his ability to speak fluently in English, in his column *Kykies in die Volksraad* (Glimpses of the House of Assembly) of 28 August 1925. When Reitz on 29 August launched an attack on J.G.N. Kemp, the Minister of Agriculture, for cronyism in his appointments and dismissals of officials, it was Pirow that came to his defence, describing his statements as thoroughly misleading. His combative reputation would eventually lead to the *Cape Times* dubbing him the "young gladiator of the Nationalists".[50]

Pirow's parliamentary performance meant that within months observers predicted a bright future for him. In 1925, the German foreign ministry observed that he was considered as a future South

48 B. Schoeman, *My lewe in die politiek* (Johannesburg, 1978), p. 79.

49 *Cape Times*, 7 August 1924.

50 M. Shain, *A perfect storm: Antisemitism in South Africa, 1930–1948* (Johannesburg, 2015), p. 9.

African prime minister.[51] Ironically, by then Pirow was starting to lose interest in the House of Assembly.

Life as a backbencher can be boring, especially for an energetic person such as Pirow whose legal services were in demand. The high regard in which he was held in legal circles was reflected when he became a King's Counsel (KC) in 1924. He was one of the youngest ever silks in South Africa. He increasingly focused on his thriving practice at the Pretoria Bar where he secured an enormous fee of 3000 guineas for one of his briefs in 1925.[52] His success at the Bar made it possible for him at the end of April 1925 to accompany Ben Pienaar, a friend and South Africa's continental trade commissioner, on a European tour that included Germany, Italy and the Soviet Union.

As a private citizen he paid all costs out of his own pocket. In an interview with Reuters in London on his return from the Soviet Union, he made it clear that he was more than ever convinced that no sane man would ever attempt to introduce Bolshevism into South Africa, but he did admit that he was very favourably impressed by the Soviet Union as a "disciplined, sober, and hard-working state". He warned that Russia was finding its feet again as a military power, and he encouraged South African trade with the Soviets. The editor of the *Cape Times* found his positive comments on the Soviet Union galling and reprimanded him in a leading article. In a sarcastic tone it was pointed out that his visit to Moscow was too short to come to such a positive conclusion, and that he was obviously ignorant of the true nature of the communist state.[53] The editor was spot-on as Markus Viljoen of *Die Burger* discovered in an interview. After a concerted effort to read up on Russian history, he was stunned to discover that Pirow knew very little about the Soviet Union, and in the printed version of the interview Viljoen effectively answered his own questions.[54] Pirow's visit to the Soviet Union had a lasting legacy as it created the perception that he had a soft spot for totalitarian regimes.

51 C. Marx, *Oxwagon sentinel: Radical Afrikaner nationalism and the history of the Ossewabrandwag* (Pretoria, 2008), p. 263.

52 National Archives Pretoria (hereafter NA), J.C. Smuts papers, Vol. 288, A.L. Cohen – Smuts, 3 December 1925.

53 *Cape Times*, 22 and 23 July 1925.

54 J.M.H. Viljoen, *'n Joernalis vertel* (Cape Town, 1953), p. 80.

During the 1926 parliamentary session Pirow only spoke four times in the House of Assembly, and these were not speeches but mere statements. For the 1927 parliamentary session he made only three speeches. One of them was in support of the Iron and Steel Industry Bill, which the *Cape Times* (1 March 1927) praised as "full of interesting points of detail". For the rest of the time he used his speaking opportunities to bash the SAP. This led to J.W. Jagger, SAP MP for Cape Town Central, accusing him of always abusing opponents.[55] In the 1928 parliamentary session he did not make a single speech. All his energy went into his legal practice.

In one such prominent court case he secured the acquittal of a farmer, Sam Gafenowitz, who had been charged with murder after he had killed a number of his workers when he fired a double-barrel shotgun into a group of them having a drunken brawl.[56] He also successfully represented the Commissioner for Inland Revenue against Mr Justice F.E.T. Krause, who had claimed that the Income Tax Act of 1925 was not applicable to judges.[57] The next year he changed sides by appearing against the Commissioner in *Leyds v. Commissioner for Inland Revenue* (1929). He successfully argued that the award of a lump sum of money to Dr. J.W. Leyds, former State Secretary of the South African Republic, for past services was not subject to income tax. Observors regarded his win as his most notable legal victory.[58]

In April 1929, he appeared as the defence counsel in the Nafte murder trial, a sensational case that gripped the attention of the country. Jack Nafte, a rich Bethal farmer, was charged with murder of a young farm worker, Sixpence Temba, who had died after a savage and cruel assault by him. Mr Justice Saul Solomon, who did his utmost to protect a black witness in a packed and hostile courtroom in which fellow farmers were outraged that one of them could be on trial, took exception to Pirow's closing argument. He interpreted it as a suggestion that no jury consisting of farmers could ever convict

55 House of Assembly Debates, 28 February 1927, Col. 814.

56 Bresler, *Tilt the sack*, pp. 144–145.

57 E. Kahn, "A trimestrial potpourri", *The South African Law Journal*, Vol. 105, No. 4, 1988, p. 819.

58 "The Minister of Justice", *The South African Law Times*, Vol. 1, No. 1, January 1932, p. 5.

a fellow farmer for killing a black labourer. Pirow immediately objected that he had not made such a statement, and although the judge withdrew the claim, during a break in court proceedings a fuming Pirow went for a long run of several miles to regain his temper. To the surprise of all – including Hjalmar Reitz, Pirow's junior counsel – the jury, disgusted by their client's sadism, convicted Nafte of culpable homicide and not murder. He was convicted to seven years' imprisonment with hard labour and ten lashes with a cane to experience some of the pain he had inflicted on his victim.[59]

These legal appearances raised Pirow's profile amongst the public, but according to Leslie Blackwell, SAP MP for Kensington, he was an almost unknown personality in the House of Assembly on the eve of the 1929 general election.[60] In the pre-election session, Pirow only made one speech in defence of the trade treaty with Germany by bashing the SAP for its emphasis on economic links with Britain that was seen as selling out South African interests.

Although his fellow NP MPs frowned upon his poor parliamentary attendance, it was Pirow's reputation as a disruptive presence that harmed his standing in the party. By hitching his ambitions to Roos's political wagon, he was obliged to support him in his power struggle with Dr D.F. Malan, the Minister of Health, Interior and Education and leader of the Cape NP, and his only serious rival as a possible successor to Hertzog. The dour, slow-moving and highly competent Malan had a fervent belief that he had a special calling to serve God and the Afrikaner. His status as a clergyman – Dutch Reformed Church ministers were treated like demi-Gods by their congregations – turned him into a formidable and respected public figure. He fiercely resented British cultural hegemony, especially the dominance of the English language, and concluded that political power had to be obtained without compromise, or the Afrikaner faced extinction. His status as an outspoken champion for the Afrikaner led to his appointment as the first editor of *Die Burger* and as the leader of the Cape NP. For him Roos was erratic, unprincipled and incompetent.

59 Reitz, *The conversion of a South African nationalist*, pp. 104–105; *The Star*, 3, 4 and 5 April 1929.

60 Blackwell, *African Occasions*, p. 156.

Roos on the other hand viewed Malan with equal contempt as a pedantic bumbler, but what he really resented was that he was replacing him as Hertzog's confidant.[61] To support Roos in his power struggle with the Cape NP leader, Pirow attempted to damage Malan's reputation for competency in 1925. In an interview with *Ons Vaderland* he claimed that his constituency had a lack of district surgeons as Malan did more for black people than white people in the northern Transvaal. He furthermore objected that SAP-supporting doctors continued to be district surgeons in Soutpansberg. A furious Malan responded in a lengthy interview in *Die Burger* (13 January 1926) that Soutpansberg had more district surgeons than many other districts, and that Pirow was ignorant of government policy. He was adamant that he would not make medical appointments based on party loyalty. The next day, A.L. Geyer, editor of *Die Burger* who as a Malan admirer viewed Roos as too lazy, unpredictable and cynical,[62] published a lengthy lead article in praise of the Cape leader's integrity, while condemning Pirow's stance on political jobbery. A petulant Pirow responded that cabinet ministers should not see legitimate criticism as a personal attack and that they should not allow civil servants to dominate them. Geyer did not turn the other cheek and once more condemned Pirow's accusations as baseless.[63] Pirow then submitted his resignation as an MP to Hertzog, knowing that with the full backing of Roos it would not be accepted.

At a public meeting at De Wildt on 26 January 1926, he defiantly declared that cabinet ministers had to be humble and not see reasonable criticism that more should be done for poor Afrikaners as a personal insult.[64] Hertzog rejected Pirow's resignation, but he had made powerful and dangerous enemies in Malan and Geyer.

Pirow's role in the flag crisis of 1925 to 1927 aggravated Malan's enmity. In 1925 the government, with Malan as the responsible minister, initiated a process to secure a South African flag. It led to an emotional and bitter struggle as most Afrikaner nationalists wanted a

61 L. Korf, "D.F. Malan: A political biography" (D.Phil thesis, University of Stellenbosch, 2010), p. 271.

62 Western Cape Provincial Archives, Cape Town (hereafter WCPA) A.L. Geyer collection, Vol. 16, Politieke herinneringe 1923–1929.

63 *Die Burger*, 15 and 16 January 1926.

64 *Die Burger*, 25 January 1926.

flag free of any link with Britain. The English-speaking community vehemently opposed it. Pirow and Roos, motivated by a personal dislike of Malan and a feeling that he dealt with the issue incompetently, provided no support for him.[65] In September 1926, Pirow declared that the "flag question is and has always been a matter of second-rate importance, handled in its initial stages with rather less than second-rate ability". He also made no attempt to conceal his dislike of the final flag design, declaring in public, "It leaves me cold."[66]

A badly bruised Malan would never forgive Roos and his acolytes for their sniping during the flag crisis.[67] Pirow added salt to Malan's wounds when he attempted to encourage resistance in the Transvaal NP against what he viewed as his too tolerant attitude to Indians. In January 1927, Malan had secured an agreement with the Indian government not to introduce legislation dealing with Indian matters to secure its support in repatriating as many of them as possible.[68] In a leading article on 24 March 1927, *Die Burger* pointed out that Pirow was absent in the House of Assembly when the issue was discussed and condemned him as disloyal and disruptive.

Pirow's support of Roos's attempts to create a new centre party also raised doubts about his loyalty to the NP. For Roos, party-political strife between the SAP and NP had left numerous national questions unresolved. As the Balfour Declaration of 1926 – which had secured for the British Dominions equal rights in status with Britain – had settled South Africa's constitutional position, the NP had to reunite with the SAP, as long as the former Unionists in the party were excluded. Behind the scenes he reached out to J.H. Hofmeyr, a leading SAP member and the highly regarded Administrator of the Transvaal, and seen as a possible prime minister, to bring about a new party. Roos argued that the future did not belong to Smuts and Hertzog but to him, Hofmeyr and Pirow. In public Hofmeyr expressed support, but the strong enmity in the NP and SAP towards any political rec-

65 H. Saker, *The South African flag controversy 1925–1928* (Cape Town, 1980), pp. 51, 249.

66 J.H. le Roux, P.W., Coetzer, *Die Nasionale Party, Vol. II, Die eerste bewindsjare 1924–1934* (Cape Town, 1980), pp. 220, 270.

67 D.F. Malan, *Afrikaner-volkseenheid en my ervarings op die pad daarheen* (Cape Town, 1959), pp. 75, 112–117.

68 Korf, "D.F. Malan: A political biography", p. 273.

onciliation made a new centre party impossible. Roos, while seeking a reason to abandon his plan, was fortunate that Smuts provided him with one when on 12 November 1927 he expressed his caution to a new party that would exclude the former Unionists. Roos claimed that Smuts's caution was a rejection of his noble ideal of a new party and signified the end of his attempts to achieve one.

Pirow, realising that Roos's standing in the NP had been damaged, used the debate on Article 4 (setting out the ideal of a republic) in the party's constitution to deflect criticism. After the Balfour Declaration, Hertzog felt that the issue of republicanism had to be shelved. Article 4 had to be adapted to acknowledge that South Africa had sovereign status within the British Empire. Roos on the other hand wanted to retain Article 4. In December 1927, Pirow at a public meeting in Johannesburg stated that the ideal of a republic always had to be part of the NP's principles.[69] Hertzog, feeling that his stance could harm the NP publicly, reprimanded him.[70] Hofmeyr shrewdly observed that Pirow's outburst on Article 4 was an attempt to disarm Roos's critics and to restore confidence in the "Lion of the North's" leadership.[71] That Article 4 was not a case of principle was evident in Roos and Pirow's meek submission when the congress of the Transvaal NP in August 1928 accepted the adaptation of the article with a large majority.

In an interview with *The Star* (13 September 1928) Pirow made it clear that he disagreed with the party on the Balfour Declaration, but that he accepted that he would not live long enough to see the party convert to its 1914 stance on secession. Many NP MPs were unconvinced by Pirow's stance on republicanism as they felt that he was not a true Afrikaner. That he was raised with German as his home language, educated in Germany, and that he was a member of the German Evangelical Lutheran Church meant that in the eyes of many Afrikaners he was not one of them. Hertzog felt that he was in essence a German.[72] Paul Sauer, a prominent Cape MP, defined it as

69 *Cape Times*, 23 December 1927.

70 J.H. le Roux, P.W. Coetzer, *Die Nasionale Party. Vol. III, Die eerste bewindsjare 1924–1934* (Bloemfontein, 1982), pp. 138–139.

71 Saker, *The South African flag controversy 1925–1928*, pp. 248–249.

72 J.H. le Roux, P.W. Coetzer, A.H. Marais, *Generaal J.B.M Hertzog: Sy strewe en stryd, Vol. II* (Johannesburg, 1987), p. 679.

Pirow's *Duitsheid* (German attitude).[73] It was not only Afrikaners, sensitive about their sense of identity, that had this perception. After a meeting in 1938, Sir Neville Henderson, Britain's ambassador in Berlin, was struck by what he described as Pirow's German mentality.[74] For Piet Meiring, a prominent Afrikaner journalist, it was obvious that with his German background Pirow had a sense of inferiority to Afrikaners, and that he felt uncomfortable in the presence of orthodox Afrikaners.[75]

By 1928, Pirow was fully aware of his isolation in the NP, especially as Roos's political star was fading fast. His chances of becoming prime minister became increasingly remote as his bored, irresponsible, cynical attitude to state affairs, and neglect of his portfolio, had alienated Hertzog and the rest of the cabinet. By January 1928, he was a marginalised figure, and tired of politics.[76] In November 1928, he informed Hertzog that he wanted to retire from politics. Hertzog responded that his resignation before the 1929 general election would harm the NP and that he had to do so after the election. This would leave Pirow isolated in a party where the political star of Malan was on the rise while Hertzog viewed him as a troublemaker. After Pirow's clash with Malan on Indian legislation, Hertzog was incensed and confronted him in the NP's parliamentary caucus and hardly greeted him afterwards. He was an autocratic party leader, obsessive about loyalty, promoting only those whom he felt were 100 per cent loyal to him.

Pirow was not the person to allow acolyte entrapment to harm his political ambitions. Realising that he had hitched his wagon to a doomed political star, he started to reach out to Hertzog by volunteering his legal expertise in dealing with constitutional matters. After 1928 he became an ultra-loyal supporter of the prime minister while they spent many hours together in drawing up a constitution for South West Africa, and in drawing up the Bill to remove blacks from the common voters' roll in the Cape.[77] Their increasingly close relationship created some suspicion amongst NP MPs, especially as

73 D. and J. De Villiers, *Paul Sauer* (Cape Town, 1977), p76.

74 NA Kew, FO 371/21682, Henderson's note of the meeting, 11 November 1938.

75 Meiring, *Tien politieke leiers*, pp. 74, 95.

76 Brits, "Tielman Roos se rol in die Suid-Afrikaanse politiek, 1907–1935", p. 219.

77 Pirow, "Drie manne uit die dae van samesmelting", p. 9, 11.

it was clear that Pirow had set out to cultivate the prime minister's friendship with flattery – and Hertzog had a reputation that he was easily flattered.[78]

Hertzog's biographers – J.H. le Roux, P.W. Coetzer and A.H. Marais – are of the opinion that Pirow's political ambition was indeed a factor in their close relationship.[79] That he had become part of Hertzog's inner circle by March 1929 was reflected in a letter he wrote to the prime minister on reading of the resignation of Sir Pierre van Ryneveld as head of the air force. Pirow urged Hertzog not to rush with a new appointment as he wanted to share some thoughts with him on the issue.[80]

That Pirow had become a favourite of Hertzog was evident in the 1929 general election. In his recollections it is claimed that he had decided to leave parliament, and that this led to his decision to oppose Smuts in his Standerton seat, a contest he knew he could not win. The reality is more complex. It seems that his Soutpansberg constituency felt that he was too absent as an MP and they wanted a more hands-on one. In August 1929, Blackwell in a statement in the House of Assembly claimed that the Soutpansberg NP association was so disappointed in him as their representative that he was informed that his continued presence in the constituency was not desired. Blackwell was an abrasive character and he loathed Pirow. The result was that they regularly clashed during debates. But for once Pirow remained quiet when Blackwell taunted him about Soutpansberg's alleged rejection of him.[81]

From contemporary newspaper reporting it is evident that Pirow expected to be elected in Standerton as the constituency was on the list of seats the NP hoped to capture from the SAP. By 1929, rural Afrikaners were no longer willing to support the SAP, especially in the wake of Smuts's opposition to the attempt to remove black people from the common voters' roll in the Cape Province. Hertzog had tabled a Bill in 1929 that would have allowed the Cape franchise to

78 WCPA, A.L. Geyer collection, Vol. 3. Political notebook, 20 February 1934.

79 J.H. Le Roux, P.W. Coetzer, A.H. Marais, *Generaal J.B.M Hertzog: Sy strewe en stryd, Vol. II* (Johannesburg, 1987), p. 582.

80 NA Pretoria, J.B.M. Hertzog papers, Vol. 95, Pirow – Hertzog, 15 March 1929.

81 House of Assembly Debates, 2 August 1929, Col. 388.

be terminated. The Bill lapsed as it failed to get the required majority. For party-political reasons the SAP had opposed the Bill – the abolition of the franchise for black people would have involved the loss of SAP-held seats to the NP in the Cape Province. Desperate to secure the two-thirds majority, the NP decided to focus on the SAP's protection of the Cape franchise in what became known as the black peril election.

While Smuts as the leader of the SAP had to campaign nationally, Pirow with the assistance of the NP's effective party machine, solely focused on Standerton. For John Martin, chairman and managing director of the Argus newspaper group, and an admirer of Smuts, it was clear that there was "a carefully planned and most determined onslaught" on the leader of the opposition in his constituency.[82] Defeating Smuts would be a feather in Pirow's cap and enhance his career. He was in effect in a win-win situation as a defeat would not signify the end of his career. He knew that Hertzog would find a seat for him. During the election there was speculation in the SAP press that he would succeed Roos who had left for Europe in February to secure treatment for a kidney problem. Pirow, feeling that victory was within his reach, urged Hertzog to visit Standerton when he noticed that the constituency was not on the prime minister's programme of election meetings.[83] Hertzog responded positively and addressed a mass meeting in Standerton on 26 May, accusing Smuts of selling out the future of white people with his defence of the Cape franchise.

Pirow took the battle to Smuts with enthusiasm in a campaign that was described as one of "the fiercest electoral battles ever fought in South Africa".[84] His determination to win was evident when on driving from Bloemfontein to Standerton to address a public meeting, he found the Vaal River in flood. He promptly swam across and delivered his speech.[85] Pirow, who described it as a battle in which no quarter was asked for or given, made extensive use of black peril tactics. He accused Smuts of being in favour of the vote for black women: "What a lovely state of affairs it will be when aya [deroga-

82 NA Pretoria, J.C. Smuts Paper, Vol. 226, John Martin – Smuts, 18 June 1929.
83 NA, Pretoria, J.B.M. Hertzog papers, Vol. 95, Pirow – Hertzog, 15 April 1929.
84 Blackwell, *African Occasions*, p. 156.
85 *Rand Daily Mail*, 3 July 1930.

tory term for a black woman] goes to the polling booth with a little monkey on her back."[86] Pirow urged Hertzog to cancel a proposed meeting with black leaders at Herschel in the Cape Province as he feared that even the slightest form of benevolent paternalism towards black people could undermine his chances of victory in Standerton.[87] His campaign was so effective that some observers concluded that Smuts's seat was in danger.[88] On election day a confident Pirow informed the party headquarters in Pretoria that he was ahead of Smuts as far as votes were concerned. Smuts hung onto his seat by a small majority of 173 votes. Personal loyalty to him as a South African War hero had pulled him through.

Letters in the Smuts papers reflected the anxiety and relief of supporters that he had survived Pirow's onslaught.[89] Nationally the SAP had taken a beating as the NP had increased the number of its seats from 63 to 77. Although a loser on the day, Pirow came out of the election with an enhanced reputation. The day after the election it was speculated in the press that he was earmarked for a cabinet position as the new Minister of Justice. When Roos resigned from the cabinet and parliament, Hertzog promptly offered him the portfolio.

Pirow's appointment – at 38 he was the youngest cabinet minister South Africa has ever had at that stage – raised some eyebrows. Many NP MPs disliked him for neglecting his parliamentary duties, for being disloyal and disruptive, and for not being a true Afrikaner. Even amongst Pirow's friends and fellow Roos disciples, there was a feeling that he did not deserve the promotion. In the lead was Hjalmar Reitz, the NP MP for Brits, who felt that it should have been him. He was the son of the former Free State president F.W. Reitz, a veteran of the South African War, one of Hertzog's earliest supporters, a member of the freedom delegation to Versailles, a high-profile attorney and advocate with a doctorate in law from a Dutch university, and an experienced politician. Reitz was disappointed not to be appointed, but the harsh reality was that he was a Roos loyalist, and

86 A. Paton, *Hofmeyr* (London, 1964), p. 283.
87 NA Pretoria, J.B.M. Hertzog papers, Vol. 95. Pirow – Hertzog, 15 April 1929.
88 A. Barlow, *Almost in confidence* (Cape Town, 1952), p. 318.
89 NA Pretoria, J.C. Smuts Paper, Vol. 226, John Martin – Smuts, 18 June 1929 and C.J. Krige – Smuts, 16 June 1929; Vol. 225. R. Close – Smuts, 26 June 1929.

Hertzog was determined to neutralise this group. He was offered a judgeship in South West Africa. Although he remained in parliament, he would be, as the other Roos acolytes, marginalised and ignored.

The unease with Pirow's promotion was reflected in the lukewarm response of *Die Burger* and also *Die Volksblad*, the party's mouthpiece in the Orange Free State. *Die Burger* pointed out that he had not made his mark in parliament, but conceded that he was very intelligent. For *Die Volksblad* he was such an unknown person that the paper published a factually incorrect biographical sketch of him.

In accepting the appointment, Pirow made a great show of loyalty to Roos. He informed Hertzog that he could only accept the post if his mentor gave his blessing and cabled him on whether he approved of his appointment. Roos advised him to accept the post. In return he promised Roos that if he wanted to return to politics, he would resign and make way for him in the cabinet.[90] He indeed made the promise and told Harry Morris that he was only keeping Roos's seat in the Palace of Justice warm for his return.[91] All of this was a calculated move by Pirow to counter the perception that he was an opportunist. He knew that Roos would never veto his appointment, while the show of loyalty to his old mentor could only raise his standing in the eyes of Hertzog. Even a close friend such as Hans van Rensburg, a former private secretary of Roos and an official in the Department of Justice, felt that his continuous reference to Roos's telegram was a bit excessive.[92] This contributed to the perception that Roos had forced his appointment on Hertzog. The *Cape Times* of 24 January 1930 mockingly referred to him as "the chosen pet of Mr. Roos".

After Pirow had appointed Roos as a judge to the Appeal Court in Bloemfontein in November 1929, he felt that he had repaid his debt to his old mentor and they started to drift apart. A father-son-relationship developed between him and Hertzog. They went on walks together, he was a regular houseguest, and he became someone the premier could share his problems and legislation with, or just discuss a book he had read.[93] To maintain his close relationship with the

90 Pirow, "Drie manne uit die dae van samesmelting", pp. 8–9.
91 Morris, *The first forty years*, p. 55.
92 *Die Burger*, 21 October 1957.
93 Pirow, *James Barry Munnik Hertzog*, pp. 136–138, 216.

prime minister, he altered his stance on republicanism. In November 1932, he proclaimed:

> I happen to be a Republican, but having said that, let me also add that nobody in his sense will imagine that it is going to be a practical issue in our generation, or as far as I know, at all.[94]

In the process, his former close relationship with Roos became a source of embarrassment. Within months there were rumours that Roos, unhappy and frustrated as a judge, planned a political comeback. This placed pressure on Pirow as Hertzog suspected him of not being honest about his relationship with his former mentor. The prime minister, who loathed Roos as an intriguer, made it clear to Pirow that he would never allow him back into cabinet. Pirow promised Hertzog that if his former mentor should attempt a political comeback, he would fight him with all his might.

94 Calpin, *There are no South Africans*, p. 215.

# 3

# A rising star, 1929–1933

To take up his position as Minister of Justice, Pirow became a member of the Senate. Provincial colleges, consisting of the members of parliament and the provincial council members, elected the senators. However, our senators were nominated by the Governor General on the advice of the government because of their thorough acquaintance with the reasonable wants and wishes of the "coloured races in South Africa". On 22 July, one of these senators was prompted to resign and replaced by Pirow. The SAP was outraged and demanded from Hertzog to explain Pirow's "thorough acquaintance" with the interests of the "coloured races". The prime minister's glib answer, "that acquaintance which is possessed by every enlightened son of South Africa who takes an intelligent interest in the people of South Africa and their welfare", added fuel to the flames.[95] Deneys Reitz mocked with relish his status as a nominated senator. Blackwell indicted his senatorship as a blatant disregard of the constitution as he had never shown the slightest desire to defend the interests of the black majority, going so far as to declare that no black person should ever be allowed to drive a car.[96]

As a government minister Pirow could participate in the House of Assembly debates but could not vote in divisions. On 3 August,

95 *Cape Times*, 3 August 1929.
96 House of Assembly Debates, 2 Augustus 1929, Col. 391–394.

he made his ministerial maiden speech. It was a real test as he had to introduce a new trade treaty with Germany since the responsible minister, F.W. Beyers, the Minister of Mines and Industries, had just resigned from parliament for health reasons. Pirow rose to the occasion, impressing the sceptical *Die Burger* and hostile *Cape Times* with his skills in mastering the fine detail of the agreement. He also had a confident start as the Minister of Justice and the *Cape Times* (13 August 1929) conceded that he was "showing great promise as a Minister".

In September a parliamentary seat was found for Pirow when the sitting MP for Gezina in Pretoria resigned his seat in exchange for a diplomatic post. The voters of this part of Pretoria were working and lower middle-class Afrikaners and a significant number were poor whites. It was a safe NP seat and Pirow, still finding his feet in his new portfolio, was frustrated not to be elected unopposed in the by-election on 23 October as the SAP decided to contest the seat. J.H. Schoeman, a farmer from outside Pretoria and a former NP member – he had opposed Smuts in the 1920 general election – was nominated as the party's candidate. He fought an aggressive campaign as a champion of poor whites, condemning Pirow as a wealthy advocate who could not relate to the poor. His candidature offended the NP whose rowdies continuously disrupted his public meetings.

Pirow treated Schoeman with contempt, ridiculing him as a feeble joke, an unbalanced turncoat without any steadfast principles. He also exploited the racial prejudices of the voters of Gezina by informing them that he had ordered the police to prevent black people from wandering around in Church Street on Sundays or to congregate around Paul Kruger's statue, as this was an insult to the memory of the late president. Pirow won the election with ease, securing 1391 votes to the 653 of Schoeman. After the result was announced, a bruised Schoeman refused to congratulate him. The SAP-supporting *Pretoria News* expressed the hope that Pirow on returning to the House of Assembly would at last take parliament seriously.[97]

As Minister of Justice, Pirow was the political head of South Africa's legal system as well as of the South African Police, a paramilitary force responsible for law and order. For Pirow the police was

97 *Pretoria News*, 9, 11, 12, 13, 15, 16, 22 and 24 October 1929.

a force to not just deal with crime, but especially to maintain white supremacy. To do so the police had to be tough and well trained, and he set out to root out slackers with compulsory physical refresher courses. The fitness demands set by him were so demanding that it led to injuries and resignations, and questions being raised in parliament.[98]

The first opportunity for Pirow to show his mettle as the Minister of Justice was in November 1929 with a massive raid of heavily armed police on Durban to collect unpaid poll tax amongst black workers. The low poll tax returns in the port city was the result of a boycott of municipal beerhalls. The Durban municipality had a monopoly on providing sorghum beer for the local black population and used the income of these sales to cover the costs for their housing and administration. In June 1929, black anger and frustration with low wages, poor living conditions and the harsh municipal control led to a boycott of the beerhalls. Between 17 and 18 June, the boycott degenerated into violent racial clashes and the deaths of two white and five black people. Pirow was determined that the boycott movement and black defiance had to be crushed. For him and Colonel I.P. de Villiers (Commissioner of the South African Police) – both 38 years old and eager to prove themselves worthy of their positions – Durban provided the opportunity to justify their appointments. The problem was that Durban was not under the jurisdiction of the South African Police. In terms of the old Natal Police Act of 1894, Durban had its own municipal police force. The avoidance of national poll tax payments in the port city provided the opportunity to intervene. Pirow arranged for a task force of 695 police officers to enter Durban on 14 November 1929 to demand proof of poll tax payments from black men. Without a receipt of payment, a person was to be arrested.

To attend the raid, Pirow flew on 13 November with Major A.A. Cilliers in a two-seater SAAF plane to Durban. Over the Drakensberg mountain range strong winds and fog forced Cilliers to make a landing in the Orange Free State. They succeeded in reaching Durban only later that afternoon. The next day the police armed with truncheons, pickaxe handles, rifles with fixed bayonets, pistols as well as two mounted Vickers machine guns on mule wagons, descended

98 W.A. Bellwood, *South African backdrop* (Cape Town, 1969), p. 47.

on Durban. A total of 2319 black people were arrested, but that the aim of the raid was to intimidate the black population was evident in the behaviour of the police. De Villiers set the example by flooring a black man with a single punch for reacting slowly to an order. Following his example, policemen assaulted and humiliated black workers with impunity whether they had paid the poll tax or not, and a number of them had to receive medical treatment. During the raid, teargas was used for the first time in South Africa when a canister was flung – to the great merriment of policemen and journalists – at a group of peaceful black citizens. Pirow flew back to Pretoria later that day, convinced that the raid was a great success and that force was the only way to deal with black defiance. More importantly, the raid had raised his profile in the country. The Durban press was ecstatic in praising his strong leadership and his nerve to fly to Durban, but outside of the port city the raid was perceived as an overreaction.

Some SAP-supporting newspapers raised doubts about Pirow's inexperience, overconfidence and his ability to hold such a responsible position as the Minister of Justice. These concerns were valid ones as the raid bolstered the beerhall boycott movement by fuelling black resentment. For Pirow this defiance was proof of communist agitation and led to him amending the Riotous Assemblies Act in 1930. This amendment allowed the government to ban alleged communist agitators from certain areas without any trial and appeal, without having to provide reasons to the banned person. This made possible the banning of the trade unionist A.W.G. Champion – who was not a communist – from Durban.[99] Eventually state repression ended the black resistance to the municipal administration in Durban.

Pirow's role in the suppression of the unrest in Durban was a true reflection of his attitude to the black majority. He had no interest in their plight or difficulties. His only aim was to implement the laws of the state. He made this brutally clear to W.M. Macmillan, a liberal historian at the University of the Witwatersrand, in a meeting on 31 October 1931. Macmillan, a campaigner for the socio-economic upliftment of blacks and the defence of the Cape franchise, concluded that the Minister of Justice's "solution" to the race problem was to

99 F.A. Mouton, "Die slag van Durban: Die massiewe polisie-optrede van November 1929 in Durban", *Kleio*, XXI, 1989, pp. 47–57.

goad blacks into resistance so that they might be dealt with.[100] Resistance was not even necessary for Pirow to apply the law without mercy. This was evident in his treatment of black farm labourers.

To secure cheap labour for white farmers he introduced the Native Service Contract Bill of 1932, which made provision for the whipping – not exceeding five strokes – of juveniles under the age of 18 who broke their contracts with farmers. Pirow claimed that he did not approve of corporal punishment, but that he could not outstrip public opinion and had to consider existing conditions for farmers. Furthermore, he claimed that blacks did not object to corporal punishment when they knew they deserved it, and he made it clear that he would have preferred if there was no age restriction to the whipping.[101] With Smuts in the lead, the whipping clause led to howls of outrage in parliament, as well as from the English-speaking churches. In the House of Assembly Pirow ridiculed his critics, but that he was stung by these attacks was evident in his address to the Transvaal Agricultural Society's annual conference in Pretoria in September 1932. He urged white farmers to treat their workers fairly to counter any possible communist agitation, but it had to be strictly paternalistic, based on the colour bar, as farmers had to form the middle ground between the dangers of liberalism and communism. He viewed liberal demands by people such as Macmillan to improve the treatment of black people as dangerous as it fuelled black agitation.[102]

Addressing white mine workers in Benoni on 12 October 1932, he condemned white people who "spoiled the natives" by demanding higher pay and better amenities for blacks. For him the main source of black agitation was the colour-blind franchise in the Cape Province:

> Many of those who were always talking of the native not getting justice had their eye on the native vote in the Cape. Until that sort of thing was changed there could never be a sound outlook on native policy...[103]

---

100 W.M. Macmillan, *My South African years: An autobiography* (Cape Town, 1975), p. 213.

101 House of Assembly Debates, 4 February 1932, Col. 640, and 24 February 1932, Col. 1436.

102 *Die Burger*, 7 September 1932.

103 NA Kew, DO 35/333/3, High Commissioner's dispatch, 19 October 1932.

White people were also the victims of Pirow's robust attitude to law and order as was reflected in his response to the illicit diamond dealing in the state-controlled diamond diggings in the northwestern Cape and the difficulty to secure convictions before juries. His solution was simple: He drafted all the police force's best boxers into the area, encouraging them to beat up suspected dealers and force them out of the area. He also had an armoured car made with a mounted machine gun to confront illegal diamond dealers who used weapons to resist arrest.[104]

The English-medium press, although disapproving of Pirow's harsh ways to maintain law and order, became intrigued by him as he was so different from his cautious, grey and dour fellow cabinet ministers. On 7 July 1930, Arthur Barlow described Pirow in the following glowing terms in a profile for the *Rand Daily Mail*:

> This young man at times has an electric current running through his veins, and I still believe that he is going to do more to discipline, and thus save, the Afrikaner than anyone else. [...] If "Ottie" Pirow has a fair amount of luck, he will yet be Prime Minister of the Union ... He is probably the greatest South African of his generation.

Barlow was a former Labour Party MP who had lost his seat in 1929 and had to return to journalism to make a living. As a supporter of the Pact and a friend of Roos, he could be suspected of being sympathetic to Pirow. The same could not be said of the *Cape Times*, a passionate defender of British interests in South Africa and which viewed NP MPs as reactionary and backwoodsmen. Even this vitriolic prejudice did not prevent the newspaper from praising Pirow's abilities. His lengthy speech in support of the amendment to the Riotous Assemblies Act was according to the *Cape Times* (14 February 1930) "admirably delivered", and attractively presented. On 6 March 1931, the newspaper gushed over the way he introduced the Female Jurors Bill:

> The Minister has a delightful way of proposing a Bill. He speaks with crystal clarity. He wastes no words, and he has a wonderful gift of concealing a certain vein of cynicism under a much more obvious surface of frank and direct statement. The House invariably listens to him with interest, if not always with agreement.

104 Pirow, *James Barry Munnik Hertzog*, p. 125.

One newspaper that remained lukewarm towards Pirow was *Die Burger*. Geyer could not forget his behaviour as a Roos acolyte. Malan's aloofness towards Pirow was so obvious that on 25 October 1932, the British High Commissioner reported in his weekly confidential dispatch to London that his relations with Pirow were no more cordial than they had been with Roos.[105]

There was one challenge that Pirow's supreme self-confidence, energy and oratory could not deal with: the economic difficulties facing the country after the collapse of the New York stock exchange on 25 October 1929. The subsequent Great Depression severely affected the South African economy as it lowered diamond and wool prices. The economic hardship was aggravated by the country being in the grip of a devastating drought, ruining many farmers. The Hertzog government's refusal to follow Britain in abandoning the gold standard in September 1931 aggravated the situation. For N.C. Havenga, Minister of Finance, and Hertzog, supported by Pirow, the gold standard was a symbol of South Africa's economic independence. This stance encouraged the outflow of capital and hampered exports, especially agricultural products. Havenga, a conservative and orthodox Minister of Finance, whose main aim was a balanced budget, attempted to support farmers with subsidies and protective rates, but it was to no avail as the number of bankruptcies amongst farmers increased drastically. Many impoverished rural Afrikaners had to move to the cities where they could not find any employment.

By 1931, with the government faltering in its response to the economic crisis and with farmers, the bedrock of the NP's support, in economic ruin, the SAP was smelling victory. Smuts seized the high ground to condemn Hertzog as destroying the economy by clinging to the gold standard. The poor state of the economy combined with Smuts's attacks had a demoralising effect on NP MPs. To rally his party, Pirow launched a scathing attack on Smuts during the budget debate of 20 April 1931, casting sneering doubts on his abilities as leader of the opposition. It was a rousing performance, reviving the drooping spirits of NP MPs.

Pirow used the same tactic in January 1932 when Smuts was at his merciless best in flaying the government's economic record. With the

105 NA Kew, DO 35/333/3, High Commissioner's dispatch, 25 October 1932.

government benches visibly shaken, Pirow rose to make indiscriminate personal attacks on the SAP, raising at once the spirits of his own party. During the budget debate on 11 April 1932, he once more attacked Smuts. In a speech, which according to the parliamentary representative of the *Cape Times* was notable more for polemics than for economics, he condemned him for using South Africa's problems for electioneering purposes. He claimed that Smuts with his attacks on the gold standard was deliberately and recklessly damaging his own country's reputation. His speech brought joy to the gloomy NP benches.

Pirow wanted to do more than just bash the SAP as he desired the government to be more interventionist to stimulate economic growth. For him Havenga was financially too timid and conservative to deal with the economic crisis facing the country. How eager he was to get involved in economic affairs was evident in his involvement in the garment workers' strike in September 1932. He visited a factory in Germiston and ended the strike when management agreed to take the strikers back on their old salaries, on the condition that he would appoint a commission to investigate their situation.[106]

With the South African economy in a deep crisis, electoral support for the NP declined. This was evident in the Germiston by-election of 30 November 1932. Pirow fought hard in the campaign. On 5 November, he addressed with great passion a meeting of over 2000 people to convince them that the government was doing its utmost to address white poverty. It was to no avail since the SAP won the by-election with a large majority in a former Pact seat that the party had not even contested in the 1929 parliamentary election. Hertzog was shaken by the defeat.[107]

The large SAP majority in Germiston convinced Roos that it was the right time to resign from the bench, bypassing Hertzog who blocked his return to politics. On 21 December, he announced his return to politics to save the country by bringing about a coalition government, and the devaluation of the South African pound. His resignation unleashed a political firestorm. The English-medium press portrayed him as the messiah that would topple the government

106 *Die Volksblad*, 5 September 1932.

107 H.J. May, *Red wine of youth* (Cape Town, 1946), p. 38.

and save the country from economic despair. A number of Roos's acolytes – Hjalmar Reitz, A.S. van Hees (NP MP for Brakpan) and H.H. Moll (NP MP of Christiana) – rushed to his side. Pirow kept his distance as he realised that with the NP and its supporting press condemning Roos as a political traitor, a puppet of the mining magnates and exchange-rate speculators, his former mentor's comeback was doomed. In his recollections, he would claim that he had ended his friendship with Roos, misled and used by false friends, for not confiding in him his true intentions of a possible return to politics.[108] He furthermore claimed that this break was one of the most traumatic events of his public career.[109]

It can be accepted that the break with Roos was not easy for Pirow, but as a shrewd and ambitious politician, he knew that siding with him would be political suicide.

Roos's actions led to a financial panic and increased cash withdrawals from banks. On 27 December 1932, Hertzog and Havenga eventually abandoned the gold standard. The economy immediately started to recover, but Hertzog and the NP had suffered a moral blow, bolstering the perception that the government was not competent enough to deal with the economic challenge. In January 1933, travelling by train to Cape Town for the parliamentary session, Pirow was in a state of deep despondency. He made it clear to Hans van Rensburg that the government would not be able to weather the storm, and that the SAP would secure power. For him the train journey was like a French Revolution tumbril on the way to the guillotine.[110] By then Roos had approached the SAP with the offer of a coalition government as his followers in the NP parliamentary caucus could bring the government down. In return, he wanted to be the prime minister and the cabinet had to consist of six members each for the SAP and NP, and one Labourite.

For Smuts, Roos was a charlatan who was in no position to assist the SAP in defeating the NP and he refused his offer. He exploited Roos's return to reach out to Hertzog on 24 January 1933 in a parliamentary motion, urging him to resign and to form with the SAP

---

108 Pirow, "Drie manne uit die dae van samesmelting", pp. 8–9.
109 *Die Nuwe Orde*, 16 May 1946.
110 Van Rensburg, *Their paths crossed mine*, pp. 58–59.

a "National Government" to resolve the economic crisis. Hertzog rejected the motion in an emotional speech. Pirow in a supporting speech turned to his favourite tactic of accusing the SAP of opportunism: that Smuts, knowing that he could not win the next election, attempted to secure political power through the backdoor with his motion. *Die Burger* (25 January 1933), usually lukewarm towards Pirow, warmly praised his hatchet job on Smuts.

Hertzog's aggressive performance in parliament did nothing to lessen the pressure from farmers on him to alleviate their poverty, while in private he had lost confidence that his government could deal with the economic crisis.[111] Havenga also felt that farmers placed unreasonable pressure on the cabinet for financial support, and that a strong government was needed to deal with these pressures.[112] Furthermore, Hertzog feared the possibility that a Roos and Smuts coalition could defeat the NP in an election – a defeat that would hand over the country to the SAP in which the pro-imperial Unionist element still had considerable influence. To outmanoeuvre Roos and to prevent an SAP government, he decided to reach out to Smuts.

On 25 January, Hertzog instructed Pirow and Havenga to meet with Patrick Duncan, Smuts's right-hand man, with the message not to close the door on possible cooperation between the two parties. In his recollections, Pirow claimed that he was astonished, but after Hertzog had explained to him that the state of the country made cooperation with Smuts necessary, he gave his full support.[113] The reality was that it did not take much to convince him as he felt that the eventual defeat of the NP was inevitable, and he had no desire to be a powerless backbencher.

Stunned by the drastic developments, *Die Burger* would claim that Pirow had pushed Hertzog to negotiate with the SAP. The role he played in convincing reluctant NP MPs to support coalition talks encouraged the view that he was manipulating the prime minister. His methods created lifelong enmity amongst some MPs. His initial

111 A. van Wyk, *Die Keeromstraat-kliek: Die Burger en die politiek van koalisie en samesmelting, 1932–34* (Cape Town, 1983), p. 41.

112 P. van Breda, "Die politieke loopbaan van N.C. Havenga, 1910–1954" (D. Phil, University of Stellenbosch, 1992), p. 116.

113 *Die Nuwe Orde*, 13 June 1946.

tactic was that he was helping Hertzog to set up the demands for a coalition, and that it was a clever ploy to kill any desire for such a government as the demands were of such a nature that the SAP would never accept them. He told J.G. Strijdom, MP for Waterberg and an outspoken opponent of coalition, that the overture was an attempt to counter Smuts's coalition plans and to alienate SAP Afrikaner supporters from Smuts. Strijdom was disgusted, condemning it as dishonest politics. It furthermore fuelled his doubts about Pirow being a true Afrikaner if he was willing to negotiate with the bitter enemies of the Afrikaner.[114] When it became evident that there would be a coalition, Pirow urged Transvaal NP MPs to accept the coalition as it would ensure that their seats in a coming election would be uncontested.[115]

With the Liquor (Amendment) Bill, Pirow in this period also brought about the enmity of Dr N.J. van der Merwe, NP MP for Winburg, a former DRC minister and a stern Calvinist, by attempting in the face of Afrikaner church opposition to liberalise the trade in alcohol. This Bill stipulated that trading hours would be extended and that it would be possible for wine farmers to sell directly to consumers. It also allowed farmers in the Transvaal to provide their workers with limited amounts of wine and beer. Pirow sneeringly referred to "petty and vexatious" restriction on hours of sale. Van der Merwe was outraged and launched a passionate denunciation of Pirow, the evils of the drink trade, and a defence of the churches.[116] Van der Merwe was a dangerous enemy as he was the leader of the republicans in the NP, a leading figure in Afrikaner cultural organisations, and an outspoken opponent of a coalition government. Another fervent opponent of coalition was Pirow's sister, Sylvia Moerdyk, chair of the Transvaal NP and a member of the party's central executive, who had become estranged from him.

Roos had also turned into an enemy after Pirow had called him a traitor in reaching out to the SAP. At a mass public meeting in Benoni in February 1933, he made it clear that he would not serve in any

114 J.L. Basson, *JG Strijdom: Sy politieke loopbaan van 1929 tot 1948* (Pretoria, 1980), pp. 44–46.

115 WCPA, A.L. Geyer collection, Vol. 3, Political notebook, 30 April 1933.

116 G.D. Scholtz, *Dr. Nicolaas Johannes van der Merwe 1888–1940* (Johannesburg, 1944), p. 158.

The "coming man" – Pirow and the coalition cabinet, 1933. Back (left to right): Two officials, C.F. Clarkson, R. Stuttaford, D. Reitz, J.C.G. Kemp, A.P.J. Fourie, J.H. Hofmeyr and an official. Front (left to right): P.W.G. Grobler, P. Duncan, J.B.M. Hertzog, Lord Claredon, J.C. Smuts, N.C. Havenga, O. Pirow.
*From: At van Wyk collection.*

coalition cabinet with Pirow or Hertzog. In reality, there was not the slightest possibility of him being offered a place in the government as both Smuts and Hertzog were determined to keep him out.

The coalition government, sworn in on 31 March, consisted of a cabinet of 12 members, six each for the SAP and NP. To secure legitimacy for the government, a general election was announced for 17 May in which the two parties would not oppose each other. D.F. Malan, who had accepted the coalition with reservations, refused to serve in the government. Smuts became Minister of Justice and Pirow was moved to the portfolios of Railways and Harbours (SAR&H) since C.W. Malan, the previous minister, had just died, as well as of Defence since Colonel F.H.P. Creswell, leader of the Labour Party, was left out of the government.

The Railways portfolio was one of the most important and challenging positions in the cabinet, especially as the Department was functioning at a financial loss. The Defence portfolio was just as demanding seeing that the UDF was in a poor state after being neglected for many years. The standing army was small: In 1927, the UDF consisted of 151 officers and 1259 men and was dependent on the ACF, part-time soldiers, for the defence of the country. The reason for this state of affairs was that geography, and the British domination of the continent after World War I, had given South Africa safe land borders, while the Royal Navy with its base at Simon's Town was responsible for the defence of the coastline.[117] It was therefore unnecessary to maintain a large army. The UDF only had to be sufficient to deal with any internal unrest. The permanent force was so small that during the Rand Revolt of 1922, the UDF had to rely on ACF soldiers to suppress the uprising. Austerity measures during the Great Depression reduced the UDF to an insignificant force as it led to the disbandment of 49 ACF units and 54 Defence Rifle Associations (the commandos). Between 1930 and 1934, the army could not afford even small-scale training exercises while the quantity of cartridges provided to the commandos was halved. Ill-equipped, with a shortage of uniforms and consisting of mainly untrained ACF troops, the UDF was not fit for purpose and Pirow was set to remedy the situation. This meant that the UDF had to be built up almost from scratch.[118]

Within days of his appointment as the Defence Minister, Pirow had to decide on the forming of a Special Service Battalion (SSB) in the UDF to assist poor white youths. On 17 March 1933, General A.J.E. (Andries) Brink, Chief of the General Staff and Secretary of Defence, had submitted a detailed plan for such a battalion to Creswell. Brink's plan was inspired by the example of the "Returned Soldiers Battalions" after World War I and "Citizens Military Training Camps" in the United States of America (USA).[119] With his eye on the ballot box and eager to proof the coalition's determination to deal with poverty amongst white people, Pirow accepted the proposal.

On 18 April, the formation of the SSB was announced. The battalion would consist of 1500 young, unmarried men between the ages of 17 and 22 with a minimum educational qualification of Standard 6 who found it difficult to find employment. The mission of the SSB was to create better citizens by preventing the younger generation,

---

117 I. van der Waag, "South African defence in the age of total war, 1900–1940", *Historia*, 60/1 (2015), p. 145.

118 I. van der Waag, *A military history of modern South Africa* (Johannesburg, 2015), pp. 141, 156.

119 W. Otto, "Die geskiedenis van die Spesiale Diensbataljon, 1933–1939", (MA Thesis, University of Pretoria, 1972), pp. 25–28.

lacking organisation and discipline, from developing bad characteristics. The ideal was that the SSB should be a pool of recruits from which the UDF, Police, Prisons Department and other government departments such as the SAR&H could draw suitable and disciplined young men.[120] The enlistment would be for one year, but recruits could be discharged after six months if employment had been secured. The SSB was promptly swamped with applications. On 1 May 1933, the SSB became formally part of the UDF. That same day the top structure of the UDF was reshaped with the replacement of the Chief of the General Staff, General Andries Brink, a South African War veteran without any proper education,[121] with the significantly younger and university-educated engineer Sir Colonel Pierre van Ryneveld. (Brink remained the Secretary of Defence to deal with the administrative side of the UDF.) Van Ryneveld was promoted to the rank of Brigadier General.[122] Courageous, highly intelligent and dynamic, Van Ryneveld had distinguished himself as a decorated ace pilot in France, and then established himself as a pioneer aviator. In 1920, he was knighted after he and Quintin Brand became the first pilots to fly from London to South Africa. The same year he was appointed as the founder commander of the SAAF. In 1927, he became the first person in South Africa to do a parachute jump. He was Pirow's type of officer, especially as they shared a belief in air power and the need for the expansion of the SAAF. However, the British were less impressed as they felt that he was a "man with singularly little military experience for the position he holds".[123]

Highly regarded as a robust and energetic campaigner, Pirow played a leading role in the election campaign. In the Transvaal he made sure that only those who supported coalition were nominated as official NP candidates.[124] Unopposed in Gezina, he campaigned

120 NA Kew, DO 35/334/3, High Commissioner's dispatch, 14 June 1935.

121 I. van der Waag, "Smuts's generals: Towards a first portrait of the South African high command, 1912–1948", *War in History*, 18(1), pp. 45–46.

122 I. van der Waag, "The Union Defence Force between the two world wars, 1919–1940", *Scientia Militaria: South African Journal of military studies*, 30/2 (2000), pp. 204, 207.

123 NA Kew, CAB 63/69, "The military defence situation of South Africa", July 1934.

124 Le Roux, Coetzer, *Die Nasionale Party Vol. III, Die eerste bewindsjare 1924–1934*, pp. 330–331.

for other coalition candidates. In the Salt River constituency in Cape Town, he produced a rousing performance to get Harry Lawrence, a formidable SAP critic of the NP, re-elected against a strong Labour Party opponent.[125] He was also used as a battering ram against Roos and his ragtag group of followers.

By April 1933, Roos was a political wreck, broken in spirit. Overnight his popularity had evaporated. The English-medium press that had hailed him breathlessly as the saviour of South Africa had promptly dropped him with the forming of the coalition government. This left Roos, who was battling poor health, politically isolated and in a financially desperate situation. He had to return to the Johannesburg Bar to make a living. It was a humiliating comedown after being a Minister of Justice and an Appeal Court judge. Despite his dismal circumstances Roos decided to oppose Piet Grobler, leader of the Transvaal NP and a member of the government in Rustenburg, but he had no clear policies apart from claiming that he was obliged to protest the intolerance of NP leaders in bringing about coalition. At a public meeting in Pretoria, he vented his bitterness and anger about how the coalition was brought about, condemning the role of Pirow as the tyranny of "*daardie klein Hitler*" (that little Hitler).[126] (Adolf Hitler as leader of the Nazi party had come to power in Germany on 30 January 1939 and started a dictatorship.) Roos was eager that Van Hees – whose parliamentary career had been destroyed by rallying behind Roos – should oppose Pirow in Gezina, but nothing came of this plan.

By nomination day it was clear that Roos and his few followers were no threat to the NP. But Pirow had to prove his loyalty to Hertzog and he showed no mercy to Roos and his old friends, including Hjalmar Reitz who was standing as a Roosite in Jeppe. He campaigned in Rustenburg, praising Grobler and the coalition government to the skies.[127] This was seen as a ruthless kicking of a down-and-out Roos.[128] At Fordsburg revengeful supporters of Roos attempted to break up a public meeting addressed by Pirow. The result was a melee in which sticks, bottles, a bicycle chain, eggs and

125 L. Lawrence, *Harry Lawrence* (Cape Town, 1978), p. 73.
126 *Die Volksblad*, 13 April 1933.
127 *Rand Daily Mail*, 9 May 1933.
128 Bresler, *Lineage of conflict*, p. 149.

other missiles were used. It took 25 policemen to restore some order for Pirow to speak. Struggling to make himself heard, he exclaimed that anyone that voted for Roos was committing treason against the NP.[129]

Roos went down to a crushing defeat in Rustenburg while only two Roosites were elected at the cost of the ailing Labour Party. One of them was Hjalmar Reitz, who was bitter about Pirow's role in the destruction of his hero. He told Pirow, who was a big-game hunter with a house full of mounted heads of animals he had shot, to mount Roos's head amongst his collection so that he could gloat over it after dinner.[130] The popularity of the coalition was reflected in its landslide victory, securing 136 of the 150 parliamentary seats.

After the election Smuts and Pirow reached out to Roos – claiming that it was with the concurrence of Hertzog – on the possibility of him joining a new party if the NP and SAP should merge. It can only be assumed that Pirow attempted to mend broken fences with Roos and to keep him under control as a potential troublemaker. For Smuts it was possibly an attempt to bring him into the coalition as a counter to Hertzog, since the NP had a majority of 75 seats to the 61 of the SAP. Roos was supportive of merging his supporters with the NP and SAP in a new party,[131] but nothing came of the plan. In May 1934, Roos founded the stillborn Central Party. He died in 1935 – an impoverished and broken man.

Pirow did not attend the funeral of the man to whom he owed his legal and political career, leaving many Roos disciples disgusted with him.

129 *Rand Daily Mail*, 13 May 1933.

130 Reitz, *The conversion of a South African nationalist*, p. 89.

131 NA Pretoria, J.C. Smuts papers, Vol. 235, Roos – Smuts, 5 December 1933.

# 4

# Hertzog's enforcer, 1933–1934

From day one the coalition government was an efficient, harmonious one. Pirow got on well with the SAP ministers. Patrick Duncan found him an intriguing and refreshing figure. To Maud Gascoyne-Cecil, the Countess of Selborne, he described Pirow as a person with "a keen forceful mind with something of the Bismarckian outlook, including the habit of blurting out things which other people may be thinking but not saying, and the spoken word comes as a shock to them."[132] Even Smuts was eventually won over, informing the British politician Leo Amery that Pirow was "very intelligent and able".[133] However, he was concerned that he was too pro-German. In September 1934 he warned Sir Maurice Hankey, Secretary to the British cabinet, to be careful with the information he shared with Pirow as he was not sure how closely he was acquainted with Germany's diplomatic representative in South Africa.[134] J.H. Hofmeyr, who as South Africa's leading white liberal had viewed Pirow as "amoral",[135] found him "a good colleague in cabinet".[136] What espe-

---

132 D. Lavin (ed.), *Friendship and Union: The South African letters of Patrick Duncan and Maud Selborne 1907–1943* (Cape Town, 2010), p. 615.

133 J. van der Poel (ed.), *Selections from the Smuts papers, December 1934–August 1945* (Cambridge, 1973), p. 38.

134 NA Kew, CAB 63/69, M.P.A. Hankey – R. MacDonald, 7 September 1934.

135 Egeland, *Bridges of understanding*, p. 104.

136 Calpin, *There are no South Africans*, p. 262.

cially impressed his new cabinet colleagues was his energy in dealing with his demanding portfolios.

At the end of May 1933 Pirow had to deliver the Railway budget – a budget that reflected the dismal financial state of the SAR&H with a deficit of £3 694 000. To deal with the challenges and problems facing his portfolio, he undertook to use his visit to Germany and Britain as part of the South African delegation to the World Economic Conference in London, to secure appointments to a commission of inquiring into, and advising him on all aspects of the South African railway system. *Die Burger* was outraged as such a commission was a pet project of the SAP, one which C.W. Malan had always rejected. For editor Geyer the proposed commission reflected Pirow's willingness to go out of his way to accommodate the SAP. As Pirow had left for London on 2 June, he was absent when the House of Assembly discussed the Defence budget.

Paul Sauer, who resented the contemptuous and autocratic way Pirow treated NP backbenchers, used the founding of the SSB to settle a score with him. His speech oozed loathing for a man he did not see as an Afrikaner:

> The hon. Minister of Railways is, I would not like to say, contemptuous, but he is very near it. He has got Prussian antecedents, and he does not believe much in democracy ...[137]

He then proceeded to claim that the SSB could be the nucleus of a Nazi corps, sneeringly demanding to know whether the young men of the SSB would wear the black or brown shirts of the fascists, or red shirts to commemorate Pirow's visit to communist Russia. Although other MPs praised the SSB to the skies, Sauer did harm Pirow's reputation as it created the perception that he had a soft spot for authoritarian ideas.

Pirow's visit was awaited with some concern in London as Sir Herbert Stanley, the British High Commissioner in South Africa, had warned that he was "very un-British". Stanley emphasised that Pirow was drawing up plans that would ensure that the SAR&H would control all internal airways, leaving him in control of military and civilian aviation in the country. It was feared that with his German

137 House of Assembly Debates, 12 June 1933, Col. 731.

background British aircraft producers, competing with Germany's Junkers Company, would struggle to sell aircraft to South Africa. He urged London to pay special attention to Pirow.[138]

The Germans had the same idea and they went out of their way to impress Pirow.[139] He was treated as a formal guest of the German state and Hermann Göring, head of the German Air Force, provided him with an official car, aide and driver.[140] Pirow also met Hitler at Berchtesgaden after the warmest of recommendations from the German foreign ministry.[141] Göring relayed to Pirow that he had made a good impression on Hitler, who had allegedly commented that of all the foreign visitors he had met, Pirow was the one he remembered most fondly.[142] He had indeed made an impression as in November 1934, S.F.N. Gie, South Africa's diplomatic representative in Nazi Germany, was asked to convey the German dictator's greetings to Pirow.[143] In his recollections, Pirow would enthuse about his first impression of Hitler who according to him spoke as a revolutionary, the language of the twentieth century. He gushed that Hitler was the greatest man of his age, maybe of the last thousand years, and that he was swept off his feet when he had met him.[144]

This was not the perception he had conveyed in the 1930s. On his return to South Africa on 4 September 1933, he refused to share his views on Hitler with awaiting journalists, but in private he more than once told his friend Piet van der Byl that he thought Hitler was a "bloody lunatic".[145]

Back in South Africa, Pirow had little time to focus on his portfolios as he had to support Hertzog in the growing civil war in the

138 NA Kew, Avia 2/1879 File 29827/Part II, Dispatch from the High Commissioner, 15 August 1933.

139 NA Kew, Avia 2/1879, File 29827/Part II, Society of British Aircraft Construction – Lieutenant Colonel F.C. Shelmerdine of the Air Ministry, 5 December 1933.

140 *Die Nuwe Orde*, 14 February 1946.

141 Marx, *Oxwagon sentinel*, p. 264.

142 K. Bourne and D.C. Watt (eds), *Studies in international history* (London, 1967), p. 404.

143 NA Pretoria, PM 4/2/12 Vol. 1, S.F.N. Gie – Dr. Bodenstein, 7 November 1934. (I am grateful to Frik Nothling for this document.)

144 *Die Nuwe Orde*, 21 and 28 February 1946.

145 P. van der Byl, *Top hat to velskoen* (Cape Town, 1973), p. 139.

NP. The success of the coalition government had convinced the prime minister of the viability to create a new party to reconcile Afrikaners and English speakers to encourage a South African identity. With Hertzog loyalists in charge of the NP in the Transvaal and Orange Free State, there was little opposition in these provinces to a possible merger with the SAP. The Cape Province with a hostile and popular Malan in the lead was a different matter. Malan fervently believed that without a strong political base the Afrikaner would be too weak to withstand the economic and cultural domination of the English-speaking community with its British backing.

Pirow accompanied Hertzog to Port Elizabeth to attend the Cape NP's conference between 4 and 6 October 1933. The conference treated Hertzog with contempt and aggression. Pirow attempted to support him, but he was refused permission to speak. The Cape NP rejected with a large majority any possible merger with the SAP. A humiliated Hertzog left Port Elizabeth in a huff.

Accompanied by Pirow and Havenga, he toured the Cape Province in the first part of December 1933 to address a succession of public meetings in an attempt to convince local nationalists to refute the conference decision. It was an exhausting tour as Malan's supporters treated Hertzog with disdain as a traitor. However, Pirow thrived on confrontation. Wennie du Plessis, Hertzog's private secretary, described him as, "Pirow with his teutonic combativeness who eagerly got involved in any promising fight with his strong political fists" (translated). Hence, Pirow stood shoulder to shoulder with Hertzog in facing these hostile crowds.[146]

During their 1934 parliamentary session, Pirow continued his battle with Malan and his followers. In March, Hertzog delegated to him the task to pilot the Status of the Union Bill, the Royal Executive Function and Seals Bill, and an amendment to the South Africa Act through parliament. After the Statute of Westminster of 1931, Hertzog desired to endorse South Africa's constitutional position within the British Empire. The Statute gave legislative effect to the Declaration of Balfour of 1926 and confirmed South Africa as a sovereign

146 Teutoniese donsop-gewilligheid van 'n Pirow wat graag met sterk politieke vuiste in enige belowende geveg ingeklim het. W. du Plessis, *Die goue draad: Op die trekpad van 'n nasie* (Johannesburg, 1970), p. 86

state united by a common allegiance to the British Crown. The three Bills formally removed the powers of the British parliament and monarch in making decisions that affected South Africa.

The British sovereign was compelled to accept the advice of his South African ministers affecting the country, and that the agent of the sovereign in South Africa was the Governor General, appointed by the South African government.

Piloting the Bills through parliament was a challenging task as Pirow had to pacify the hard-line republicans in the NP and the small, but vocal, British imperialist element in the SAP consisting of C.W.A. Coulter (MP for Cape Town Gardens), J.S. Marwick (MP for Illovo), with Colonel Charles Stallard (MP for Roodepoort) as their leader. The British-born Stallard, a veteran of the South African War, had settled in the Transvaal to practise as an advocate at the Johannesburg Bar. He fought with distinction in France during World War I, receiving the Military Cross, and showed the same valour and determination to maintain the closest constitutional link with Britain. With Coulter and Marwick, he opposed the loosening of constitutional ties with Britain as they feared that it could lead to secession from Britain and in turn it would diminish the status of English speakers as British subjects. Stallard felt that Hertzog was hand in glove with Malan to create a large Afrikaner block and to split the English-speaking section. Governor General Lord Claredon, although not in complete agreement with Stallard, was also unhappy with the wording of a clause dealing with his power to execute and sign instructions on behalf of the King.

Pirow, despite two visits by Malise Hore-Ruthven of the Governor General's office, refused to tinker with the clause. Sir Herbert Stanley took this badly and perceived it as a sign that the Hertzog government feared Malan and his supporters, while relying on the docility of English speakers.[147]

Malan and his followers felt that Hertzog, influenced by Pirow, was selling out the interests of Afrikaner nationalism to pacify the pro-British SAP. This suspicion was bolstered by the prime minister's silence during the parliamentary debates. According to Stanley,

147 NA Kew, DO 35/133/1, File 4579/29, Sir Herbert Stanley – Sir Edward Harding, 28 April 1934.

he kept quiet (as Duncan and Smuts had urged him to do) as they feared that he could say something on the spur of the moment, or in the heat of the battle, that could harm the progress of the Bills.[148]

The reality was that it was not necessary for him to be involved, as Pirow loyally reflected his stance on South Africa's sovereignty. The combination of his silence and Pirow's arrogance in his dealings with Malan, Sauer and Swart did much to alienate these men and to create the perception that he was dictating to Hertzog on what should be in the Bills.[149] What irked republican NP MPs was his contemptuous attitude towards them. He treated Frans Erasmus, MP for Moorreesburg and Malan's right-hand man in the Cape NP, with disdain while handling Stallard with courtesy and respect.

In *Die Burger* an outraged Geyer proclaimed that the Status Bill was a farce as Pirow was too eager to soothe the feelings of the imperialists. For Geyer this was final proof that Pirow was a too-clever-by-half opportunist. He vented his disgust in his political notebook:

> … the most cunning knave – in a political sense – in the cabinet. A man that can even answer more ambiguously than Smuts, evading difficult points, and can bluff unashamedly. But P [Pirow] views parliament with too much contempt. (translated)[150]

Geyer took his revenge by placing a cartoon in *Die Burger* on 2 May 1934 to portray the Status Bills as having been set and approved by British imperialists.

Pirow, on introducing the Status of the Union Bill, argued that the Bill merely affirmed the already existing constitutional situation and was designed to remove all doubts concerning South Africa's sovereign independent status. His speech was approved by most of his fellow MPs. The passing of the Bills raised Pirow's standing amongst SAP MPs as he had showed himself to be more than an energetic administrator or a caustic debater. More importantly, he had proven

148 NA Kew, DO 35/133/1, File 4579/3, Sir Herbert Stanley – Sir Edward Harding, 27 April 1934.

149 WCPA, A.L. Geyer papers, Vol. 3, Political notebook, 7 and 27 April 1934.

150 … die mees geslepe skelm – in die politieke sin – van die Kabinet, die man wat selfs gladder as S [Smuts] dubbelsinnig kan antwoord, moeilike punte ontwyk, onbeskaamd kan bluf. Maar P [Pirow] het te veel minagting vir die Parlement. WCPA, A.L. Geyer papers, Vol. 3, Political notebook, 16 June 1934.

himself loyal to the constitutional link with Britain as he made it clear that republicanism was not practical politics:

> I am also at heart a republican, but like many voters, I realise that a republic will not be practical politics in our lifetime, or perhaps in that of our children.[151]

As a result, he was seen as free of the rivalries that existed between English speakers and Afrikaners since the South African War.[152]

Smuts was not too impressed. "On constitutional matters Pirow is a fool", he informed Leif Egeland, a newly elected SAP MP.[153] Obviously Smuts was still smarting after his bruising contest with Pirow in Standerton.

While piloting the three Bills through parliament, Pirow had to cope with his two ministerial portfolios. His main aim was to improve and modernise the struggling railway system – a challenge he approached with gusto, especially as Hertzog allowed him complete freedom on how to manage his portfolio. He also had the advice of a Commission of Experts which included Sir Guy Granet, chairman of the London, Midland and Scottish Railway, and Herr Meyer of the Reichsbahn.[154] As a first step he invested and expanded the railways' rolling stock and improved the management of SAR&H. His interventions had an immediate impact. By April 1934, the Department expected a surplus of £1 000 000 which Pirow planned to use for the modernising and enlargement of the Cape Town harbour.[155] He also used the railways to improve the socio-economic position of poor whites by securing higher wages for them. Havenga first wanted to balance the budget before increasing state salaries.

Pirow used his regular walks with Hertzog to secure the prime minister's support, and Havenga had no choice but to concede.[156] On 31 January 1934, Pirow announced that he had budgeted money to provide financial relief for railwaymen who were prematurely retired during 1930–1933. Furthermore, he recruited more than 10 000 tem-

151 NA Kew, DO 35/334/2, High Commissioner's dispatch, 30 October 1934.

152 ACA UFS, Pirow collection, File 7, Unidentified newspaper clipping of 10 June 1936.

153 Egeland, *Bridges of understanding*, p. 104.

154 *Cape Times*, 17 August 1933.

155 *Cape Times*, 13 and 15 March, 12 April 1934.

156 Pirow, *James Barry Munnik Hertzog*, pp. 214–217.

porary white workers and provided financial assistance for housing, medical services and pensions for employees.[157]

That he had won over hostile railway workers was evident in March 1934 at a public meeting in Salt River. Until 1929 this constituency with its large number of railway workers was a Labour Party fortress. On entering the hall, and when he stood up to speak, he was loudly jeered. But after he made it clear that he would restore as many of the cuts as soon as possible, and that he would place the railwaymen and their families before any thought of wiping out the accumulated deficit, he was enthusiastically applauded and secured a vote of confidence in the government.

As part of Pirow's attempt to modernise the transport system, he created the South African Airways (SAA) as a part of the SAR&H. In August 1929, Union Airways Ltd, owned by Major A.A. Miller, a South African pioneer aviator, started a passenger and postal service between Cape Town, Port Elizabeth, East London and Durban. On the grounds of efficiency and public safety, the government took over the insolvent Union Airways at the end of January 1934. For Pirow the aeroplane was a symbol of modernisation and power. Turning Union Airways into a state project was to show Afrikaners that the government was reducing South Africa's dependence on Britain, and to convince English speakers that South Africa was becoming a sovereign country and a leading power. For him nothing "did more for the prestige of a great power than to show itself regularly and efficiently on the move in established air services".[158] He also wanted a large civilian airline that in any future war in Africa could act as troop carriers.[159] Furthermore, a South African airline with routes to British colonies was needed to encourage the settlement of a permanent white population in the continent as "transportation was the basis of the white man's civilisation in Africa".[160]

157 P.W. Coetzer, J.H. le Roux, *Die Nasionale Party, Vol. IV, Die "Gesuiwerde" Nasionale Party 1934–1940* (Bloemfontein, 1986) p. 163.

158 R.L. McCormack, "Man with a mission: Oswald Pirow and South African Airways, 1933–1939", *Journal of African History*, 20, 1979, p. 545.

159 NA Kew, Avia 2/1879, File 29827/Part III, Memorandum by P. Liesching, 17 September 1934.

160 NA Kew, Avia 2/1879, File 29827/Part IV, High Commissioner's dispatch, 11 September 1936.

On expanding air links for SAA into Africa at the cost of Imperial Airways, a British company that dominated air traffic in Africa, the British found Pirow a tough and ruthless negotiator. He set high standards for the procurement of aircraft. On a visit to South Africa, Sir John Siddely, a prominent aero-engine manufacturer, found Pirow "a rude and impossible man".[161] Pirow's stance was that British planes were inferior to those manufactured by Germany, while the Junkers planes met Pirow's requirements and insistence that the SAA fleet had to be convertible to bombers.[162] British hopes that SAR&H officials could influence Pirow to purchase British aircraft were to no avail. According to the office of the British High Commissioner, the General Manager of SAR&H, T.H. Watermeyer, viewed the SAA as farcical in terms of a business proposition, but that he was unable to stand up to Pirow.[163]

Pirow's German background and the presence of Germans in managing SAA led to accusations in *Aeroplane*, a British periodical, that a German cabal with Pirow in the know was running the airways with hostile intentions to Imperial Airways. On 1 June 1934, Stallard raised these allegations in parliament. Pirow dismissed them as scurrilous and entirely without any foundation.

Pirow also stamped his personality on the UDF. Although he had no military background while Van Ryneveld was a forceful character, notoriously autocratic and stubborn, Sir William Clarke, the British High Commissioner, observed that "Mr. Pirow is certainly more than a match for Van Ryneveld".[164] That Pirow was determined to set the pace in the UDF was evident in April 1936 when he was invited by the British government to discuss defence matters in Britain. Despite the urgings of the High Commissioner, he refused to take along a UDF staff officer. He was adamant that although Van Ryneveld was a hardworking officer and a first-rate pilot, he was not conversant with the detailed aspects of defence. Pirow argued that a

161 NA Kew, Avia 2/1879, File 29827/Part IV, Record of a conversation that took place between Sir John Siddely and the staff officer (Intelligence), Major R.W. Spraggett, MC, RM, on 6 March 1936.

162 McCormack, "Man with a mission", p. 549.

163 NA Kew, Avia 2/1879, File 29827/Part IV, Sir W. Clark – Sir H.A. Batterbee, 27 August 1936.

164 NA Kew, DO 35/186B/11, Sir W. Clarke – Sir H. Batterbee, 27 August 1935.

staff officer would in all probability be biased in support of one particular aspect of defence according to his own point of view, while he as the minister wanted a clear mind in London.[165] Pirow was such a domineering personality that the perception developed in London that Van Ryneveld could not stand up to his minister and that he was without initiative.[166]

The challenge to Pirow's attempt to revamp the UDF was not the generals but the white voter who was unwilling to pay more taxes for such a project. A large standing army was seen as a waste of money for a country without any enemies. Even in British circles there was a feeling that a large defence force in South Africa was unnecessary. For G.A. Wallinger, a member of the High Commissioner's staff, the desire for such a force was a result of "Pirow's undoubted megalomania".[167]

In addition, many Afrikaners felt that the traditional commando system, made up of volunteers, was more than enough to protect the country. Any professional standing army could be an instrument for British imperialism. For republican NP MPs this meant that the SSB was an unsuitable institution for South Africa and an attempt to militarise the Afrikaner youth as potential cannon fodder to fight for the British Empire in any future war.[168] This opposition concerned Sir Maurice Hankey who visited South Africa in September 1934. In a confidential report to Sir Harry Batterbee, Assistant Permanent Secretary for Dominion Affairs, he expressed doubts about the nature of the SSB and speculated that the accusation of militarism could come to haunt Pirow:

> I have a notion, also, that in time people will kick against his "militarism", which, as I reported in my memo for the Defence services, is tantamount to enforcement of the compulsory citizen service law. Pirow is undoubtedly aiming at the creation of a much stronger military spirit than at present exists in the Union. If he can maintain the present policy for ten years he will succeed.[169]

165 NA Kew, DO 35/186B/11, Record of an informal conversation that took place in Cape Town between the commander-in-chief (Vice Admiral F.L. Tottenham, CB, CBE) and the honourable O. Pirow (Minister of Defence) on 20 May 1936.
166 Van der Waag, "Smuts's generals", pp. 48, 55.
167 NA Kew, DO 35/186B/11, G.A. Wallinger – C.R. Price, 19 July 1935.
168 *Die Burger*, 27 January 1934.
169 NA Kew, DO 35/334/3, M.P.A. Hankey – Sir H. Batterbee, 14 September 1934.

To secure public support for an enlarged and modernised UDF, Pirow was obliged to exploit the fear of a black revolt amongst white people. He focused on one of the reasons for the founding of the UDF: the fear of a potential black uprising in Africa, north of the Limpopo, against colonial rule that could imperil the "white civilisation" in South Africa. In July 1933 at a Committee of Imperial Defence meeting in London, he pointed out that although it was not governmental policy, it was possible that South Africa could provide military assistance in the British colonies of Kenya, Uganda and Tanganyika in "a case of protecting whites against natives". Van Ryneveld, who was present at the meeting, told British officials that Pirow's "plea for cooperation in defence of the white civilization of Africa was really a political cry to justify the retention of the Union Defence Forces".[170] Pirow explained to Major A.N. Williams of the Royal Marines, the Royal Navy's intelligence officer and liaison officer with the UDF in South Africa, his "political cry" in more detail:

> He said that France and Italy had a large number of trained native troops which must receive consideration, but that as far as the native was concerned he did not think they constituted a real threat. He had, however, to provide in South Africa a local idea which would fire the imagination of the young South African and get the necessary support. It would be no use for him, as Minister of Defence, to give as a raison d'etre for the retention of the Defence Force, a Locarno war in Europe or a remote war in the North West Frontier of India.[171]

Pirow also confided in Colonel G.M.J. Molyneux, a leading figure in the Natal SAP, that he did believe in the existence of the "black menace", but in order to create a strong permanent force in the UDF to counter a genuine threat from a rising Japan, he had to make public play with black peril tactics.[172]

Pirow started a propaganda campaign about a potential black uprising north of the Limpopo, which could imperil the "white civilisation". Such an uprising could be unleashed by the French policy

170 NA Kew, CAB 63/69, "The military defence situation of South Africa", July 1934.

171 NA Kew, DO 35/186B/11, Report by Major A.N. Williams, R.M. of an interview between the Minister of Defence, Union of South Africa, and the staff officer (Intelligence) Cape Town, with the subsequent action, 17 April 1934.

172 NA Kew, DO 35/186B/11, G.A. Wallinger – C.R. Price, 19 July 1935.

of arming black people and extending equal political rights to them in its colonies.[173] Furthermore, he emphasised the growing military might of imperial Japan and that a Japanese victory over Western colonial powers in Asia could create the opportunity for a black uprising against the colonial powers, unleashing an invasion of South Africa. He reasoned that the country could be in the frontline if the British base in Singapore should fall to Japanese aggression.[174]

The "maintenance and supremacy of our white civilisation" against the threat of a possible invasion by "the black masses to the north", became the essence of Pirow's five-year reorganisation plan for the UDF. This plan, compiled with the assistance of Van Ryneveld and Andries Brink, was presented to parliament on 2 May 1934. The focus of the plan was to create a strategy that would link up the UDF with Britain in Africa to counter any black uprisings. The most sensible way to defend South Africa would be to assist Britain with a mobile force protected by air support. (Here Pirow envisaged that in a war between Britain and Japan, South African troops would be deployed to replace the British forces transferred to the Far East. He was willing for the SAAF to be sent up to the Suez Canal in defence of South Africa.)[175] This meant that the air force had to be enlarged as it also had to defend the country against any possible foreign maritime attacks.[176]

The five-year plan was a significant change to South Africa's security strategy. Up to 1933, the NP government's strategy was limited to the land defence of the Royal Navy base in Simon's Town in terms of the 1922 agreement with Britain. There was a determination not to use the UDF outside of South Africa as it was feared that it could be used to support the British Empire in the case of a European war. The change in South Africa's security strategy convinced Major Williams that Pirow was a "whole-hearted Imperialist", working hard to make South Africa a valuable link of the Empire, and that there was the possibility that South Africa might participate in a war against Japan. Although he accepted that the country would be reluctant to partici-

173 NA Kew, DO 35/334/3, M.P.A. Hankey – Sir H. Batterbee, 14 September 1934.
174 NA Kew, Avia 2/1879, File 29827/Part III, Memorandum by P. Liesching, 17 September 1934.
175 NA Kew, DO 35/334/3, G.A. Wallinger – Batterbee, 24 September 1935.
176 J. Ellis, "Oswald Pirow's five-year plan for the reorganisation of the Union Defence Force, 1933–1939", *Scientia Militaria, South African Journal of Military Studies*, 30/2 (2000), pp. 224–225.

pate in a war against Germany, Williams thought that if the Germans attacked Great Britain, South Africa would come to its assistance.[177] Sir Herbert Stanley was more sceptical, viewing Pirow's eagerness to participate in the defence of Britain's East African territories as an attempt to draw this area into South Africa's sphere of influence.[178]

The "black menace" threat made it possible for Pirow to get his reorganisation plan for the UDF approved by parliament and to secure the first increase since 1924 for the Defence budget. The budget would increase every subsequent year.[179] He used the same approach in his attempts to secure aircraft and poison gas from Britain as air power – using gas and bombs was the most effective and humane way to deal with "native troubles".[180] In September 1934 in a confidential conversation with P. Liesching, political secretary to the High Commissioner, he made it clear that South Africa had to have access to poison gas:

> Personally he was not content to envisage with equanimity the bayoneting of Europeans by Askaries in a war, if the latter could be disposed of by the use of gas. His desire, he said, was to have in South Africa a very small nucleus of chemical experts and the necessary formulas, so that supplies of gas could be developed locally in the event of war.[181]

In London, the Dominions Office viewed Pirow's "black menace" warnings with amusement. As Batterbee explained to Sir William Clark:

> Incidently we have in the past been rather inclined to smile at Pirow's idea of the possibility of a great native uprising in Africa. Regarding it as a form of auto suggestion on his part, carefully nurtured for propaganda purposes.[182]

---

177 NA Kew, DO 35/186B/11, E.J. Harding – Col. Sir Maurice Hankey, 11 April 1934.

178 NA Kew, DO 35/186B/11, Sir Herbert Stanley – H. Batterbee, 16 April 1934.

179 Van der Waag, "The Union Defence Force between the two world wars, 1919–1940", pp. 205, 208.

180 T. Dedering, "Air power in South Africa, 1914–1939", *Journal of Southern African Studies*, 41/2 (2015), p. 462.

181 NA Kew, Avia 2/1879, File 29827/Part III, Memorandum by P. Liesching, 17 September 1934.

182 NA Kew, DO35/186B/11, Batterbee – Hankey, 10 October 1935 with a draft of the letter to Sir Clark attached.

Pirow also used "black menace" tactics to secure support for Hertzog's campaign to merge the SAP and NP, as the unification of Afrikaners and English speakers was essential to secure a white South Africa. The two parties merged, or fused as it was popularly known, to create the United Party (UP) on 5 December 1934. Malan refused to join the new party and became the leader of the remaining rump of the NP. This ultra-nationalistic party, supported by *Die Burger* and *Die Volksblad*, became known as the purified NP. With messianic fervour the NP set out to portray the UP as a puppet of British imperialism, selling out the interests of Afrikaners. For Smuts the merger of the two parties was a less painful process as most English speakers viewed Stallard as a charming but hair-splitting eccentric whose political ideals belonged in the previous century. In October 1934, only a small group followed him out of the SAP to form the Dominion Party (DP) with the sole aim of defending the constitutional link with Britain.

Hertzog was exhausted by the trauma surrounding coalition and fusion politics and he became increasingly dependent on Pirow, who felt that the premiership was within his grasp. Pirow knew that the prime minister was determined that Smuts should not be his successor. To strengthen his position he worked behind the scenes to convince leading and influential English-speaking business leaders such as Abe Bailey, a mining magnate, and John Martin of the Chamber of Mines and the Argus Press group, that with Hertzog's retirement, Smuts also had to leave the political scene because Havenga had to be the prime minister.[183] This was a ruse, as the much loved and respected Havenga had no ambition to be the premier. His sole ambition was to serve Hertzog with whom he had fought with distinction in the South African War – he was wounded on three separate occasions.

Pirow also launched a charm offensive in parliament to secure the allegiance of UP MPs. The surly, abrasive loner without any sense of humour disappeared to be replaced by a warm and engaging person. Ben Schoeman, MP for Fordsburg, found him a pleasant person with a refreshing personality and a fine sense of humour, and became

183 *Die Nuwe Orde*, 30 May 1946.

a loyal follower.[184] He was especially successful in cultivating the friendship of English-speaking former SAP MPs who until 1933 had viewed him as a self-advertising egotist, always trying to override them in a dictatorial way.

According to B.K. Long, a prominent English-speaking MP after the 1938 election, Pirow was a mixer, happy to "gather a little crowd around him, stand them drinks, tell them stories and be on genial, hail-fellow-well-met terms with them." Personally, he found Pirow admirable company, intelligent with a bubbling sense of fun, irreverent and mercurial in repartee.[185] The result was a number of unlikely friendships. Piet van der Byl, former SAP MP for Bredasdorp, an affluent anglicised Afrikaner who was a Cambridge University blue in rowing, a staunch defender of the constitutional link with the British Empire and vehement opponent of the NP, became one of his closest friends. Van der Byl admired Pirow's fine brain and basic personal integrity.[186] Leif Egeland, a liberal SAP MP from Durban, also became a fervent admirer.[187]

Outside of parliament, Pirow went on a charm offensive with loyalists to the British Empire. Colonel G.M.J. Molyneux, a veteran of the South African War and World War I, chairman of the UP in Natal and one of Durban's most revered and influential citizens, became a close personal friend. The High Commissioner's office was amused that a mature person such as Molyneux could have "such violent hero-worship" for Pirow.[188] He was not the only hero-worshipper as Vice Admiral Sir E.R.G.R. Evans, officer-in-command of the Royal Navy's Africa Station, regarded Pirow as his greatest friend in the southern hemisphere: "His company to me was like a glass of champagne after a successful Admiral's inspection."[189]

However, the main target for Pirow's charm offensive was English-speaking journalists whom he played like a master. Apart from respecting him as an extraordinary capable man, they enjoyed his

184 Schoeman, *My lewe in die politiek*, p. 79.
185 B.K. Long, *In Smuts's camp* (London, 1945), 67.
186 Van der Byl, *Top hat to velskoen* (Cape Town, 1973), pp. 75–77.
187 Egeland, *Bridges of understanding*, p. 103.
188 NA Kew, DO 35/186B/11, Wallinger – Price, 19 July 1935.
189 R. Pound, *Evans of the broke: A biography of Admiral Lord Mountevans K.C.B, D.S.O, LL.D* (London, 1963), p. 219.

accessible, affable and stimulating personality, and more importantly, his willingness to share confidential information in off-the-record conversations. His warm relationship with them was reflected in a formal dinner for journalists in the parliamentary dining room at the end of the 1933 parliamentary session. After he went on for some length about physical fitness, Billy Knox, news editor of the *Cape Argus*, challenged him to a walk around Table Mountain. He accepted the challenge on condition that the five other journalists at the table joined them. After dinner in the dark, cold and rain they proceeded with the walk. All the way Pirow joked, talked and told stories about the Bushveld. Arriving at Groote Schuur hours later, he allowed the exhausted journalists to sleep in his ministerial residence. When they woke up late the next morning, they found that he had already left for parliament hours ago.[190]

It was these type of activities as well as his honesty about his own flaws – in the words of his bitter enemy Leslie Blackwell he could be "disconcertingly candid" about them[191] – that made him the blue-eyed boy of the English-medium newspapers.[192] One editor began a leading article, "We do not like Mr. Pirow – we respect him!"[193] Determined to secure Pirow as prime minister, journalists of the English-medium press went out of their way to enhance his reputation as an efficient minister. In the lead were D. Friedmann of the South African Press Association (SAPA),[194] W.A. Bellwood of *The Star*, George Heard of the *Sunday Times* and Arthur Barlow of the *Sunday Express*. Barlow was a brilliant journalist, but also a bitter and vindictive person who felt that life had not rewarded him with the prizes he deserved. He could be a dangerous enemy and he could flay people with sadistic pleasure in his columns. However, Pirow had immunity as Barlow had a physically handicapped son for whom Pirow had secured a job as a librarian at the Supreme Court in Cape Town.[195] This act of kindness left him eternally grateful.

190 *Cape Argus*, 12 October 1959.

191 *Blackwell, Farewell to parliament*, p. 74.

192 Bellwood, *South African back-drop*, p. 57.

193 Calpin, *There are no South Africans*, p. 260.

194 University of the Witwatersrand (hereafter Wits), D. Friedmann papers, Vol. 1, Unpublished memoirs, pp. 45–46.

195 Barlow, *Almost in confidence*, p. 231.

Pirow also won over his fellow UP MPs with his reputation as a man's man. As a former amateur boxer, he regularly sparred with Willy Greenfield, parliament's watchman and fireman.[196] He also had a reputation as a fearless hunter who shot elephant, lion and buffalo. At a banquet for Pirow in London in November 1938, Charles te Water, South Africa's High Commissioner, announced that he had just shot his 60th lion and that Pirow was "the sort of companion one would choose in the veld, endowed with courage and reliability, with a dash of impetuosity."[197]

His image as a man of action and courage was bolstered by his status as a qualified pilot. He was notoriously reckless and found it difficult to find anyone willing to fly with him. But the fact that he could pilot a plane made him an exceptional figure in the eyes of his fellow MPs.

Pirow's popularity in the UP parliamentary caucus made him the odds-on favourite to succeed Hertzog. Hankey in his report to Batterbee in September 1934 confirmed that Pirow's punch and drive meant that he was tipped as a future prime minister, but that he personally had doubts:

> He [Pirow] knows his own mind and has immense courage – two of the principle attributes of a statesman – but my doubt is as to whether he has the political judgement.[198]

Hankey was referring to what he regarded as Pirow's irrational obsessions about the French in Africa and the black peril. Pirow's fellow UP MPs had no doubts about his judgement and viewed him as Hertzog's anointed successor.

196 S. Haigh, *Strangers may be present*, p. 90.

197 ACA UFS, Pirow collection, File 3, *South Africa: A weekly journal for all interested in South African affairs*, 19 November 1938.

198 NA Kew, DO 35/334/3, M.P.A. Hankey – Batterbee, 14 September 1934.

# 5

# The crown prince, 1935–1936

With the opening of the 1935 parliamentary session, the UP had an overwhelming majority of 119 MPs to the 19 of the NP, four of the DP, and the four of the Labour Party. And yet, although small in parliamentary numbers, the NP with the support of the Afrikaans churches, cultural organisations, intellectuals and newspapers was a serious threat to the UP's Afrikaner support base. Malan honed in on the Achilles heel of the government: South Africa's position in a European war involving Britain. While the majority of English speakers were of the opinion that the country would be obliged to side with Britain, most Afrikaners supported neutrality. Hertzog and Smuts, fearing a split on the issue in the UP, referred to it as an academic one that did not require a formally defined party policy. Instead, a promise was made that with the outbreak of any war involving Britain, parliament would have the final say in determining the country's role. This pacified most of the UP supporters but left an opening for Malan to claim that the government with its support of the Simon's Town Agreement was part of a British imperial defence scheme and would automatically be dragged into any British war.[199]

Pirow was determined to neutralise Malan's fear mongering. On 4 February 1935, in a speech in Cape Town to the Imperial Press Conference, a conference representing journalists from the British

199 *Die Burger*, 6 and 9 February 1935.

Commonwealth, Pirow made it clear that South Africa's defence policy would not be part of a general scheme of British imperial defence. A rash commitment to war on behalf of Britain could only embitter relations between Afrikaners and English speakers, leading to large-scale disturbances, possibly civil war. South Africa could only participate in a war where the true interests of the country made it inevitable.

Some of the British delegates were shocked by Pirow's stance, condemning it as "packed with treason", "hostility in every word" and condemned him as a "rebel to the backbone". The *Cape Times* (6 February 1935) came to his defence and stated that South Africa had the right to determine its own defence policy. Pirow also had the support of Duncan who felt that the speech reflected reality and the evolved position of the Dominions in the Empire.[200]

Stallard was incandescent, claiming that neutrality would bring ruin to kith and kin beyond the seas, and disgrace upon South Africans. Although most English speakers viewed the DP as anachronistic, their British heritage and the constitutional link with Britain remained important to them. Aware of this sentiment Stallard set out to convince electors in the predominantly English-speaking constituencies in Cape Town, the Eastern Cape, Natal and Johannesburg that the UP was turning South Africa against Britain. In pressing these attacks, the hope was that English-speaking MPs such as Blackwell would defect to the DP. On 19 February 1935, Stallard initiated a parliamentary debate, claiming that South Africa was an integral and indivisible part of the British Empire and therefore obliged to stand or fall with Britain in any conflict. He repudiated Hertzog's stance that South Africa had the absolute right to neutrality if Britain was involved in a war and insisted that the country had to be part of a British imperial defence scheme. In his dispatch to London, the British High Commissioner reported that Stallard initially had the support of former SAP MPs while speaking, but that he lost their attention when he referred to Britain as "home".[201]

Malan was far more effective in his focus on Afrikaner UP MPs. He pointed out that South Africa could not remain neutral if a foreign

200 Lavin, *Friendship and Union*, p. 588.

201 A.J. Fick, "Die Dominiumparty van Suid-Afrika, 1934–1938", (D.Litt et Phil, University of South Africa, 1979), p. 329.

force attacked the Royal Navy at Simon's Town, shelling a South African port town and coastal gun batteries manned by South Africans. It was a difficult argument to refute and Pirow's response was to play the man and not the ball, accusing him of opportunism and hypocrisy. He hammered on the fact that Malan during his years in the cabinet between 1924 and 1933 had never raised any concerns about the Simon's Town Agreement as a threat to the country's neutrality and that it was only a pretext to split Afrikaners and English speakers into two racial camps to the electoral benefit of the NP.[202]

Although his assault on Malan raised the morale of UP MP's in the House, it could not neutralise the NP's effective use of the Simon's Town Agreement to harm the UP amongst Afrikaners. The NP portrayed Pirow's desire for closer defence ties with British colonies as proof of South Africa being part of an imperial defence plan. Malan rejected his warnings of attacks by "black hordes" from the north as ridiculous. Especially the Japanese threat was condemned as a scare story to convince Afrikaners to give up their freedom by seeking protection from the British Empire.[203] Pirow was so sensitive to this type of criticism that he refused to have British army officers seconded to the UDF.[204]

In its determination to portray Pirow as a puppet of British imperialism, the NP's spokesman on defence, Frans Erasmus, condemned him for allowing regiments such as "The Imperial Light Horse" and "The Duke of Edinburgh's Own Rifle", as well as foreign garments such as the Scottish kilt, in the army. Pirow defended the continued use of these regimental names in the name of tradition and pointed out that he had gone out of his way to create a South African identity in the UDF. Up to his appointment, only English was used in the UDF and he brought in the policy that Afrikaans and English would be used every alternate month.[205]

He also encouraged Afrikaner involvement in the UDF with the creation of Afrikaner-dominated ACF units, namely the President Steyn, Delarey, De Wet, Louw Wepener and the Botha regiments.

---

202 House of Assembly Debates, 19 February 1935, Col. 1800–1806.

203 *Die Burger*, 9 February and 18 November 1935.

204 NA Kew, DO 35/186B/11, Record of Sir John Maffey's meeting with Pirow, 23 June 1936.

205 R.C. Hiemstra, *Die wilde haf* (Cape Town, 2001) p. 197.

Furthermore, the selection boards for officers' training in the UDF went out of its way to appoint Afrikaners. This was made possible by the strict adherence to the bilingualism requirements which excluded many promising English-speaking candidates.[206]

Pirow's position was also strengthened with the success of the SSB, securing him extensive grassroots support in the Afrikaner community. Pirow cynically noted that while some NP MPs publicly condemned the SSB they made sure to secure places for friends and relatives in the battalion. That most Afrikaners supported the battalion was evident in the fact that even a hostile *Die Volksblad* (11 April 1935) praised the SSB for uplifting young South Africans.

In contrast to the NP, the DP hounded Pirow as an underminer of any British influence in South Africa. On 22 March 1935, Stallard demanded a parliamentary select committee to investigate the management of the SAA as it allowed F. Hoepfner, a representative of the German Junkers firm, to be in its service. For him, this German presence led to the "Junkerising of our air service" at the cost of British firms. Pirow defended himself in the House and dampened the criticism,[207] but some former SAP MPs demanded a parliamentary select committee to investigate Stallard's claims. Hertzog ended the agitation by reminding the committee that it was a matter of showing confidence in his leadership. But that these accusations caused the UP some harm was evident in the April 1935 East London North by-election. The constituency was a former SAP electoral fortress, and despite Pirow doing his utmost to rally support for the UP, the DP won the seat.

After Sauer had condemned the founding of the SSB as Nazi-inspired, combined with the growth of small but vocal domestic Nazi groupings, the so-called Shirt movements, Pirow also had to face accusations that he had fascist sympathies. In April 1935, H.D. Esterhuyse, a UP organiser from Calvinia, was so concerned about the accusations that Pirow desired a dictatorship that he demanded to know whether he supported the principle of a *volksregering* (people's government). Through Louis Esselen, General Secretary of the party, Pirow assured him that he was indeed a supporter of democracy.[208]

206 Van der Waag, "South African defence in the age of total war", p. 153.

207 House of Assembly Debates, 22 March 1935, Col. 3644–3654.

208 Unisa, UP archive, Central Head Office, File 15.1.5, I.J. Kok – Esselen, 26 April 1935.

In June 1935, the UP MP Morris Kentridge made an accusation of fascist tendencies after Pirow had made two speeches in Johannesburg about the economic challenges facing the country. Although he made it clear that he did not propagate a society based on fascist corporations, he did advocate a stronger governmental involvement in commerce and a system based on corporative lines. He suggested that what worked well in the professions could work equally well in every other sphere of national activity. He defined it as "ordered self-government among all sections of the economic system", which would especially assist the economically hard-pressed middle class.

Kentridge objected to the suggestion that the middle class should be disciplined in corporations as it was a fascist-inspired system. This led to the *Pretoria News* of 18 June 1935 carrying a leading article, "Is Mr Pirow a Fascist?" The newspaper, accepting Pirow's repudiation of fascist inspiration, answered with a resounding "no". For the *Pretoria News* his ideas on social reconstruction was based on the success of the SSB that had given backbone to a section of the population which needed it.

His stance on order and discipline, as well as his ideas on social reconstruction based on economic progress as a social interest, shared alike by the state and private enterprise, were hailed as interesting ones. In its leading article on 20 June, the editor praised Pirow as an energetic and dynamic minister attempting to resolve the country's economic woes in a period of worldwide chaos in which the old economic textbook had become out of date. The *Rand Daily Mail* (22 June 1935) entered the fray by rejecting his proposed plans as too simplistic, drastic and dangerous, but it did accept his claim that his ideas were not fascist-inspired. The newspaper declared its admiration for his energy and reputation for getting things done.[209]

The accusations of fascism also fell flat as Pirow reflected no anti-Semitic tendencies. He was in fact seen as a friend of the Jewish community. In January1930, he had addressed a public meeting in Bethal where he made it clear to the local Jewish community that the NP had no intention of changing the immigration laws to curtail the influx of Jews from eastern Europe. In his view Jews were the only immigrants "who did not become a burden on the state". Confronted

209 NA Kew, DO 35/334/3, High commissioner's dispatch, 25 June 1935.

by extreme right-wingers on the alleged economic influence of Jews, he made it clear that he was opposed to blaming poverty on Jews and that he refused to judge a person according to his religion.[210] During the Germiston by-election of 1932 he had campaigned diligently for H.J. Schlossberg, the NP's Jewish candidate. In 1934, against the background of rising anti-Semitism in South Africa, he made it clear to Sarah Gertrude Millin, a prominent Jewish author, that the persecution of Jews was "despicable, in fact as cowardly and despicable".[211]

Pirow's condemnation of political intolerance with anti-Semitism did not apply to the black majority, especially with regard to the Cape franchise. To his joy, a fusion government made possible the removal of black people from the common voters' roll in the Cape. For Smuts the establishment of the UP meant that the Cape franchise was dispensable in electoral terms. In February 1936, Hertzog tabled the Representation of Natives Bill which would place Cape black voters on a separate voters' roll with the right to elect three white representatives in the House of Assembly, two white provincial councillors in the Cape Province, and four senators representing the entire black population. For Pirow this Bill would lay to rest the grim ghost of black domination, and the fear that – according to him – was the reason for the oppressive attitude towards blacks. The Representation of Natives Bill would enable black and white to exist side by side without animosity and inimical intentions. Together they would build up South Africa. Malan did not share this sanguine view as he felt that the Bill did not go far enough to secure total segregation. Apart from demanding the removal of coloured people from the common voters' roll, he rejected black representation in the House of Assembly, believing that it would encourage radicals to demand more rights, while their white parliamentary representatives would act as agitators.

Pirow condemned Malan's stance as mere opportunism to bring the UP into disfavour with the electorate. NP MPs were outraged and bombarded his speech with interjections. When the Speaker ordered them to be silent, Malan and four other NP MPs left the House in

210 Shain, *A perfect storm*, pp. 9, 92.
211 Wits, S.G. Millin papers, C, Pirow – Millin, 7 February 1934.

protest. The NP eventually supported the Bill, but Pirow's hostility would remain unforgiven. *Die Burger* (26 February 1936) reckoned that he had lowered himself to the political gutter with his behaviour.

Hertzog had little time to celebrate the acceptance of the Representation of Natives Act, as possible foreign aggression against South Africa became a serious concern after the Italian invasion of Abyssinia (Ethiopia). Addis Ababa was occupied in May 1936, turning this independent African state into an Italian colony. Hertzog was deeply concerned about Italian aggression and was willing to cooperate with Britain to counter it.[212] He had the full support of Pirow who realised that due to the technological advances in aviation the Witwatersrand could be bombed by long non-stop flights from Madagascar, Tanganyika, the Congo and Angola in the near future. The country could no longer feel secure in its geographical isolation.[213] To counter any foreign threat, South Africa had to create a modern air force.

After World War I the main aim of the SAAF was internal security and white hegemony, for example the bombing and machine gunning of rebellious African groups such as the Bondelswart Nama in South West Africa, and to crush the revolt of white miners in Johannesburg. For this the obsolete aeroplanes of the SAAF were adequate, but not for dealing with a modern air force such as that of the Italians. Pirow became convinced that if the SAAF had a thousand modern planes, no foreign country would venture an attack on South Africa. To make this a reality, he announced a scheme to train a thousand pilots over five years with the commensurate expansion in the strength of the air force and the creation of four new airfields.[214]

To implement this scheme the state subsidised flying clubs to train civilians. The aim was to recruit university students. On completion of their training, these new pilots would be contractually obliged to undergo part-time military training and to be placed on the SAAF Special Reserve.[215] This initiative combined with the improvement

212 Le Roux, Coetzer, Marais, *Generaal J.B.M. Hertzog* II, p. 638.

213 T. Dedering, "South Africa and the Italo-Ethiopian war, 1935–6", *The International History Review*, 35, 5, 2013, p. 1019.

214 *Cape Times*, 30 April 1936.

215 J.W. Illsley, "Aerial symbiosis: The interrelationship between military and civil aviation in the Union of South Africa, 1912–1940" (MA, University of Pretoria, 2018), pp. 126–130.

of the infrastructure of the UDF, and the training of its members led to the military correspondent of the *Cape Argus* writing a series of articles that would be published in 1937 as a booklet *The nation on guard: An exposition of South Africa's defence policy*. The journalist was full of praise of Pirow's "tireless zeal and impatience" in improving the UDF from its "quite useless proportions" in 1933.[216]

Pirow found it difficult to spend the money provided by parliament to modernise the UDF. This was because Britain, increasingly concerned about the growing might of Nazi Germany, refused to sell any modern armaments. In 1935, a total of 400 Bren guns were ordered, but after two years only 15 had been delivered.[217] Not even Smuts with his high standing in London could convince Hankey to provide the UDF with the machine guns.[218] Britain's refusal to provide modern aircraft to South Africa was a source of great frustration for Pirow.[219] His relations with British officials became increasingly strained at what he perceived as London's attempts to prescribe to him how he should use the Defence budget. This was evident in his efforts to secure a 15-inch gun battery for the defence of Cape Town. The British War Office and the Committee of Imperial Defence felt that 9.2-inch guns were more than adequate to deal with any hostile naval raiders. Pirow had set his heart on the bigger guns and he was determined to get them, as Admiral Evans warned the High Commissioner:

> Mr. Pirow is a man of action who likes the big thing and who has little use for half measures. Also, he is a great admirer of South Africa and would strongly resent any remark which might be interpreted as belittling his country.[220]

When Admiral F.L. Tottenham, Evans's successor, pointed out that a 15-inch gun battery would be impractical and too costly, Pirow

216 Anon., *The nation on guard: An exposition of South Africa's defence policy* (Cape Town, 1937), p. 52.

217 Van der Waag, "The Union Defence Force between the two world wars, 1919–1940", p. 208.

218 NA Kew, DO 119/1052, Hankey – Smuts, 9 December 1935.

219 NA Kew, Avia 2/1879, File 29827/Part IV, Record of a conversation which took place between Sir John Siddely and the staff officer (Intelligence), Major R.W. Spraggett, MC, RM, on 6 March 1936.

220 NA Kew, DO 119/1052. Admiral E.R.G. Evans – High Commissioner, 10 September 1935 with an attached memorandum on discussions with Pirow.

claimed that such guns were a case of political necessity: The UP was on the crest of the political wave and the party would win the next election, but it was impossible to say what would happen after that. Fearing the potential growth of the NP with the claims that the UP was a puppet of British imperialism, he wanted big defence measures to counter purified propaganda:

> He said that a few mere 9.2's and the modernisation of the existing mountings only meant money spent and little to show for it, and would lead to continual trouble in the "House" [parliament]. He wanted to do something entirely different, something "a la americain", something big, something which would appeal to the people.[221]

Ultimately, the 15-inch guns had to serve as proof that the UDF was not in the service of the British Empire but was the defender of South Africa's neutrality. Pirow's stance also reflected that he was in complete charge of the UDF. According to British officials at the meeting, Van Ryneveld showed signs of distress when his minister showed interest in the political rather than the strategic aspect of coastal defence, but he kept quiet.[222] Smuts, although aware that the British government opposed Pirow's demand for 15-inch guns as too costly and unnecessary, did not oppose it.[223]

To defuse the tensions between Pirow and British officials concerning the defence requirements, he was invited on 7 April 1936 by the British government to visit London to discuss defence matters.[224] For the NP the invitation was proof that he was a pawn of British imperialism. On 6 May, *Die Burger*, apart from a leading article expressing outrage that he was so eager to accept the invite, placed a Boonzaier cartoon of a John Bull figure instructing a cringing and obliging Pirow to rush to London. During the Defence budget of 14

221 NA Kew, DO 35/186B/11, Record of an informal discussion which took place between the Minister of Defence (Mr O. Pirow), Major General A.J.E. Brink DTD, DSO, Brigadier General Sir Pierre van Ryneveld, KBE, DSO, MC, and the commander-in-chief: Africa Station at Admiralty House, Simonstown on 7 May 1936.

222 NA Kew, DO 35/186B/11, M.E. Antrobus – M. MacDonald, 15 May 1936.

223 NA Pretoria, J.C. Smuts papers, Vol. 238, Hankey – Smuts, 27 November 1935; Vol. 239, Hankey – Smuts, 3 July 1936.

224 NA Kew, DO 35/186B/11, Antrobus – Pirow, 19 May 1936.

Cartoon by Boonzaier in *Die Burger,* 6 May 1936.
John Bull instructs Pirow to visit London.

May, the NP claimed that Pirow's London visit signified that South Africa would inevitably be dragged into any European war involving Britain. Malan mocked Pirow's visit as a case of going "home" and that he was betraying South Africa's precious neutrality.

Pirow, sensitive to the accusation that he was not a true Afrikaner, responded, in the words of the *Cape Times*, like a hurricane. After accusing NP MPs of lacking brains, he once more abused Malan as a hypocrite and opportunist for never raising any concerns about the Simon's Town Agreement as a cabinet minister. Malan's response that he was kept in the dark about the true meaning of the agreement led to Pirow demanding an apology to the House as he was attempting to mislead members. An outraged C.R. Swart, NP MP for Ladybrand, retaliated that Pirow's London visit was on the instructions of "His Master's Voice". The debate had intensified the NP's loathing of Pirow. In *Die Burger* (15 May 1936) Geyer warned that in the future there will be a day of reckoning in which he will have to account for his abusive behaviour. Determined to settle a score with him the newspaper reported his arrival in London on 8 June on its front page under the heading, "*Minister Pirow by sy hoofkwartier*" (Minister Pirow at his headquarters).

In London Pirow was given red-carpet treatment. Lord Claredon, the Governor General in South Africa, urged King Edward VIII to take note of Pirow:

> He is a very able little man and, although a German by birth and a Republican at heart, is sound from an Imperial point of view… He has however to contend with political difficulties here in so far as many Imperial questions are concerned, but is none the less anxious and ready to co-operate: indeed his courage and determination have enabled him to go farther than many of us thought it possible. Sooner or later he will undoubtedly become Prime Minister of the Union: he is therefore well worth taking notice of…[225]

Claredon's advice was taken to heart and meetings were arranged for Prime Minister Stanley Baldwin and the King to meet Pirow. Pirow was determined to make a good impression to secure modern armaments for the UDF and to bolster his standing as Hertzog's successor. To do so he asked Van der Byl to accompany him as an unofficial aid. It was a shrewd move as Van der Byl, a World War I veteran with a distinguished military record and a reputation as a loyal supporter of the British Empire, went out of his way to convince the British of Pirow's good intentions. Van der Byl's friend, Sir Campbell Stuart, a prominent businessman, arranged a banquet in Pirow's honour with 70 guests which included newspaper editors, the First Sea Lord, the Secretary of War, the Chief of the Imperial General Staff, the King's private secretary, and prominent businessmen. Van der Byl helped Pirow to prepare his speech, emphasising that up until the implementation of the Statute of Westminster, Pirow had been anti-British, but since then he was neither anti-British nor pro-German but entirely pro-South African. However, as South Africa's interests were tied up with those of Britain, he would work closely with London:

> South Africa and the British Empire have ninety-nine and nine-tenths of their interest in common today, so we stand together. The whole strategy of the Empire has changed. Cape Town is now once more a half-way house to the east and to Singapore. South Africa being hostile to England is unthinkable, and we should have to have a civil war before that.[226]

225 Royal Archives, Windsor PS/GVI/C 051, The Earl of Clarendon – King Edward VIII, 1936, 001, Clarendon to Edward VIII, 28 May 1936, p. 6. (I am grateful to John Lambert for this document.)

226 M. Kentridge, *I recall: Memoirs of Morris Kentridge* (Johannesburg, 1959), p. 291.

The audience was impressed and the *Daily Telegraph* (10 June 1936) published a glowing profile of Pirow. In the *Spectator* (12 June 1936) B.K. Long, a former editor of the *Cape Times*, wrote a laudatory profile praising Pirow as an outstanding minister and a future prime minister. For Van der Byl it was clear that Pirow's intelligence, clear mind, quick decisions and frankness had made a good impression, that he had the world at his feet, and had established himself as a future prime minister.[227] For the next three weeks the British authorities shared military secrets with Pirow, hosted visits to military bases and factories, allowed him to view weapons still on the secrets list and meet senior political and military figures.[228] He used this opportunity to convince the War Office that Cape Town had to be defended by a 15-inch gun battery. The British government was fully aware of Pirow's eagerness to boost his image with grand designs. This was articulated in a profile the Dominion Office provided to Edward VIII before their meeting:

> Mr. Pirow is known to be exceedingly ambitious and to see himself as a future Prime Minister of the Union. He believes in advertisement and has frankly American ideas. Of publicity as an aid to the success of his schemes, for which to him the recommendations is their power to capture public imagination. What always appeals to him is something big, e.g. speed in the air (he is an enthusiastic airman and pilot) and power and range in guns (he is an advocate of 15 inch guns for the Capetown defence).[229]

To boost his credentials as Hertzog's successor and to secure his goodwill in any future European conflict, the British government approved his request for 15-inch guns. To protect the city during the period it would take to install such a gun battery, the monitor HMS *Erebus* was offered on loan to South Africa. The *Erebus* with its two 15-inch guns, launched in 1916, was a stable gun platform, in effect a floating gun battery, designed with a shallow draft to provide artillery support for land operations. As the *Erebus* needed refitting, it was only used for gunnery training and it would take a while before it could sail to South Africa.[230]

227 Van der Byl, *Top hat to velskoen*, pp. 139, 141–142.

228 NA Kew, DO 35/186B/11, R.A. Wiseman – Antrobus, 9 July 1936.

229 NA Kew, DO 35/186B/11, The honourable O. Pirow, Minister of Railways and Harbours and of Defence of the Union of South Africa.

230 D. Visser, "Anglo-South African relations and the Erebus scheme", *Scientia Militaria. South African Journal of military studies*, 35/1 (2007), pp. 73, 90.

It quickly became clear that the refitting and maintenance of the *Erebus* would be more costly than anticipated. In addition, it was realised that if the *Erebus* was moored in Cape Town harbour, her firing range would be limited and a hostile cruiser would be able to remain out of range and shell the city at leisure. As it was essential for Pirow to present to parliament a complete scheme for the defence of Cape Town, he demanded support and assistance from Britain to ensure that the use of a monitor was a viable protection scheme. The High Commissioner in Pretoria promptly urged Malcolm MacDonald, Secretary of State for Dominion Affairs, to provide support: "It is important that we should do our best to meet the wishes of Pirow who would be rather seriously embarrassed politically in the event of the scheme collapsing."[231] MacDonald concurred and wrote to Sir Samuel Hoare, First Lord of the Admiralty, to give the most sympathetic consideration to Pirow's requests: "I need not say how important it is from the political point of view that we should do everything that we can to help him."[232]

The British government's willingness to provide arms remained limited to the *Erebus* as the Air Ministry refused Pirow's request for modern aircraft.[233] In Pretoria the High Commissioner, worried about the political ramifications, urged MacDonald to secure twelve new training aircraft for the SAAF to prevent Pirow's much acclaimed programme of pilot training being impeded.[234]

In London the British establishment's adulation of Pirow, combined with his supreme self-confidence, led to some embarrassment as he proposed himself as a mediator between Germany and Britain. He sent a detailed message to Hertzog expressing anxiety about anti-German feelings in Britain regarding German re-armament. Through Gie and Hertzog, he proposed that he and Lord Halifax, leader of the House of Lords, should go on a peace mission to Berlin to relieve Anglo-German tension. Hertzog communicated this pro-

231 NA Kew, DO 35/186B/11, Telegram from the High Commissioner, 2 November 1936.

232 NA Kew, DO 35/186B/11, M. MacDonald – Sir Samuel Hoare, 5 November 1936.

233 NA Kew, DO 35/186B/11, Visit of Mr. Pirow. Note of the last meeting between the Secretary of State and Mr. Pirow on the 1st July, 1936.

234 NA Kew, DO 35/186B/11, Telegram from the acting High Commmissioner, 23 September 1936.

posal to Emile Wiehl, Germany's diplomatic representative, who forwarded it to Berlin. Pirow's behaviour was not out of the ordinary as Britain was in the grip of what the historian Tim Bouverie describes as "that curious phenomenon of the appeasement years: the amateur diplomats".[235]

From 1934 a string of politicians, businessmen, journalists and cultural figures – to the frustration of British foreign affairs and its ambassador in Berlin – would visit Germany to secure meetings with Hitler in an attempt to improve relations. The difference with Pirow was that he wanted to act as a representative of the British government. The German foreign ministry was shocked and annoyed by Pirow's presumptuous attitude,[236] while the British government was equally unimpressed. The British excuse to prevent Pirow's mission was that an Italian delegation was in Germany at the time. It was claimed that because of strained relations with Italy as a result of sanctions imposed by Britain, it would be diplomatically awkward for both the British and Italian missions to be in Germany at the same time.[237] To the relief of the British government nothing came of the proposed mission.

Pirow returned to South Africa on 1 July, travelling with various civilian airlines via Amsterdam, Budapest and Athens to Cairo in Egypt. From Cairo he was to return to South Africa on an SAAF flight. This flight provided an opportunity to win the friendship of Stallard, one of his severest critics. Although an eccentric with political views stuck in the Victorian age, Stallard's military record, charm and affability ensured that he was viewed with much affection in the English-speaking community. Securing Stallard's friendship would strengthen his attraction to these voters and soften the DP's criticism. His efforts as Minister of Defence to take leaders of opposition parties into his confidence about defence matters made it possible to secure a place for Stallard on the SAAF aircraft to Cairo.[238]

---

235 T. Bouverie, *Appeasing Hitler: Chamberlain, Churchill and the road to war* (London, 2019), p. 47.

236 NA, Pretoria, PM 4/2/12 Vol. 1, S.F.N. Gie – J.B.M. Hertzog, 16 June 1936; Bourne and Watt, *Studies in international history*, pp. 409–411.

237 W.R. Kienzle, "German policy towards the Union of South Africa, 1933–1934", (Ph.D., Pennsylvania State University, 1974), pp. 20–21.

238 NA Kew, DO 35/335/1, Letter from the High Commissioner's office – Dominion Office, 17 July 1936.

Stallard loved every second of the flight and stay in Cairo. Pirow had won him over, and they became close friends.[239] Apart from Pirow genuinely enjoying Stallard's company, their friendship also had the benefit that DP criticism of his portfolios became less hostile.

On his way to South Africa Pirow had a stopover in Nairobi where he made it clear to the colonial authorities that South Africa would work for a common defence policy with British Africa. These were no empty words as was evident in a conference he had in Pretoria with generals Andries Brink, Manie Botha and Jack Collyer on 18 August 1936. It was concluded that to defend South Africa against any possible Italian aggression, or that of Germany to recapture her lost colonies by force, initial resistance had to be offered as far north as Tanganyika.[240]

To prepare the UDF for fighting in this region, Pirow instructed Collyer, a former mounted infantryman with 50 years' service in Africa and the UDF's Chief of Staff during World War I, to produce a "Manual for Bush Fighting". In January 1937, Colonel George Brink, who was appointed to assist Collyer, warned that such a manual was undesirable and would prove a too formidable task. He suggested that a critical history of the UDF's campaign in German East Africa during World War I would be of greater value to prepare UDF officers for service in Africa. The result was *The South Africans with General Smuts in German East Africa* by Collyer in 1939.[241]

Pirow's visit to Britain, despite the embarrassment of the proposed mission to Germany, had met all the expectations of the British. According to Leo Amery, a leading British politician, he had made "a very favourable impression here".[242] This was an opinion

239 Unisa, UP archive, C.F. Stallard papers, Correspondence July–September 1936, Stallard – Pirow, 20 July 1936, 7 and 23 September 1936; Correspondence October–December 1936, Stallard – Pirow, 20 November 1936.

240 Department of Defence Documentation Centre (hereafter DOD), CGS 944/2, Memorandum in connection with matters discussed with the Minister by Major General Brink and BDR; Generals Botha and Collyer at Pretoria on Tuesday 18th August, 1936. (I am grateful to Evert Kleynhans for this document.)

241 E. Kleynhans, "Bush fighting? The Union Defence Force, interwar defence schemes and the evolving South African threat perception", (Paper delivered at the symposium "The aftermath of the First World War in southern Africa: Repercussions and transformations", Unisa, 12–13 November 2018.)

242 J. van der Poel, *Selections from the Smuts papers, Vol. VI, December 1934–August 1945* (Cambridge, 1973), p. 45.

shared by the influential Hankey.[243] He blotted his copybook in London with an interview on his arrival in South Africa in which he hinted that he wanted Germany to return to Africa as a colonial power to maintain a white civilisation in Africa. Pirow was adamant that although South West Africa and Tanganyika would never be returned to Germany, the country should be compensated for this loss in other parts of Africa.

Pirow seemingly did not think it was a controversial statement since he had found that some influential figures in Britain shared this view. Edward VIII had made it clear to him that he was willing to give German colonies back to Germany in a bid to secure peace in Europe.[244] This was not the view of the British government or of public opinion. The *News Chronicle* (15 July 1936) was disgusted, condemning him as too pro-German, an oppressor of Africans, and as a "dangerous little man".

An irate Baldwin was obliged to state in the House of Commons that Pirow was only reflecting his personal views. Although Smuts cynically observed that Pirow's stance was one of cheap generosity to compensate Germany at the cost of others for refusing to return South West Africa,[245] it did him no harm amongst conservative white people concerned about their future in Africa. The English-speaking community also did not see his stance as a pro-German or a pro-fascist one; especially as he warned in a speech to the Caledonian Society in Pretoria in November 1936 that the flaws in democracy – selfishness, individualism, promiscuity and inefficiency – had to be confronted as it made democracy vulnerable to the challenges of fascism and communism.[246]

---

243 NA Pretoria, Smuts papers, Vol. 239, Hankey – Smuts, 3 July 1936.

244 *Die Nuwe Orde*, 24 January 1946.

245 Van der Poel, *Selections from the Smuts papers, Vol. VI, December 1934–August 1945*, p. 401.

246 *Die Suiderstem*, 30 November 1936.

# 6

# The gladiator, 1937–1938

Pirow's British visit had a profound effect on him. Duncan noted that he had returned from London "full of ideas for more defences, bigger guns, faster airplanes, new gas methods."[247] To implement these ideas he commissioned Colonel George Brink to visit Britain, Germany, France and Italy to study their armed forces. On his return, he was appointed Director of Army Organisation and Training. He was promoted to Deputy Chief of Staff in 1938 and played a leading role in reorganising the army and improving its training.[248] Pirow also brought about far-reaching changes in the high command of the UDF. General Andries Brink, who had retired in August 1937, was replaced by advocate A.H. Broeksma, KC, a civilian and friend of Pirow, as the Secretary of Defence. The UDF was divided into two with the retired Andries Brink's appointment as Chief Commandant of the commandos.

To deal with the shortage of weapons and military equipment, Pirow also set up a War Supplies Board in May 1937. The first step of the Board was to initiate the process to establish a small arms ammunition factory.[249]

Although obsessed with his ideal to create a modern and power-

247 Lavin, *Friendship and Union*, p. 615.

248 Van der Waag, "South African defence in the age of total war", pp. 152–153.

249 C. Birkby, *Uncle George: The Boer boyhood, letters and battles of Lieutenant-General George Edwin Brink* (Johannesburg, 1987), pp. 95–96.

ful UDF, Pirow could not afford to neglect the demands of party politics. Because he was seen as Hertzog's successor, the local associations of UP-held parliamentary constituencies continuously begged for the prestige of a visit by him. In August 1935, P.N. Basson of Prins Albert in the Cape Province complained to Louis Esselen that they have been waiting for two years for a visit.[250] The usually calm and efficient Esselen eventually became flustered with this stream of requests, as Pirow with two demanding portfolios found it difficult to find time for public meetings.[251] His presence at UP public meetings, or social occasions, became even more valued. When he was able to visit a constituency, the public meetings he addressed were packed with hundreds of people. The combination of his charm and oratorical skills secured him a growing army of grassroots supporters in the UP. By then he had even won over Esselen, Smuts's ally and friend, who addressed him as Ottie, a name used only by Pirow's closest friends.[252]

Pirow's status as a prime minister-in-waiting was bolstered by his leading role after Edward VIII abdicated on 10 December 1936. For Hertzog the abdication provided an opportunity to strengthen South Africa's sovereign status and the divisibility of the Crown: that the loyalty of South Africa was not to Britain but to the king of South Africa. Pirow piloted His Majesty King Edward the Eight's Abdication Bill and the Coronation Oath Bill through parliament. Both the NP and DP attempted to use these Bills to divide the UP and to attract potential supporters. For Malan the Bills had to include a resolution reaffirming the right of any member of the British Commonwealth to withdraw from it.

The DP opposed the Bills as a thinly disguised attempt to establish the claim of the South African parliament to proclaim its own king, and when the time was ripe, the power to depose him. By then the DP was no longer a threat to the UP. The party had fared dismally in the 1936 provincial council elections, winning only eight seats: one each in the Transvaal and Cape Province and six in Natal. Pirow,

250 Unisa, UP archive, Central Head Office, File 15.1.2 (Part 1), P.N. Basson – Esselen, 31 August 1935.

251 Unisa, UP archive, Central Head Office, File 15.1.5, Esselen – D. Erasmus, 26 April 1938; and File 43.1 (Part 1), Esselen – P. White, 30 July 1935.

252 Unisa, UP archive, Central Head Office, File 15.1.10, Esselen – Pirow, 25 January 1938.

fully aware that he needed the support of English-speaking UP MPs to be prime minister, wanted to affirm that he was not anti-British. This meant that he responded with patience and respect to the jingoistic paranoia of the DP. He told the journalist Horace Flather that in his Bills he would include one or two clauses that he did not particularly care for so that he could drop it if the DP opposed them.[253] This cynical approach intensified the NP's loathing of him.

The NP MPs were not the only ones offended by Pirow's behaviour and Hofmeyr increasingly became alienated. In the 1936 parliamentary recess, the NP in an attempt to portray the UP as a liberal party campaigned for a law to prevent interracial marriages. To neutralise this threat, some UP MPs demanded a Bill to prohibit such marriages as well as one to bar Indian traders from employing white women. Hofmeyr, in an interview with the *Sunday Times* (14 February 1937), made it clear that the cabinet did not back these demands.

Pirow, realising that this statement would play into the hands of the NP, responded in an interview with *Die Suiderstem* (16 February), a UP supporting Afrikaans newspaper, with a promise that by the end of the parliamentary session no white woman would be in the service of an Asian. Fearing damage to party unity, Hertzog and Smuts ordered Pirow and Hofmeyr to draw up a formula that would satisfy both sides. When left on their own, Pirow turned to Hofmeyr and nonchalantly said: "What shall we say to save the country?" When Hofmeyr told this to Alan Paton, his future biographer, Paton noted the amount of admiration, and even of envy, in his voice.[254] The two antagonists agreed on a formula of a select parliamentary committee to investigate the issue of a Bill to prevent white women from being employed by Indians.

The NP proclaimed the compromise as a defeat for Pirow and a warning that there was no place for Afrikaners in the liberal UP. In reality the situation was the exact opposite, as Hofmeyr was isolated in the cabinet, and Smuts and Esselen had to go out of their way to save him from himself.[255] The compromise only postponed the showdown between the two antagonists because in April the select

253 H. Flather, *The way of an editor* (Cape Town, 1977), p. 101.
254 Paton, *Hofmeyr*, p. 261.
255 Unisa, UP collection, Central Head Office, File 15.1.9, L. Esselen – J. Martin, 21 February 1937.

committee recommended a White Women's Employment Bill in line with Pirow's wishes. Hofmeyr refused to proceed with such legislation. In the cabinet Kemp, Grobler and Pirow insisted that it should be implemented but, concerned about party unity, Hertzog decided to shelve the Bill.

This led to a clash in the cabinet, and Hertzog demanded that the three ministers back down. Pirow refused to do so and it was only after the prime minister threatened to cancel his planned visit to London to attend an imperial conference for prime ministers that Pirow capitulated. Hofmeyr, in a "private and urgent" but not posted letter to Smuts, made it clear that he was wounded by Pirow's behaviour as it had embarrassed his efforts to find a solution on the issue of white women working for Indians.[256] Esselen, deeply concerned about party unity, feared that it would take some time to heal the breach between Pirow and Hofmeyr,[257] and by June 1937 observed that their relationship was getting worse.[258]

Pirow's assertiveness must be seen against the background of an increasingly aggressive and confident NP targeting him. He could not afford to be seen as accommodating to Hofmeyr. Determined to cut him down to size, the NP consistently attacked his stewardship of the SAR&H portfolio, claiming that he was a pawn of British imperialism as he did too little to support Afrikaner railway workers. His launch of the development programme to enlarge Cape Town harbour at a cost of £2 250 000 in order to deal with the growing number of vessels visiting the port city was condemned as being part of the British imperial defence plan. Pirow's response was to mock these attacks by questioning the intellectual abilities of NP MPs, and to portray Malan as an opportunist and a liar for claiming that as a member of the NP government he was kept in the dark about what the Simon's Town Agreement entailed.

As usual, this accusation outraged NP MPs and led to another bad-tempered Defence budget vote on 8 May 1937. Erasmus argued that as the money budgeted for the UDF had expanded from £760 000

256 Wits, J.H. Hofmeyr papers, Dg File 2, Hofmeyr – Smuts, 27 May 1937.

257 Unisa, UP collection, Central Head Office, File 15.1.9, L. Esselen – J. Martin, 15 April 1937.

258 Unisa, UP collection, Central Head Office, File 43.1 (Part 1), L. Esselen – F. Joubert, 2 June 1937.

in 1932 to £1 666 090, it signified that South Africa was to be in service of the British Empire.

The NP's concern about South Africa's possible involvement in a future British war was not baseless. Pirow in a farewell meeting with Wiehl, who was recalled in September 1937, made it clear that in the case of British involvement in a continental war, it would be natural that South Africa and other Commonwealth nations would eventually be dragged into the conflict.[259] In parliament, Pirow sidestepped this issue by reducing the budget debate to a mudslinging contest. He did so by being his abusive best, treating Erasmus as a buffoon who was completely ignorant of military affairs. In the House the NP's loathing of Pirow reached boiling point. *Die Burger* (12 May 1937) published a cartoon of Pirow as an inflated bullfrog armed with a sword.

Cartoon by Boonzaier in *Die Burger*, 12 May 1937, depicting Pirow as a bullfrog.

The 1937 parliamentary session was a bruising one that enhanced Pirow's reputation as a political gladiator and confirmed his status as Hertzog's successor. In April 1937, MacDonald informed his British cabinet colleagues:

> Mr. Pirow's views are of considerable importance as he is a dominant personality in South African politics and likely eventually to become Prime Minister of the Union.[260]

259 Kinzle, "German policy towards the Union of South Africa", p. 25.

260 *Rand Daily Mail*, 29 January 1968.

After the parliamentary session, Pirow went on a political tour of the Free State where the NP was making worrying progress. He addressed a succession of public meetings to explain why the government did not ban racially mixed marriages and defended its stance on neutrality. On the demands for legislation to prohibit racially mixed marriages, he proclaimed that it was a ghastly insult to Afrikaners to claim that white people needed a law to stay racially pure. On neutrality in a war involving Britain he used his tried and tested method of bashing Malan's stance on the Simon's Town Agreement as opportunistic.[261]

Malan retaliated by accusing Pirow of being a weakling for failing to stand up to Hofmeyr's liberalism. He depicted Hofmeyr as a circus lion tamer leading Pirow by a rope symbolising British imperialism and racial equality and that he was sacrificing the interests of the Afrikaner to maintain the unity of the UP. He also went out of his way to portray Pirow as an abuser of power by returning to their 1925 clash on district surgeons in Soutpansberg when he had opposed his demands to dismiss doctors simply because they were not supporters of the NP. For him any party using such methods had to come to a fall.

*Die Burger* also hammered away by claiming that he was influenced by the alien ideology of fascism and in doing so he was not a true Afrikaner. On 7 July 1937, the newspaper published a cartoon of railway workers being obliged to give him a Nazi salute.

Cartoon by Boonzaier in *Die Burger*, 7 July 1937.
"Hail Pirow" – Pirow greeted with the Hitler salute.

261 *Die Suiderstem*, 28 May and 7 June 1937.

In reality, Pirow went out of his way to distance himself from national socialism. He opposed high-profiled national socialist activities amongst Germans in South West Africa and complained to Wiehl in February 1937 that the Nazification of all German cultural activities in South Africa made his participation in them impossible.[262] He also publicly declared his support of democracy. On 6 June 1937, he announced "that South Africa will never depart from its democratic system, and it will be deplorable, therefore, if that system is undermined or rendered impotent."[263] But those concerned about his German background noted that in a speech in October 1937 to Afrikaner students he referred to democracy as encouraging selfishness, exploitation and sterility. He felt that it was a waste of time and that the idealistic alternatives were communism and fascism. Although he rejected communism, he remained silent on fascism.[264] However, at a public meeting in January 1938 at Piet Retief, he made it clear that although national socialism was the best system for Germany, the importation of such a system into South Africa would lead to civil war within four weeks, and that South Africa's democratic system could be improved but not by the means of foreign systems.[265]

Pirow, aware of what a dangerous enemy Malan was, attempted to smooth relations by inviting him, together with Stallard, to accompany him on a three-week official tour of Africa to negotiate air routes and postal contracts for SAA. He was to visit Angola, French Equatorial Africa, the Belgian Congo, Uganda and Kenya. Malan refused the invite, but Stallard, an old and lonely bachelor, joined him. By then their friendship had led to some concern in the DP as Marwick felt that his party leader was too close to Pirow.[266] The SAA Junkers 52 departed from Pretoria on 9 August and returned on 27 August. The various colonial governors treated Pirow with full military honours. Although Stallard did not participate in the meet-

262 Bourne and Watt, *Studies in international history*, pp. 405–406.

263 Calpin, *There are no South Africans*, p. 391.

264 R. Ovendale, *"Appeasement" and the English-speaking world: Britain, the United States, the Dominions, and the policy of "appeasement"*, (Cardiff, 1975), p. 53.

265 *Cape Times*, 31 January 1938.

266 Unisa, UP archive, C.F. Stallard papers, Correspondence July – September 1937, Stallard – Marwick, 6 August 1937.

ings, Pirow allowed him to consult confidential documents and the minutes.[267]

Pirow returned to South Africa with the bolstered idea that all the territories he had visited, except those of the French, were areas where a white population could flourish and had to be kept for them if the Afrikaner wanted to survive.

The 1938 parliamentary session, with a general election scheduled for 18 May, was a short and volatile one. The NP, loathing Pirow as too clever-by-half and too arrogant – his smirking and contemptuous attitude drove them mad – attacked him relentlessly. He was condemned as an inefficient and absent Minister of the SAR&H because he was more interested in the Defence portfolio.

He was also condemned as too autocratic after withdrawing the Spoorbond as a representative organisation of Afrikaner railway workers – the NP manipulated the union for political purposes. H.F. Verwoerd, the editor of the newly established NP-supporting *Die Transvaler* (10 January 1938), asserted that Pirow had declared war on the Afrikaner railway worker as he did too little to improve their financial position while ignoring the policy that all railway workers had to be fully bilingual. The NP's favourite tactic was the accusation that he only cared for the interests of the British Empire. His purchase policy for locomotives was held up as proof. As part of Pirow's modernising plan for the railways, the government invited tenders for the purchase of locomotives. The German quote was £2000 per locomotive cheaper than the British one. Sensitive to the concerns of English speakers in the UP, Pirow ordered 45 locomotive engines from Britain and 116 from Germany.[268] The NP was outraged about the British order and lambasted Pirow in a free-for-all parliamentary debate. Pirow's response was to mock the intelligence and abilities of NP MPs, claiming that their contributions would shame a school debate.

On 23 March 1938, Pirow's career nearly came to a premature end when he was involved in two crash landings. The Airspeed En-

267 Unisa, UP archive, C.F. Stallard papers, Correspondence July – September 1937, "Report of the aerial tour undertaken by the Minister of Railways and Harbours and Defence in August, 1937".

268 *The Star*, 24 November 1937.

voy that transported him to Cradock for the opening of an agricultural show was badly damaged when the undercarriage collapsed on landing in Bloemfontein. The undercarriage of the replacement Airspeed collapsed at the Cradock landing strip.[269] Although shaken by the crashes, Pirow still managed to give his speech. Despite the trauma of the day, his faith in air travel remained unshaken. He left by plane the next day to observe military manoeuvres at Piet Retief in the Transvaal.

Pirow's determination to get to the exercise reflected his obsession to prepare the UDF for what he viewed as an inevitable war to resist Japanese imperialism. For him South Africa's status as gateway to the West meant that the country would be dragged into a war when Japan turned its sights onto the Asian colonies of Britain, France and the Netherlands.[270] By then the thousand-pilot training scheme was taking off. A hundred Hawker Hart aircraft, purchased from Britain, started to arrive in the country to be used for the training of pilots. To assist with the training process, a new airbase in Pretoria, the Waterkloof Air Station, was built. This allowed the Swartkop airfield to be solely used for training purposes.[271]

After the UDF exercise, Pirow gave his undivided attention to the parliamentary election. Before nomination day some rural UP constituencies vied for the prestige to have him as their MP. Pirow remained loyal to Gezina where the NP's Theo Wassenaar, a poet and a prominent medical eye specialist, opposed him. Hertzog relied heavily on Pirow as the UP had to fight on two fronts. In predominantly English-speaking constituencies, the party had to cope with the DP, and in the Afrikaans areas with the vehement onslaught of the NP. In Natal where the DP was a threat, English speakers viewed Pirow with suspicion as being too pro-German and being soft on republicanism. He rejected these accusations with great charm and portrayed himself as a friend of Britain. According to Horace Flather, editor of the *Natal Daily News*, Pirow had the magnetic quality of leadership that captured a crowd and deceived the discriminating; he was both charming and devious. He was so charming and convincing

269 *Cape Times*, 24 March 1938.
270 *The Star*, 11 May 1938.
271 Illsley, "Aerial symbiosis", p. 142.

that Flather was without doubt that Pirow had given him his solemn assurance that if Britain went to war with Germany, South Africa would fight beside her.[272]

It was a far more challenging task to face the NP onslaught. In the Transvaal Pirow's public meetings were packed with NP supporters who disrupted proceedings by accusing him of being a sell-out to British imperialism. He was also accused of doing too little to protect the white minority with stricter segregation laws. Leading these attacks was Verwoerd in *Die Transvaler* who accused Pirow of being arrogant, self-important with dictatorial tendencies and a tool for Jewish capital. At a meeting in Braamfontein in Johannesburg, Pirow was questioned on whether he was aware of the Jewish problem in the country. He denied the existence of such a problem.[273]

In Gezina, Wassenaar portrayed Pirow as a leader in a party dominated by Jews, capitalists, liberals and imperialists and that he was an "arch enemy of Afrikanerdom in the Railways", while he was responsible for not taking legal steps against the evil of racially mixed marriages. Wassenaar's energetic campaign forced Pirow to return to Gezina to address a series of public meetings in order to secure his own election.

Pirow took the battle to the NP by stating that republicanism could plunge South Africa into a civil war as English speakers would not accept a republic. On the issue of racially mixed marriages, he exploited the NP's so-called "bastard placard". The poster showed a black man, a white woman and racially mixed children, the result of miscegenation as a product of the UP's policy of not prohibiting mixed marriages. Pirow with great emotion accused the NP of circulating a mortal insult to "our woman-hood".

At a public meeting in Potchefstroom, packed with hostile NP supporters, he asked the audience to stand up and repudiate this shameful libel on South Africa's white mothers and daughters. This tactic was so successful that nothing came of the NP's attempt to pass a motion of no confidence in the government.[274] Meeting after meeting Pirow would silence NP disrupters by hammering on the fact that

272 Flather, *The way of an editor*, p. 101.

273 *Die Transvaler*, 13 April 1938.

274 Pirow, *James Barry Munnik Hertzog*, p. 210

the poster was an insult to white women and did incalculable harm to the reputation of white people amongst the black community. Pirow also boasted with great effect how he had used the SAR&H and the UDF to address the poor-white problem, and that voters had to vote UP if they wanted continued assistance.

The political tide was with Pirow. His reputation as a dynamic Minister determined to eradicate white poverty, combined with his strict stance on segregation, meant that the NP's accusations were ignored while his exploitation of the "bastard" poster threw the NP campaign off stride.

In Gezina he held his seat with a comfortable majority, securing 3436 votes to the 1529 of Wassenaar. For *Die Transvaler* (19 and 20 May 1938) Pirow's victory was made possible by the support of Jewish financial power that provided his campaign with 200 cars to convey voters to the polling booth. It was claimed that the Jewish community in Johannesburg alone provided his campaign with 30 cars. In a leading article on 20 May, Verwoerd declared the UP victory "*'n Joodse oorwinning*" (A Jewish victory).

The UP returned to parliament with a massive majority of 111 seats. For the DP the election result was catastrophic, as it had won only eight seats. The party had been reduced to a provincial one, as its representation was limited to Natal, more accurately to Durban and its surrounding areas. A victim of the party's poor performance was Stallard who had failed to hang onto his Roodepoort seat. The NP had secured 27 seats, but this was not a true indication of the strength of the party. The party did far better with the vote count than the count in seats, especially in rural areas. Hertzog was shaken when he held on to his Smithfield constituency by a narrow majority.

Hertzog's determination to counter the growth potential of the NP, combined with his desire to see the Afrikaans song "Die Stem van Suid-Afrika" (The Call of South Africa) becoming the national anthem in combination with "God Save the King", led to a crisis in the UP a few days after the election.[275] He had initiated the convention to play both "Die Stem" and "God Save the King" at official occasions such as the opening of parliament in 1938. This led to un-

275 W.K. Hancock, *Smuts: The fields of force 1919–1950* (Cambridge, 1968), pp. 293, 295–296.

ease amongst the UP's English-speaking supporters who were concerned that "Die Stem" could supplant "God Save the King", which they regarded as the national anthem. On Union Day, 31 May 1938, when the unification of 1910 was celebrated, these concerns reached boiling point during a military parade at Roberts Heights, the headquarters of the UDF.

Pirow and Hertzog as well as thousands of spectators attended the occasion. Just before Hertzog's arrival it was noticed that the furled Union Jack was removed and that during the ceremony only the South African flag was unfurled. While "Die Stem" was played as a general salute, "God Save the King" was omitted. The reason was that in terms of the Flag Act, only the South African flag was allowed on UDF property, while the playing of "God Save the King" was stipulated by the provisions of the King's regulations applicable to the UDF. This meant that with a formal military parade "God Save the King" could only be played if the King, or his representative, was present and no such official was at the parade. Pirow had instructed the playing of a portion of the music of "Die Stem" as a fitting compliment to Hertzog who was taking the general salute. Ignorant of the reasons for the absence of the Union Jack and "God Save the King", English speakers felt insulted, with the English-medium press fanning this anger.

The indignation of English speakers was evident in a Transvaal Provincial Council by-election in Turffontein, Johannesburg. In the general election the UP had won the seat by a majority of 2082 votes, but in the by-election on 1 June lost the seat by 567 votes to the Labour Party.[276] This anger was also reflected in the cabinet. Hofmeyr felt that Pirow's flag instruction had been stupid and provocative.[277] R. Stuttaford, Minister of the Interior, promptly resigned, although he later withdrew his resignation.

Smuts viewed the whole incident as a blunder by Pirow that nearly led to the breakup of the government.[278] Despite the emotions surrounding the flag crisis, it did little damage to the UP as Pirow – after Malan raised the incident in the House of Assembly – gave a detailed

276 Blackwell, *Farewell to parliament*, pp. 19–22, 25–26.

277 Paton, *Hofmeyr*, p. 284.

278 NA Pretoria, Smuts papers, Vol. 292, Smuts – S.G. Millin, 4 June 1938.

explanation of events. This led to a compromise that in the absence of a national anthem "Die Stem" and "God Save the King" would be played on formal occasions.

The NP attempted to portray the compromise as a humiliation to Pirow. *Die Burger* claimed that he was a weakling that had failed to stand up for Afrikaner interests. On 8 June, the newspaper published a cartoon with Pirow as a boxer that had suffered a knockout defeat at the hands of Stuttaford. This was wishful thinking as most Afrikaners did not see him as a weakling or a puppet of British imperialism and approved of his efforts to encourage a South African identity amongst English speakers.

Cartoon by Boonzaier in *Die Burger*, 8 June 1938.
Pirow once again knocked out.

Determined to demolish Pirow's standing amongst Afrikaners, Malan on 25 July targeted Pirow's stewardship of the SAR&H by demanding a judicial inquiry into allegations of improper influence by him. In a measured and effective speech, he pointed out that a number of senior SAR&H officials had charges of theft and malpractices drawn up against them, but that with Pirow's knowledge, an attempt had been made to delay the normal operation of the law against them. Pirow, feeling that he was accused of being part of a conspiracy to defeat the ends of justice, emotionally lashed out at Malan, challenging him to repeat his accusations outside of parliament. Strijdom was also sneered at with "I do not want to take advice from a little countryside attorney."[279] He was so volatile that the Speaker reprimanded him for using unparliamentary language.

Pirow's admirers felt that it was an embarrassing performance. The NP relished his discomfort and continued to press him on his role in the affair. By 1 August, a calmer Pirow could explain to the House that nothing untoward was taking place and that the law was taking its course, but the NP did succeed for once to cut him down to size. Ironically, the NP did Pirow a favour as the aggression towards him encouraged a sense of unity in the UP after the flag and anthem crisis.[280]

Pirow's embarrassing response to Malan was erased by his impressive performance in the Defence budget debate of 7 September 1938. In a speech lasting an hour and a half, he promised that the UDF would be prepared for a bushveld war against any northern invader. To counter any threat from the sea, he promised that the coastal gun batteries at Cape Town would be adapted from 9,2 inches to 15 inches, making the city safe from any attack by a hostile battleship. He pointed out that the shortage of arms and equipment in the UDF was considerable and that to remedy the situation would be costly. Another challenge was that South Africa remained dependent on Britain for the provision of modern and heavy weaponry and that the British government, with the growing threat of Nazi Germany, was only prepared to sell obsolete arms.[281] Pirow also addressed ac-

279 House of Assembly Debates, 25 July 1938, Col. 27.
280 Unisa, UP Archive, Louis Esselen papers, Pirow – Esselen, 27 July 1938.
281 J. Ellis, "Oswald Pirow's five-year plan for the reorganisation of the Union Defence Force, 1933–1939", *Scientia Militaria, South African Journal of Military Studies*, 30/2 (2000).

cusations that he had German sympathies by forcefully denying that he was pro-Nazi:

> I am not pro-Nazi and I am not anti-Nazi. I am once and for all in favour of our democratic system, and I do not get hot and bothered about what is going on in other countries.[282]

Pirow's performance had affirmed his status as the UP's crown prince. F.N. Broome, the newly elected UP MP for Pietermaritzburg District, was in awe of his debating abilities and dynamic approach to his duties.[283]

Pirow's position in the government was bolstered by Hofmeyr's resignation from the cabinet in September. Attie Fourie, the Minister for Commerce and Industries, had lost his seat in the general election. To reward Fourie's loyalty – he was the only senior Cape NP MP to support a fusion government – Hertzog was determined to keep him in the cabinet. But as Fourie was unable to find a parliamentary seat, Hertzog was obliged to appoint him on 9 September to a Senate seat reserved in terms of the constitution for a person that had a "thorough acquaintance with the reasonable wants and wishes of the coloured races". Hofmeyr viewed such a Senate seat for Fourie as a breach of the constitution. Pirow, who in 1929 was appointed to the cabinet in the same way, took exception and in a caucus meeting launched a violent attack on Hofmeyr who subsequently resigned from the cabinet.

This left Smuts isolated as he had lost his strongest ally in the government. Pirow was the acting Minister for Mines, Social Welfare and Education until a replacement could be found. The ease and confidence with which he handled the budget debates of these portfolios raised his standing in the UP.

Hofmeyr's resignation was overshadowed by the gathering of war clouds in Europe with Hitler's demand that Czechoslovakia should cede the Sudetenland region with its ethnic German majority to Germany. For South Africa it raised the spectre that the country could be sucked into a European war as a British ally. On 24 September, Malan initiated a parliamentary debate on South Africa's neutrality. He

282 House of Assembly Debates, 7 September 1938, Col. 2347.
283 F.N. Broome, *Not the whole truth* (Pietermaritzburg, 1962), p. 170.

urged the government to alter its defence policy regarding Simon's Town, as the agreement made it impossible for South Africa to remain neutral in any war involving Britain. Pirow once more sneeringly bashed Malan's stance as hypocritical and opportunistic while he insisted that South Africa could defend the British naval base and remain neutral.[284]

Geyer, outraged by Pirow's sarcastic treatment of Malan, thundered in *Die Burger* (26 September 1938) that he was a political clown. Behind the scenes, a concerned Hertzog compiled a memorandum affirming South African neutrality that was approved by Pirow, Havenga and Smuts, the inner circle of his cabinet. The full cabinet approved the statement on 28 September.[285] The next day the Munich agreement between Germany, France and Britain allowed Germany to annex Sudetenland, dispersing the war clouds. The Sudeten crisis had convinced the government that if a European war had erupted, the country was ill prepared to defend itself and the decision was made to send Pirow to London to secure armaments. On 24 September 1938, he announced in parliament that he was to visit Britain to negotiate with the British War Office for military supplies.

For Pirow the visit provided an opportunity to offer his services to British Prime Minister Neville Chamberlain to act as a mediator with Hitler to prevent a war. In 1945, with his political career shattered, he would claim that he had offered his services on the urging of Smuts who was part of a conspiracy by British intelligence and Foreign Affairs to destroy him as a rival for the premiership and to undermine the case for neutrality.[286] As shown by Pirow's efforts in 1936, he did not need Smuts's encouragement to be a mediator between Britain and Nazi Germany. He also knew that in a European war it would be difficult for South Africa to remain neutral. When the journalist David Friedmann asked him whether the country would be drawn into a major war, he responded that with the importance of the Cape sea route he could not see it remain neutral.[287] A war could only shatter the achievements of the fusion government and damage his chances to become the prime minister.

---

284 House of Assembly Debates, 24 September 1938, Col. 4589–3593.

285 Le Roux, Coetzer, Marais, *Generaal J.B.M. Hertzog* II, p. 643.

286 *Die Nuwe Orde*, 4 October 1945, 2 and 30 May, 12 and 26 September 1946.

287 Wits, D. Friedmann papers, Vol. 1, Unpublished memoirs, p. 56.

Pirow feared that an Anglo-German war would weaken white domination in Africa.[288] That there was no British conspiracy to destroy his credibility was evident in London's embarrassment, caution and disdain for his proposed mission.[289] London was so in the dark about Pirow's intentions that the High Commissioner had to ask Smuts whether Pirow had a government mandate to discuss Germany's colonial demands. Smuts responded in the negative, but he did request that the British government should take care to talk the matter over with Pirow.[290]

Hertzog gave his full support to Pirow's proposed role as a mediator and stated that he could use his discretion on how to proceed. The prime minister, Smuts and Havenga were the only members of the cabinet in the know. To justify a visit to continental Europe, Pirow announced that he would visit Portugal for talks on trade relations and Germany for technical matters relating to railways and aviation. Pirow requested Gie (in Germany) and Dr Rudolf Leitner (Germany's diplomatic representative in South Africa) to arrange meetings with Joachim von Ribbentrop (the German Minister for Foreign Affairs), Göring, and possibly Hitler. He had reason to hope that his request would be favourably received as he had a reputation as the South African politician with the best understanding of Germany and national socialism.

Berlin took so long to respond that Pirow left for Europe without an invitation. Before his departure, the British government through its High Commissioner in Pretoria requested him not to make any public utterances about his visit to Europe.[291] But in private Pirow informed Herr Von Dewitz (the Junkers Company's representative in South Africa) that he desired to discuss Germany's colonial claims. Von Dewitz promptly informed officials of Germany's Foreign Affairs Department of Pirow's intentions.[292]

288 W. Schellack, "The Afrikaners' Nazi links revisited", *South African Historical Journal*, 27, 1992, p. 183.

289 Bourne and Watt, *Studies in international history*, p. 421.

290 NA Kew, FO 371/21682, High Commissioner's telegram, 19 October 1938.

291 NA Kew, FO 371/21682, High Commissioner's telegram, 19 October 1938.

292 W. van der Merwe, Suid-Afrika en "appeasement": Oswald Pirow se "vredesending" na Nazi-Duitsland in November 1938, *Kleio*, 20, 1988, p. 37.

# 7

# The diplomat, October–November 1938

Pirow left South Africa on 20 October for Lourenço Marques, Mozambique, to link up with an Imperial Airways flight to London. The aircraft developed mechanical problems on landing in Brindisi, Italy. An impatient Pirow took a plane to Rome and then travelled by car to Ostia. From there he flew with an Italian aircraft to Marseilles in France where he brusquely refused an interview with a French journalist. This did not prevent the journalist to publish a story about Pirow's mission to see Hitler to satisfy Germany's colonial claims. From Marseilles, he flew with a Lufthansa flight to Lisbon over Spain that was in the grips of a civil war between the forces of the republic and those of the fascist-inspired nationalists. At the Portuguese frontier his flight was met and escorted to Lisbon by a squadron of Portuguese bombers while he was welcomed by cabinet members, several hundred spectators and with full military honours.[293]

Between 27 and 28 October, Pirow had three meetings with Dr Antonio Salazar, the Portuguese dictator, about the provision of labour from Mozambique for South Africa's mines, and regarding a formal agreement on an air link between Angola and South Africa. The importance of Lourenço Marquez to the defence of South Africa was also raised. (At Pirow's 18 August 1936 conference with UDF generals on the defence of South Africa, it was concluded that

293 *Die Nuwe Orde*, 15 and 22 November 1945.

"the presence of the Portuguese, effete and utterly useless from the military point of view, at Delagoa Bay represented the Achilles heel of South Africa.")[294] To bolster the defence of Lourenço Marques, Pirow offered to assist with the training of Portuguese pilots. They also discussed the strained state of international relations with Salazar being pessimistic about the future.[295]

In the 1940s, Pirow would claim that Salazar stood head and shoulders above all the European leaders he had met, and that he was an inspiration for his own New Order movement. This was not the case in 1938 when in a confidential conversation with Friedmann in Lisbon, he expressed serious reservations about Salazar's harsh treatment of those with opposing views and said that the Portuguese system of censorship was too extreme. In his notes of the conversation, Friedmann recorded the following statement by Pirow: "You know anyone spilling the beans in this country is liable to be shot."[296]

While in Lisbon, Pirow received a formal invitation to visit Germany. He also secured – with the recommendation of Salazar – an invite to visit General Francisco Franco, leader of the Spanish nationalist government, to investigate the effects of modern warfare. After a four-day stay in Lisbon, he flew to Salamanca where he viewed the destructiveness of modern armaments and met Franco at his frontline headquarters. In his recollections he claimed that he found the Spanish fascist dictator "charming, quick witted and brilliant".[297]

What struck Friedmann in his conversation with him on his return from Spain, was that Pirow was profoundly shocked by the horror defenceless civilians had to endure from aerial bombardment and that he had concluded that there was no adequate defence against high-speed dive bombers. Friedmann felt that Pirow was so shaken by what he had witnessed in Spain that he was a changed person, and that this explained his decision to embrace neutrality in September 1939.[298]

294 Department of Defence Documentation Centre CGS 944/2, Memorandum in connection with matters discussed with the Minister by Major General Brink and BDR; Generals Botha and Collyer at Pretoria on Tuesday 18th August, 1936.

295 *Die Nuwe Orde*, 22 and 29 November 1945.

296 Wits, D. Friedmann papers, Vol. 1, Unpublished memoirs, pp. 47–48, 60, 62.

297 Pirow, *James Barry Munnik Hertzog*, p. 232.

298 Wits, D. Friedmann papers, Vol. 1, Unpublished memoirs, pp. 48–49.

Pirow arrived in London on 1 November. By then there was a media frenzy, fed by his refusal to talk with the press. The British press was divided in its perception of Pirow. *The Times* referred to him "as a sort of mystery man, from whom great things are expected", but some newspapers viewed him as too pro-German. The *News Chronicle* referred to him as "South Africa's Prussian defence minister". The *London Evening Standard* accused him of being South Africa's Hitler, claiming that he was a fascist, that Germany was his spiritual home, and that he was in favour of Germany having her colonies back. He was also condemned for buying German aircraft instead of British ones for the SAA.

In contrast to his 1936 visit, Pirow was an unwelcome guest. As Britain was rearming herself against any possible aggression from Germany, it could not afford to sell weapons, while his self-appointed status as a mediator was a source of embarrassment. In parliament, MacDonald was obliged to answer a question on the purpose of Pirow's planned visit to Germany. His response was that he had received no information from the South African government about his intentions. And yet, the red carpet was rolled out for Pirow. As a leading figure in the South African government and a Dominion whose support would be needed in any future war with Germany, the government was determined to keep him on their side.

When his train arrived at Victoria station, MacDonald and a bevy of establishment figures welcomed him. He was granted a long meeting with King George VI, who in contrast to his brother, Edward VIII, made no pro-German statements.[299] He was also invited to attend a state banquet for King Carol of Romania at Buckingham Palace. Sir Abe Bailey arranged a special luncheon for Pirow to meet establishment figures, including Winston Churchill as the leading anti-appeaser. Addressing a dinner of the South Africa Club, attended by over 400 people at the Savoy Hotel, Pirow made it clear that the South African parliament would ensure that the participation in any European war would be based on South African interests, and not on sentiment.[300]

299 *Die Nuwe Orde*, 24 January 1946.

300 ACA UFS, Oswald Pirow collection, File 3, *South Africa. A weekly journal for all interested in South African affairs*, 19 November 1938.

Pirow had a succession of meetings with government ministers. Of his first three encounters with Chamberlain there are no official minutes and the only source is Pirow's unreliable recollections. According to him the British prime minister, whom he viewed as an honest man with a big heart, informed him that Hitler's treatment of Jews had caused a lot of ill will in Britain, but that they should have another meeting to discuss affairs.[301] To secure weapons, Pirow met with Leslie Hore-Belisha, Secretary of State for War, and General Lord Gort, Chief of the Imperial General Staff. He was disappointed to discover that they were only willing to part with obsolete weapons.[302]

In his meeting with MacDonald on 2 November, after a wide-ranging conversation on Portugal's attitude towards Germany's colonial claims, the civil war in Spain, South Africa's defence programme and the cooperation of Britain and South Africa in the defence of British territories, he requested the minister's assistance to buy modern weapons. He pointed out that he had to secure at least 1400 Bren guns, anti-aircraft guns and searchlights, or he would not be able to face parliament and the public in South Africa. To bolster his case, he argued that South Africa's neutrality was becoming increasingly theoretical as war was no respecter of persons or countries, and that the two countries should be together in a war with Germany.[303]

MacDonald, in an attempt to support Pirow, arranged a meeting with Sir Thomas Inskip, Minister for the Coordination of Defence, for the next day. During the meeting Pirow used South Africa's willingness to defend Kenya against an invasion by Italy to secure modern armaments. He also emphasised South Africa's considerable financial contribution in erecting coastal gun batteries to protect the Cape sea route, an important trade route for Britain. Inskip remained unmoved; Britain needed the required Bren guns. Apart from his quest for weapons, the meeting also dealt with Pirow's concerns for an early settlement of the colonial question with Germany. He was adamant that Tanganyika and South West Africa could not be

301 Pirow, *James Barry Munnik Hertzog*, p. 233.

302 *Die Nuwe Orde*, 3 and 10 January 1946.

303 NA Kew, FO 371/21682, "Conversation between Mr MacDonald & Mr Pirow, 2 November 1938".

returned to Germany as it would bring the Witwatersrand into aerial bombing range.[304]

Pirow also focused on his upcoming visit to Germany. Before his second meeting with Chamberlain, he met some of the premier's supporters. He attempted to convince them that Hitler should be allowed a free hand in eastern Europe as it was a choice of a war between Britain and Germany, or Germany and the Soviet Union. A war with the Soviet Union would weaken Germany and make a permanent peace agreement with Britain possible. Those at the meeting concurred but pointed out that public opinion had become increasingly anti-German after the euphoria of Munich and that some friendly gesture from Hitler was necessary to strengthen Chamberlain's position before he could make any concession. Captain V.A. Cazalet, a British parliamentarian who was passionately concerned about the plight of German Jews, convinced Pirow that such a gesture by Hitler should be the possible resettlement of Jews in a new national home, possibly Tanganyika, Madagascar or British Guinea. The problem was that they were only allowed to emigrate with a few of their possessions, and Cazalet wanted Hitler to allow them to leave Germany with half of their property. International aid could provide these refugees with the other half. Chamberlain, according to Pirow, was satisfied with his offer to discuss Cazalet's proposal with Hitler.

They then discussed Germany's objectives in eastern Europe. From this Pirow concluded that if Hitler could appease British public opinion on the German Jewish question, he may well be granted a free hand in eastern Europe.[305] While he and Chamberlain were in the process of formulating a concrete instruction for his visit to Hitler, Hirsch Grynszpan, a young and displaced Polish Jew, on 7 November 1938 shot and wounded Ernst vom Rath, a German diplomat attached to the embassy in Paris, to protest to Germany's anti-Semitism. Vom Rath died of his wounds two days later. His death unleashed *Kristallnacht*, an anti-Semitic pogrom. On the night of 9–10 November, a total of 91 Jews were murdered, synagogues were destroyed, thousands of Jewish shops were plundered and 30 000 Jews were imprisoned in concentration camps.

304 NA Kew, FO 371/21682, "Conversation between Mr MacDonald, Sir T. Inskip, Mr Pirow and Mr Te Water, 3 November 1938".

305 Pirow, *James Barry Munnik Hertzog*, p. 234.

On 10 November, Pirow had a conversation with Sir Neville Henderson, Britain's ambassador in Berlin, who was in London for health reasons. Henderson advised him to draw information out of Hitler that might serve in a way as a practical basis for future negotiations.[306] Pirow then met a gloomy Chamberlain who informed him that "I think it is quite hopeless to try anything at present" and that because of *Kristallnacht* he could no longer give him even semi-official status. Pirow offered to proceed with the Cazalet plan and would inform Hitler that if he made a gesture of friendship to Britain in the spirit of Munich, he might be given a free hand in eastern Europe. Chamberlain made no statement of support, but wished him success and stated: "Hitler knows how anxious I am that there should be a lasting peace."

Gie was requested to convey Pirow's proposal to Göring. Pirow also discussed this proposal with other British politicians in Chamberlain's circle, claiming he got the feeling that if he should have success with Hitler, the prime minister could identify himself with Pirow's proposal of giving Hitler a free hand in eastern Europe.[307]

On 15 November, Pirow once more met with MacDonald who made it clear that Britain would not bargain with Germany about refugees, and no colony would be traded for the better treatment of Jews. Hitler had to make a unilateral concession for relations to get back to what they had been before. Pirow agreed, stating that he assumed that Britain would not be prepared to discuss other questions whilst the Germans were behaving so brutally to the Jews, or until Germany had made some reparations to them.[308]

Pirow also met Lord Halifax, the British Minister of Foreign Affairs. According to Charles te Water, South Africa's High Commissioner in London, Pirow stated that he was determined to leave the German authorities under no illusion about the effect of their policy towards Jews on the public opinion in Britain, and that they should make a substantial gesture regarding Jewish refugees.[309]

---

306 NA Kew, FO 371/21682, Henderson's notes of the meeting, 11 November 1938.

307 *Die Nuwe Orde*, 24 January 1946.

308 NA Kew, FO 371/21791, File C14095, MacDonald's notes of his meeting with Pirow, 15 November 1938.

309 NA Pretoria, PM 22/3/2 Vol. 1, C. te Water – J.B.M. Hertzog, 22 November 1938.

Pirow left for Germany via the Netherlands on 17 November. On the Dutch-German border a specially arranged train awaited him. Underway in Hannover his wife – who was on holiday – joined him. The train arrived at 20:52 at Berlin's Charlottenburg railway station, brightly lit and decorated with the South African and German flags. General Wilhelm Keitel (Chief of Staff of the army), Walter Funk (Minister of Economics), Prince Otto von Bismarck (of the Department of Foreign Affairs and grandson of the Iron Chancellor) as well as a military guard of honour, welcomed him. Pirow would later claim that it was the most impressive group of soldiers he had ever had the privilege of inspecting. A representative of the Hitler youth handed Mrs Pirow flowers. The Pirows were taken to the Hotel Adlon in Unter den Linden with its luxurious rooms for state visitors. One of the military aides provided by the Germans was Colonel Max Pirow, a cousin and close friend of Pirow since their school days. Max would become a general and would be killed on the Russian front during World War II.[310]

Despite the impressive welcoming ceremony, Pirow's peace mission was unwelcome in Germany.[311] According to the British intelligence service he was viewed with some suspicion,[312] but the British embassy noted the special trouble the Germans were taking to impress him with their hospitality and display.[313] As South Africa was an important market for German goods while its neutrality in any war with Britain would be welcomed, the Nazis went out of their way to show him its military might. He met General Walther von Brauchitsch, commander-in-chief of the army, to visit an air force training camp and was taken on a flight.[314] A military parade was also arranged for him to lay a wreath at the German War Memorial in Unter den Linden.

On Friday, 18 November, he was entertained by Göring. Pirow informed him that in a war between Germany and Britain, South Africa would not enter the war immediately, but as government-embracing

310 *Die Nuwe Orde*, 31 January 1946.

311 Bourne and Watt, *Studies in international history*, p. 421.

312 NA Kew, KV 2/908, Extract from an intelligence report, 7 November 1938.

313 NA Kew, FO 371/21791, Report from Sir George Ogilvie Forbes to London, 22 November 1938.

314 *Dagbreek en Sondagnuus*, 15 February 1948.

neutrality would struggle to survive, South Africa would be fighting on the side of Britain within six months. He made it clear that South Africa would definitely be part of the British Empire for the next hundred years or so.[315] Gie, who attended the meeting, confirmed in his report to Pretoria that Pirow made it clear that the anti-British attitude of the Nazis could only be to the detriment of Germany.[316] In his 1946 recollections, Pirow claimed that Göring expressed support for his proposal on Jews but made it clear that although Hitler may ask for his advice, the final decision resided with him. Pirow would after the war claim that he left Göring in a positive state of mind and was full of admiration for the Nazi leader, gushingly referring to him as a Viking type.

That evening Pirow had a meeting with Joachim von Ribbentrop. The official German minutes of the meeting reflect that Von Ribbentrop was haughty and arrogant, and that Pirow had confronted him on the Nazis' brutal treatment of Jews. This was after Von Ribbentrop had boasted that *Kristallnacht* had at last put the Jews in their place. Pirow responded that Germany's behaviour made it difficult for those who wanted to defend the Third Reich abroad.

Von Ribbentrop also bombastically proclaimed that the colonial question was not urgent and that it could wait at least five or six years. He refused to link the colonial question to the treatment of Jews.[317] In his recollections Pirow condemned the German Minister of Foreign Affairs as disgustingly arrogant, vain and stupid.[318]

On 20 November, while waiting for his appointment with Hitler, he went to visit Dr Hans Merensky, a friend from South Africa, on his estate in Silesia.[319] He used this opportunity to do some hunting, but never stopped brooding about the importance of his visit to Hitler. On 22 November, he wrote to Esselen that his plan on settling the Jewish question was the only way to avoid a seemingly inevitable war in Europe.[320]

315 NA Kew, FO 371/21791, Malcolm MacDonald's report of a meeting with Pirow on his return from Germany, 5 December 1938.

316 NA Pretoria, PM 22/3/2 Vol. 1, Extract from a letter by Gie dated 1 December 1938. (I am grateful to Frik Nothling for this document.)

317 Van der Merwe, "Suid-Afrika en 'appeasement'", pp. 44–45.

318 Pirow, *James Barry Munnik Hertzog*, pp. 235, 238.

319 *Dagbreek en Sondagnuus*, 15 February 1948.

320 Unisa, UP Archives, Louis Esselen papers, Pirow – Eselen, 22 November 1938.

While in Silesia, his proposed visit to Hitler continued to create waves in Britain and South Africa. MacDonald, responding to questions in the House of Commons on 22 November on whether Pirow was entrusted with any mission from the British government, or whether he was directly or indirectly entitled to represent the views of the British government on colonial questions, emphatically denied that he was in any way representing the views of the government.

That he was speaking for himself was confirmed by Smuts. On 16 November, at the Natal UP's conference, he insisted that the main objective of Pirow's European visit was to discuss defence matters in Britain and that "all the rest is mere thrills". This did not prevent the Labour Party from accusing him of intending to hand South West Africa back to Germany. Even in the UP there was some concern as Morris Kentridge at a public meeting condemned Pirow for shaking "hands with men whose hands are dripping with the blood of innocent victims".[321]

On 24 November, Pirow met Hitler at Berchtesgaden where he was welcomed with a guard of honour by SS troops. Also present was Von Ribbentrop and a German Foreign Office official who took notes. In his recollections, although admitting that he found Hitler less impressive than in 1933, Pirow created the impression of a successful meeting. He claimed that they had a man-to-man conversation and that he had made an impression on the German dictator with his proposal that an agreement with Britain on the Jewish issue would lead to Britain giving Germany a free hand in eastern Europe. The meeting was so positive that if Chamberlain had asked him to return to Berlin, a breakthrough could have taken place. This would have given Germany a free hand in the east, securing Western civilisation by destroying Bolshevism.[322] Their conversation could have lasted longer if Von Ribbentrop did not remind Hitler that King Carol was waiting. Hitler then walked him to the door and took his hand in both of his, asking when they will see each other again. Pirow responded: "Herr Kanzler, that matter is entirely in your hands."[323]

In reality, the meeting was a disappointment for Pirow and his recollection bordered on fiction as the German minutes of the meet-

321 Kentridge, *I recall*, pp. 265–267.

322 *Die Nuwe Orde*, 28 February 1946.

323 Pirow, *James Barry Munnik Hertzog*, p. 238.

ing reflect that the question of a free hand in eastern Europe was not raised at all.

According to the German minutes, the meeting started with a lengthy discussion on South Africa's trade relations with Germany and the merits of the new German car, the Volkswagen. Pirow then emphasised that South Africa had a significant influence on British foreign policy, and that during the Sudeten crisis it had played a leading role in encouraging peace. Hitler responded that Anglo-German relations could not be normal if Britain continued to act as if she was the governess of Germany and that Britain had to realise that she was dealing with Europe's strongest power. Pirow retorted that as the greatest European power Germany had to take the initiative in reaching out to appeasers such as Chamberlain and Halifax, since their estrangement could only strengthen the war party in Britain.

When Pirow raised the Jewish question, Hitler reacted sharply that he resented British criticism, especially as they did not propose on how to deal with the problem and that he was determined to resolve the Jewish problem permanently. Pirow urged that Germany had to find a solution with the international community, especially with the USA and Britain. He raised the proposal of an international loan to assist the resettlement of Jews. Hitler did not reject the proposal outright but made it clear that he would not allow Jews to take capital out of Germany. Pirow responded that the scheme would not cost Germany any money as the country only had to provide its cooperation and provide a place of settlement. Hitler retorted that Germany had no colonies and that he could not convince Germans to give a place where German blood had been shed to Germany's worst enemy.

He then demanded to know why Pirow objected to South West Africa and Tanganyika being returned to Germany. Pirow explained that since 1918, South West Africa had become of strategic and military importance to South Africa, but that Hertzog was willing to compensate Germany financially. For him Tanganyika fell within the influence sphere of the Afrikaners, a white *Herrenvolk*. On Hitler wanting to know why Germany did not fit into this scheme, Pirow explained that Germans were regarded by Afrikaners as the leading exponents of white hegemony, but if the area became a German colony again, white people would identify with Germany and would not see themselves as Afrikaners.

Hitler eventually claimed that the colonial issue was not urgent and could be addressed in the next five to six years. The conversation returned to the Jewish question with Pirow urging Hitler to give his cooperation to resolve the issue. Hitler responded that the Jews did not want to leave Europe as they were part of the communist onslaught, and that they hated him (Hitler) as he had halted this process. Pirow then made a final attempt to convince the dictator to make some gesture of friendship to Britain. In some length Hitler responded with great bitterness towards Britain, claiming that he had spent years to work for better Anglo-German relations, even sending his best man (Von Ribbentrop) to London where he was humiliated by the British, while he himself had only received kicks from them.[324]

Pirow left the meeting with a deep sense of disappointment as he was shaken by Hitler's arrogance, impatience and aggression. In January 1939, he told G.H. Wilson, editor of the *Cape Times*, that while talking to Hitler he felt like a "second rate Roman Consul talking to John the Baptist".[325] A few days after the meeting he told Sir Ogilvie Forbes of the British embassy in Berlin that his conversation with Hitler had left him pessimistic. He felt that he was talking to a brick wall, and that it was as if Hitler was addressing a meeting of ten thousand people when talking to him. He claimed that Hitler occasionally thumped the table and that he then thumped the table back.

Pirow was adamant that he had made it clear to Hitler that his attacks on Britain were making the British prime minister's position very difficult.[326] Pirow later told Lord Perth, the British ambassador in Italy, that he had made no impression on Hitler and that he was up against a stonewall, but that Göring had told him that he had shaken Hitler on various points.[327] This was an obvious attempt by Göring to soothe Pirow's bruised ego. What did boost Pirow's ego was that King Carol of Romania requested a meeting with him in Munich

324 Wits, D. Friedmann papers, Vol. 1, The memoirs include the entire recording of the meeting, pp. 76–82.

325 G.H. Wilson, *Gone down the years* (London, n.d.), pp. 214, 216.

326 NA Kew, FO 371/21791, Report by Sir Ogilvie Forbes, 26 November 1938.

327 NA Kew, FO 371/21791, Lord Perth's summary of his conversation with Pirow, 28 November 1938.

because he wanted to know more about his conversation with Hitler, and to discuss the international situation.[328]

On 26 November, Pirow left Berlin for Rome with a formal send-off with a guard of honour, military band and Funk representing the German government. The Germans were not sad to see him go. His warnings that in a war with Britain, South Africa would eventually be fighting on the British side meant that he was no longer *persona grata* in Berlin. Leitner, as Germany's representative in South Africa, was instructed that for the *Reichsparteitag* in 1939 no special effort had to be made for Pirow.[329]

After the disappointing meeting at Berchtesgaden, Pirow placed his hopes on Mussolini to act as a mediator with Hitler on the Jewish question and requested a meeting with the Italian dictator. The Italians were prepared to invite him to discuss commercial affairs only, but he refused to visit Rome on this basis. After some hesitation, he was given a formal invite. Pirow in his recollections claimed that he found fascist Italy unimpressive. He condemned Count Galeazzo Ciano, Mussolini's son-in-law and Italy's Minister of Foreign Affairs, as a *twak* (trash) and an eventual traitor to Mussolini. With regard to Mussolini he noted that he was amused by the theatrics of the Italian dictator, especially his use of a hall for an office, and that he was an egoist, only interested in hearing how good he was. Mussolini, struggling to repress his yawns, showed no interest in his proposed Jewish scheme, claiming that it had nothing to do with world peace. The only time Mussolini showed any interest in their conversation was when he predicted that a European war would break out by April 1939.[330]

Pirow's description must be taken with a pinch of salt as he told Wilson in January 1939 that Mussolini was highly practical and much better informed than Hitler.[331] This is also what he told Lord Perth on 28 November. According to Perth, Pirow had urged Mussolini to persuade Hitler to be more reasonable on the Jewish problem, but that Mussolini had responded that he could not interfere in Germany's internal affairs. Despite this, Pirow continued to push the case to find a

328 *Die Nuwe Orde*, 7 March 1946.

329 Van der Merwe, "Suid Afrika en 'appeasement'", p. 53.

330 *Die Nuwe Orde*, 21 March 1946.

331 Wilson, *Gone down the years*, p. 217.

place of refuge for German Jews to settle. He proposed that sufficient money had to be raised by means of an international loan, or by some other methods. Mussolini, according to Pirow, did not dissent, and he had the impression that the dictator would go a long way to assist if Chamberlain asked him to intervene on the issue.

However, Mussolini did reject any Jewish settlement in Tanganyika. They also discussed the use of black armies in Africa. Pirow wanted an agreement between European powers whereby no such armies would be formed, as well as a further agreement to be reached that hostilities between European armies should not be extended to Africa. Pirow made it clear that South Africa was a loyal member of the British Empire and that South Africa would eventually join any war against Germany after a period of neutrality.[332]

Mussolini viewed Pirow's visit as a waste of time and Ciano in a conversation with the German ambassador, Hans Georg von Mackensen, on 28 November did not attempt to hide his contempt for the South African visitor:

> It had been impossible to conduct any serious conversations with this man who was floundering about in world history. Among other similar stupidities he had suggested that Mussolini should mediate between Hitler and the Jews. The conversation had accordingly been a short one and apart from the visit to the Duce, he had taken no notice of this strange visitor who had come here uninvited. After his talk with Pirow, Mussolini had summed up his opinion of him by saying he was an outstanding example of the rapidity with which a race living in another latitude could deteriorate. It was almost impossible to believe that Pirow's father had been German. Pirow was quite right when he always described himself as an African.[333]

After reading Ciano's unflattering observations in the published documents of the German foreign ministry (released in 1951), Pirow took his revenge in his 1957 biography on Hertzog, condemning Ciano as good-looking, vain and stupid.[334]

332 NA Kew, FO 371/21791, Lord Perth's summary of his conversation with Pirow, 28 November 1938.

333 Ovendale, *"Appeasement" and the English-speaking world*, pp. 192, 196; Wits, D. Friedmann papers, Vol. 1, Unpublished memoirs, p. 87.

334 Pirow, *James Barry Munnik Hertzog*, pp. 239.

Pirow's next stop was to be France to discuss Madagascar as a possible national home for Jews, and colonial compensation for Germany in West Africa. However, widespread industrial unrest led to the cancellation of the visit. He instead went to Belgium to discuss commercial flight links between the Belgian Congo and South Africa.

According to his recollections, he found Belgium, apart from its monarch, Leopold III, deeply disappointing. The Netherlands was another disappointment for him as the Dutch prime minister, Hendrikus Colijn, was too pro-British and pro-Jewish and not interested in world affairs.[335] Back in London on 5 December, Pirow met MacDonald and conveyed his pessimism about the situation in Europe. He affirmed that in any war with Germany, South Africa would be fighting alongside Britain within months.[336]

Two days later he met Chamberlain in a small office at the House of Commons. He found that the prime minister was more interested to hear of his meeting with Mussolini than the one with Hitler. They discussed in some depth how Mussolini could be split from Hitler. Pirow would later claim that he had urged Chamberlain to give Germany a free hand in eastern Europe, but that Chamberlain pointed out that British public opinion would not allow any further concessions.[337] The prime minister's summary of the meeting does not reflect any such discussion. According to his notes, the focus was on the German attitude towards its former colonies, the possible resettlement of Jews, and that there was a possibility that Mussolini could intervene on the issue on Chamberlain's request.[338]

In London, Pirow allowed his first interviews with the press, strenuously denying that his visit had anything to do with German colonial claims and that his sole intention was to buy weapons in Britain, and to discuss trade with Germany and Italy. On the eve of his return to South Africa on 9 December 1938, he issued a press statement that he was leaving Europe "with a feeling of almost unqualified anxiety":

335 *Die Nuwe Orde*, 28 March and 4 April 1946.

336 NA Kew, FO 371/21791, Malcolm MacDonald's report of a meeting with Pirow on his return from Germany, 5 December 1938.

337 *Die Nuwe Orde*, 18 April 1946.

338 NA Kew, FO 371/21791, Chamberlain's summary of the meeting, 7 December 1938.

> Europe is drifting into war – war which no nation wants, but against which every nation is preparing. Unless there is a complete change of outlook within the next month or two international tension will reach breaking point during the spring of next year.[339]

In addition, Pirow declared that to prevent a war, Europe had to deal with the refugee problem, which included displaced Jews. On 9 December, Pirow left London and travelled to South Africa on board the *Warwick Castle*, arriving in Cape Town on 23 December.

In terms of diplomacy Pirow's visit achieved little. His self-appointed peace mission was not welcomed in Germany, while it caused embarrassment in Britain. Chamberlain treated him as an unwelcome visitor. His summary of the meeting on 7 December reflects no warmth or appreciation for Pirow. British officials also viewed his press statement with some cynicism and disbelief. It was noted that while he encouraged countries to take in Jewish refugees, South Africa had the most illiberal immigration policy of all the Dominions. They found it hard to believe that he thought a solution to the refugee problem was a cure for Europe's ills.[340] And yet there was relief in London that Pirow accepted that in a war with Germany, South Africa would not remain neutral.

Ultimately, he had allayed fears in British circles about his loyalty to the Empire and that he was pro-German. This was evident in an article of S. Hardie Stewart, editor of *The Torchbearer*, official mouthpiece of the Junior Imperial League in the *Right Bulletin*, organ of the Right Book Club. He forcefully stated that he hoped that Pirow would be the next prime minister of South Africa as it would be a good thing for South Africa and Britain: "Mr Pirow is a true British subject. His interests are those of the British Commonwealth of Nations."[341] When Hofmeyr wrote to Sarah Gertrude Millin on 16 December 1938 that "I don't think Pirow has done himself much good in South Africa by his peregrinations through Europe. He is undoubtedly more distrusted than ever before,"[342] he could not have been more wrong. That Pirow was treated as if he was a head of

339 *Daily Telegraph*, 6 December 1938.

340 NA Kew, FO 371/21791, C 1501, Notes by Foreign Affairs officials on Pirow's press statement.

341 *Sunday Times*, 26 February 1939.

342 Wits, S.G. Millin papers, C1, Hofmeyr – Millin, 16 Dec 1938.

state in Europe, meeting leaders such as Franco, Salazar, Leopold III, Chamberlain, Hitler and Mussolini, was an achievement that boosted his image as a statesman and a future prime minister.

The world at his feet – a studio photograph by celebrity photographer Howard Coster, 1939. *From: National Portrait Gallery, London.*

# 8

# Before the storm, January–August 1939

Pirow, on arriving in Pretoria, had a lengthy meeting with Smuts to inform him of his visit. According to him the deputy prime minister was impressed and congratulated him while Hertzog also expressed his appreciation. Pirow exploited the publicity surrounding his European visit to bolster his image. He had a lengthy conversation with Wilson of the *Cape Times* who found him candid and straightforward on his experiences.[343]

On 10 February 1939, he addressed the UP's parliamentary caucus. Heaton Nicholls, the UP MP for Zululand, recorded in his diary how a complacent Pirow in a fluent, anecdotal and racy way claimed equality with the statesmen of the world, creating the perception that kings and dictators had accepted him as a confidant. The UP MPs cheered him lustily, but an unimpressed Nicholls viewed him as vainglorious.[344] Pirow also addressed the DP parliamentary caucus where, according to Blackwell, he created the perception of a common defence scheme with Britain.[345] There was such an interest in Pirow's meeting with Hitler that even the NP parliamentary caucus, in which there was the gossip that Hitler had thrown him out of the meeting as Pirow was too pro-British, allowed him to give an overview of his visit.[346]

343 Wilson, *Gone down the years*, pp. 214, 216.
344 C.H. Nicholls, *South Africa in my time* (London, 1961), p. 349.
345 Blackwell, *Farewell to parliament*, p. 72.
346 *Die Nuwe Orde*, 2 May 1946.

The vehemently anti-fascist Labour Party declined Pirow's offer to discuss his European mission in a caucus meeting. The party felt that such a step would prevent them from confronting him in parliament, and Labour MPs did so on 20 February during the Part Appropriation Bill. Duncan Burnside, MP for Umbilo, moved an amendment to the effect that the House should refuse to pass the Bill until it was furnished with the reasons for, and the results of, Pirow's tour. Burnside was a notoriously caustic debater and he laid into Pirow for making a mockery of democracy by refusing to give a statement to parliament on his visit. He condemned his visit to fascist-controlled Spain and Nazi Germany as "the most irresponsible things which have been done by any Cabinet Minister in a trying period", and in effect accused him of being a supporter of fascism.[347] His motion was seconded by Reverend Miles Cadman, MP for Durban North, who condemned Pirow's visit to Hitler as objectionable and dangerous, and viewed his willingness to shake the hands of Nazis as disgusting. Pirow lashed out at Burnside in such a sneering way that the Speaker reprimanded him for his unparliamentary language.

To counter any suggestion of being sympathetic to fascism, Pirow in a speech to a University of Stellenbosch debating society on 4 March stated that after his European visit he was more than ever convinced that a dictatorship would never succeed in South Africa.[348]

However, suspicions of fascist sympathies remained and were strengthened in 1938 with the founding of the Ossewabrandwag (OB) as an Afrikaner cultural organisation after the centenary celebration of the Great Trek of that year. The organisation rapidly evolved into a paramilitary one under the leadership of Colonel J.C. Laas, an ACF officer. By March 1939, Colonel I.P. de Villiers, the commanding officer of the South African Police, was concerned about the growth of the OB as he felt that it was Nazi-inspired and that Pirow was implicated in the movement.[349]

This suspicion was without any foundation. Pirow had no dealings with the OB and in May 1939 banned all ACF and commando officers from joining the organisation because of its militaristic na-

347 House of Assembly Debates, 20 February 1939, Col. 507–515.

348 *Die Burger*, 6 March 1939.

349 Ovendale, *"Appeasement" and the English-speaking world*, p. 221.

ture.[350] But De Villiers's concern about Pirow and the OB was an indication that the combination of his German background and his visit to Hitler did raise concerns about possible fascist sympathies.

After basking in the limelight of his European tour, Pirow had to focus on his cabinet portfolios. On 8 November 1938, Hertzog had reshuffled his government with Pirow exchanging the portfolio of SAR&H with A.J.P. Fourie's Department of Commerce and Industries. By then Pirow had achieved what he had set out to do with the SAR&H. The railways had been modernised and made more efficient, while Cape Town harbour was in the process of being enlarged. The SAA had a modern and efficient fleet of 29 Junker planes, with four Junker 90s on order. In the process SAA had become a continental airline gradually pushing Imperial Airways out of the African market as the British airline was limited to the route between Durban and Britain.[351] Domestically, a growing number of people used SAA, with a 50 per cent increase of passengers every half-year.

With his departure from the SAR&H even *Die Burger* (9 November 1939) grudgingly conceded that he had been an efficient minister. Commerce and Industries was a less stressful portfolio, leaving him with more time to spend on the UDF in an increasingly dangerous world. That he was certain that South Africa would be involved in a war in the near future was evident in a memorandum from the Quartermaster General of the UDF to the Chief of General Staff on 3 March 1939. The memo made it clear that six months would elapse after the outbreak of a war before South Africa could become involved on a major scale.[352]

To his frustration he had to waste a significant part of his energy on party-political disputes surrounding the UDF. Both the DP and the NP attempted to secure party-political advantage by criticising the military's recruitment policy. The DP reckoned the UDF was being used to benefit the Afrikaners, while the NP took the exact opposite stance, claiming that the culture of the army was too British for potential Afrikaner recruits. Pirow had to concede that urban ACF

350 *Die Suiderstem*, 8 May 1939.

351 McCormack, "Man with a mission", pp. 544, 556.

352 L. Reeves, "The war issue and the demise of the Fusion government in 1939" (MA, University of Natal, Durban, 1984), p. 156.

units were predominantly English speaking and that many urbanised Afrikaners were reluctant to join them.[353]

The big political divide was South Africa's position in a European war involving Britain. To English speakers Pirow created the perception that South Africa would stand shoulder to shoulder with Britain against Nazi Germany. When Hitler invaded and occupied Czechoslovakia on 15 March 1939, he told Bellwood that the German dictator "must have gone thoroughly mad".[354] On 18 March 1939, Nicholls confronted Pirow on his stance if Britain should enter a war with Nazi-Germany, and recorded his answer in his diary:

> My [Pirow] own position is that while I would not fight for the Empire as you would, I am going to fight for South Africa. I believe we shall have no say in the matter. The fight will be forced on us. I do not trust Hitler. I did, before he made this last move. I do not do so now and he must be resisted. But we must avoid trouble in South Africa such as we had last time.[355]

Nicholls concluded that Pirow and Hertzog would not favour neutrality if a war should result from German aggression. That Pirow was sincere was evident from notes that he provided in May 1939 for a UP pamphlet to be released after South Africa had entered a European war, to explain why the country could not be neutral if Germany had attacked Britain.[356] By then the perception that Pirow would stand with Britain was so strong that a prominent DP MP told the public of Durban that he was entirely to be trusted.[357] When Pirow addressed a public meeting in the port city, he had the audience of this jingoistic city in his hand from the moment he entered the room, and the meeting ended with thunderous clapping and shouting.[358]

Pirow boosted his anti-Nazi credentials when he insisted on sending a heavily armed police contingent to Windhoek in South West Africa to deal with a rumour of a possible uprising by local Germans on 20 April, Hitler's birthday.[359]

353 *Die Suiderstem*, 11 February 1939.
354 Bellwood, *South African back-drop*, p. 60.
355 Nicholls, *South Africa in my time*, p. 351.
356 *Die Suiderstem*, 20 March 1940.
357 Blackwell, *Farewell to parliament*, p. 72.
358 Flather, *The way of an editor*, p. 100.
359 Pirow, *James Barry Munnik Hertzog*, pp. 242–243.

During the Defence budget debate on 23 March 1939, Pirow assured South Africans that the country would be able to defend itself in a war. He gave a comprehensive survey of the measures to strengthen the country's defences, and proudly announced that the defence programme as set out in 1934 had been exceeded in most respects. Five years earlier there had been only 22 pupil pilots in the SAAF, in 1939 there were 432 and an organised reserve of 140 pilots, compared to the 46 in 1934. He said that there had been 16 ACF infantry battalions in 1934, but in 1939 they were increased to 37. Also that there were 150 000 men in the Defence Rifle Associations, the commandos, compared to 118 000 in 1934. For the first time he publicly announced, to loud approval from the House, that from 1 September the HMS *Erebus* armed with 15-inch guns, manned by South Africans, was to protect Cape Town. He pointed out the difficulty of purchasing modern weapons as Britain was only willing to sell obsolete equipment.[360]

It was a confident speech which left *Die Burger*'s parliamentary correspondent deeply impressed. Sauer, having observed that Pirow tends to flounder when he felt his pride wounded, on 2 May 1939 attacked him as a total failure as the Minister of Defence. He accused him of providing a false picture of the state of the UDF's readiness as it was not properly equipped or armed. South African troops would be mere cannon fodder if they had to meet a well-equipped force. When Pirow interjected that he agreed, Sauer responded that he had to be dismissed as he had had six years to rectify the situation.

The usually volatile Pirow did not rise to the bait and expressed surprise that after years of being accused by the NP of doing too much for Defence, he was now accused of having done too little. He thanked Sauer for undermining the NP case that he was arming the country to assist Britain in a war. He furthermore wholeheartedly welcomed Sauer's criticism as well-founded since the UDF was not ready for any major war. The biggest challenge facing the Department of Defence was a lack of money, as its budget was smaller than that of the police.[361]

On 8 May 1939, on Pirow's initiative, the government started a National Reserve registration, a voluntary registration of men, not

360 House of Assembly Debates, 23 March 1939, Col. 2273–2287.

361 House of Assembly Debates, 2 May 1939, Col. 3923–3929.

part of the ACF, who were willing to do military service in a war situation. The *Cape Times* (11 May 1939) enthusiastically reported that the Department of Defence had distributed 250 000 registration forms, while an intake of 1700 ACF recruits were accommodated to do their military training. *Die Burger* (29 May 1939), also with a tone of satisfaction, reported that only English speakers and Jews were registering. On 8 August 1939, the newspaper announced with glee that hardly any Afrikaners had registered.

The main reason for the reluctance of many Afrikaners to register was their distrust of institutions outside of the commando system. Pirow added to this distrust in his dismissive attitude to concerns about how young Afrikaner recruits were treated by UDF instructors. This was after Reverend P.J.S. de Klerk, a Pretoria minister in the Reformed Church, demanded an investigation into the alleged foul language used by instructors. Advocate A.H. Broeksma as Secretary of Defence rejected the complaint in a brusque way. Pirow defended Broeksma's behaviour and the outraged De Klerk turned to the Afrikaans press and the NP to vent his anger and hurt about his treatment.

On 12 June, Strijdom took up De Klerk's objections in parliament. For him the attitude of the Defence Department towards a church minister was something that belonged in dictatorships such as the Soviet Union which Pirow so admired. He was furthermore outraged that Pirow treated fellow Afrikaners like dirt while cultivating a close relationship with imperialists like Stallard. A riled Pirow lashed out at Strijdom's weak spot – his determination to keep his active service in the UDF during the invasion of German South West Africa in 1915 out of the public eye. Strijdom's defence was that as a member of the ACF, he had had no choice in the matter. Pirow, using as a pretext that anyone with military experience will realise that swearing is part of military life, sneeringly referred to Strijdom's participation in the SWA invasion, while pointing out that he personally had refused to do so.[362]

*Die Suiderstem* (13 June 1939) rejoiced in Strijdom's humiliation, but it was an unnecessary attack that would come to haunt Pirow. Pirow belatedly realised the harm caused by the De Klerk fracas and he organised a DRC minister, Reverend L.P. Snyman, to

362 House of Assembly Debates, 12 June 1939, Col. 6717–6723, 6717–6820.

visit the SSB at Voortrekkerhoogte (as Roberts Heights had been renamed). The minister praised the clean living of the recruits, but the damage had been done as the offended Reformed Church had been turned into a powerful opponent of the attempts to attract Afrikaner recruits for the UDF.

To boost the manpower of the UDF, Pirow initiated a process to investigate the possibility of a draft system, based on the drawing of lots for men between the ages of 17 and 25. Pirow's biggest challenge was not manpower, but to secure weapons as the British remained reluctant to sell modern armaments. As part of the measures to strengthen the defence of the country, Pirow played a leading role in the development of bush carts – a type of Scotch cart with one shaft and two large spoked wheels pulled by two oxen or mules. For a man obsessed with modernity and the desire to have the latest weapons, the bush cart seemed an odd acquisition, but for Pirow, who was convinced that in any future war the British colonies of Kenya and Tanganyika would form South Africa's defence barrier, they were the perfect means to convey material over rough terrain for bush warfare.

General Collyer who between 1937 and 1939 wrote about the history of the UDF's role in the war in German South West Africa and German East Africa, also influenced Pirow. Collyer discounted mechanised transport in Africa, and the fact that only mounted troops could be counted on.[363] This perception was enthusiastically shared by Pirow who proclaimed that since oxen could live off the local environment, it was an economic way to convey equipment, while it would not get bogged down in mud as would be the case with mechanised transport. The bush carts were formally unveiled at the Military College at Voortrekkerhoogte at the end of July 1939. It was regarded as such an important event that *Die Burger* (1 August) placed it on its front page.

On 8 and 9 August 1939, the UDF held a field exercise with 1000 men and the bush carts in the northern Transvaal near Tzaneen. Oxen were provided by the local black farmers. The objective of the exercise was to test the bush carts under active service conditions by transporting equipment over virgin bush country with no roads, while

363 Van der Waag, "South African defence in the age of total war", p. 149.

the SAAF had to find the convoy from the air. Pirow, first riding on a horse and then marching along with the troops, observed events.[364]

According to Gideon Jacobs, a young SSB recruit, the exercise was a disaster as the troops struggled to control the oxen. Many oxen panicked, broke their yokes and stampeded. Eventually some of the heavy carts had to be pulled by soldiers.[365]

Pirow declared that he was satisfied with the performance of the carts and that it would prove to be a great asset to the army. The *Cape Times* special correspondent observing the exercise bubbled over in his admiration and respect for Pirow and the UDF and declared the manoeuvres exceptionally successful.[366] An attitude shared by the editor of the *Cape Times* on 11 August in a leading article "Our Bushveld frontier":

> The combination of the primitive ox-drawn cart on the one hand, and the most modern instrument of warfare on the other may indeed point to a solution of the difficulties peculiar to military operations on our northern frontier and far beyond it. The aeroplane will be indispensable, if only for the purpose of reconnoitring, but motor vehicles and even tanks may have to make way for a sturdier, more elastic conveyance, manned by soldiers of a race that possesses a natural aptitude for what Mr Pirow yesterday called bushcraft.

After the exercise, Pirow addressed the assembled officers, promising them that from 1940 compulsory military service for boys would be implemented with that year's voluntary registration to bring the ACF regiments up to strength. He emphasised that he did not think that a war in Europe was inevitable and that nothing had happened in Europe that affected South African interests directly, or indirectly. The real threat to South Africa was the rise of Japanese imperialism which meant that in the Far East the white man's prestige had sunk to zero with repercussions for the white population in Africa, a situation the UDF would have to face.[367]

---

364 *Cape Times*, 9 August 1939.

365 G.F. Jacobs, *Beckoning horizons* (Johannesburg, 1985), p. 30.

366 *Cape Times*, 10 August 1939.

367 NA Kew, FO 371/23964, File W11507, High Commissioner's telegram, 11 August 1939.

Pirow also informed the British High Commissioner that a war with Japan was inevitable and that South Africa would have to join in. This meant that Britain had to supply South Africa with aircraft and big coastal guns for its defence. For the High Commissioner, Pirow's fear of Japan was quite fantastic and he prescribed it to his colour prejudice.[368]

In August 1939, the UDF comprised 260 officers and 4600 men (of which 2080 were in the air force), the SSB comprised 1900 men, and the ACF comprised 950 officers and 14 000 men. The air force had one Blenheim bomber, one Fairey Battle bomber, four Hurricane fighters and 63 obsolete Hawker Hartebeest planes and 230 training aircraft. With regard to armaments, the army had two obsolete medium tanks, two outdated armoured cars, two armoured trains, a number of artillery pieces with only 941 rounds of ammunition and eight anti-aircraft guns.[369]

The country had no navy, but in August 1939 it was decided to establish the South African Local Seaward Defence Corps as part of the ACF for minesweeping, anti-submarine and examination services at ports in the events of a war.[370] Although numerically small and poorly armed, the UDF had undergone a dramatic improvement under Pirow's control since 1933. The number of commissioned officers in the standing army was enlarged and the training of troops was improved. Money was provided for the field training of ACF units, while the army held large field exercises in 1937, 1938 and 1939.[371]

The one weak spot in Pirow's tenure as defence minister was the commando system. Although he had increased the spending on them from £270 000 in 1933 to £870 000 in 1937, its members remained poorly trained and armed. He added to this problem by making political loyalty of recruits, and not merit, the determining factor for the appointment of the commanding officers. He was determined to keep NP supporters out of such positions.

---

368 NA Kew, FO 371/23964, File W11507, High Commissioner's telegram, 31 July 1939.

369 E. Kleynhans, "Armoured warfare: The South African experience in East Africa, 1940–1941", (M.Mil, Stellenbosch University, 2014), p. 10.

370 I. van der Waag, "'The thin edge of the wedge': Anglo-South African relations, dominion nationalism and the formation of the Seaward Defence Force in 1939–1940", *Contemporary British History*, 24 (4), 2010, p. 435.

371 Birkby, *Uncle George*, p. 97.

Hertzog was so outraged by the political activities of Commandant J. du Toit of the Smithfield commando that he ordered Pirow not to reappoint him as the commanding officer when his term came to an end.[372] That appointments were dependent on the approval of local UP MPs was evident when Pirow wanted to know from J.M. Conradie, MP for Rustenburg, whether he would be happy with the reappointment of Major F.W. Conradie as the commander of the Rustenburg North-East commando.[373]

By March 1939, Pirow informed Nicholls, who was concerned about the reliability of the commandos in a war in support of Britain, that there were only six commando commandants whose loyalty he had doubts about.[374] And yet, despite the poor state of the commandos, Pirow had turned the UDF from a dilapidated unit into a well-trained and efficient one. As Ian van der Waag points out: "South Africa's defences reached a peak in 1939 and were in a better state of preparation than any other time in its peacetime history."[375] Evert Kleynhans, although critical of Pirow's lack of strategic planning for the UDF, concurs with Van der Waag and concludes that in terms of improvements to the military, the period between 1933 and 1939 was a "Pirowian renaissance".[376]

It was as a highly respected Minister of Defence that Pirow on Sunday 14 August represented the South African government to meet General António Oscar de Fragoso Carmona, the president of Portugal, at Komatipoort station on the Mozambique border for a state visit. His high standing with the Portuguese government was reflected in the gift the president presented him with – an Andalusian Arab stallion.

During his stay in Lisbon the year before, he was taken to the government's horse-training establishment at Mafra. A mount was provided for him and he had impressed the Portuguese with his skills

372 NA Archive Pretoria, J.C.G. Kemp Papers, Kemp – Pirow, 25 January 1939.

373 UP Archive, J.M. Conradie papers, File 9, Correspondence 1939, Pirow – Conradie, 17 July 1939.

374 Nicholls, *South Africa in my time*, p. 351.

375 Van der Waag, *A military history of modern South Africa*, p. 170.

376 E. Kleynhans, "'n Militêre debakel: Die Unieverdedigingsmag, die tussenoorlogse jare, en lesse van die Eerste Wêreldoorlog" (Unpublished paper, Geskiedenissimposium, Suid-Afrikaanse Akademie vir Wetenskap en Kuns, 25 Januarie 2019).

as an equestrian. Pirow had little time to bask in the respect of the Portuguese as the NP had turned the state visit into a party-political issue. The NP claimed that the objective of Portugal, Britain's oldest ally, was to create a naval base in neighbouring Mozambique – which had to be protected by South Africa.

Pirow rejected this as utter rubbish. But how strong the perception was that he was a pawn of Jewish-British imperialism was reflected in the arrest on a charge of criminal libel in August 1939 of Stanislow Boleslow Gricius, a blacksmith of Clocolan who had published a letter that Pirow was a Jew. He claimed that Pirow's real name was "Shapirow" and that he used his position as a cabinet minister to assist Jews in avoiding paying tax.[377]

By August 1939, a war between Britain and Germany seemed increasingly inevitable. After Germany's occupation of Czechoslovakia, Hitler turned his attention to Poland with territorial demands. In April 1939, Chamberlain, realising that Hitler had to be stopped, declared Poland's borders inviolable and guaranteed British support for Poland against any German aggression. As tensions between Poland and Germany increased, Pirow fed the suspicions of the NP that South Africa would enter a war on Britain's side. At a public meeting near Brits in August, he made it clear that he was investigating reports of army officers who have stated that they would not march further than the borders of the country in event of a war.[378]

In Europe, tension reached breaking point after Germany and the Soviet Union signed a non-aggression pact on 23 August. Pirow went to visit Hertzog on his farm near Witbank in the Transvaal to discuss the measures to be taken if a war should break out. As the cabinet had agreed in 1938 with the Sudeten crisis to remain neutral in any war, they did not anticipate a local crisis. As a precaution, South African citizens in Germany were instructed to leave the country. Two of them were his daughter Else, who had left South Africa on 11 May for a six-month stay in Germany, and his mother who was on vacation. They immediately left Germany via the Netherlands.

That Pirow felt unconcerned by events in Europe was evident in his statement to Bellwood that the Polish situation had nothing

377 *Cape Times*, 16 August 1939.

378 *Sunday Times*, 20 August 1939.

to do with South Africa.[379] However, Wilson of the *Cape Times* in a conversation with Pirow during the Polish crisis had the feeling that in a few days South Africa would be at war with Germany if Hitler carried out his intention of invading Poland.[380] It is possible that he misunderstood or confused Pirow's stance, who remained of the opinion that South Africa would enter the war after a period of neutrality. This was evident in his statement to T.C. Robertson of the *Sunday Times* that it would take at least six months before a decision would be taken to declare war against Germany.[381]

379 Bellwood, *South African back-drop*, p. 61.

380 Wilson, *Gone down the years*, p. 208.

381 *Dagbreek en Sondagnuus*, 6 September 1964.

# 9

# War and division, September–December 1939

Pirow, secure in the knowledge that his daughter and mother were safe, and that South Africa would be neutral in any European conflict, retired to his farm for a ten-day vacation. He had reason to be relaxed as his status as Hertzog's successor was assured, especially after Blackwell and Hofmeyr had resigned from the party's parliamentary caucus by the end of May. This was after they had opposed the Asiatics (Transvaal Land and Trading) Bill which restricted Indians from buying land in clearly defined areas. Hertzog was outraged and demanded that they be censured in the UP parliamentary caucus.

What Pirow did not realise was that after the Nazi occupation of Czechoslovakia in March 1939, Smuts had concluded that South Africa had to stand with Britain against Nazi Germany by entering any war immediately. By a sheer fluke, events played into Smuts's hands when parliament was unexpectedly convened to deal with the expiring mandate of the Senate. On 25 August, legal advisors of the government discovered that the Senate would reach the end of its tenure by 5 September and that the country would be without a full parliament. Smuts, as the responsible government minister, was immediately informed.

In consultation with Hertzog it was decided to reconvene parliament for a special sitting on Saturday 2 September to prolong the tenure of the Senate. On 28 August, all MPs received telegrams from the clerk of the House of Assembly instructing them to attend the special session. Esselen, using his position as Secretary General of the UP, started to canvas UP MPs to oppose a neutrality motion by Hertzog.[382]

On 1 September 1939, the German army invaded Poland. Britain and France issued an ultimatum for Germany to withdraw from Polish territory, or they would declare war on 3 September. Pirow and Hertzog were confident that the cabinet was united on neutrality. It was only in Cape Town on 2 September that they realised that Smuts was determined to reject neutrality.[383] According to Keith Hancock, Smuts's most outstanding biographer, the claim that Hertzog and his supporters in the cabinet were unaware of Smuts's new stance on neutrality is baffling, as he had made it abundantly clear in public speeches after March 1939 that Hitler had to be stopped. The reason why this did not alert Pirow was that he was also convinced that South Africa would be involved in a European war, but that local political circumstances would ensure that it would only happen after a few months.

The cabinet met on the afternoon of 2 September. Hertzog read the neutrality declaration of September 1938 and declared it as the government's policy to stay out of the war. Smuts responded that the agreement only applied to the Sudeten crisis and that the international situation had changed since Germany's invasion of Czechoslovakia. Hitler was aiming at world domination, and for the sake of South Africa, not of Britain, the country could not remain neutral.[384] He had the support of seven of the thirteen cabinet members.

The next day, after the British declaration of war on Germany, the cabinet reconvened but remained divided. The decision on whether South Africa should enter the war was referred to the House of Assembly. Hertzog informed Governor General Patrick Duncan, his former cabinet colleague, that he expected a majority of three or four votes and that after the vote he would immediately request a dissolution of parliament, and a general election.[385] Realising that the cabinet

---

382 *Dagbreek en Sondagnuus*, 6 September 1964.

383 *Die Nuwe Orde*, 4 October 1946.

384 A. van Wyk, *Vyf dae: Oorlogskrisis in 1939 – 'n spanningsverhaal uit SA se geskiedenis* (Cape Town, 1985), p. 47.

385 NA Kew, DO 35/1003/6, File W.G.3/4/1, High Commissioner's dispatch, 13 September 1939.

division meant the end of the fusion government, and confident that with the support of the NP the neutrality vote would prevail in the House of Assembly – leading to a realignment of political parties – Pirow showed once more his ability to trim his sails to prevailing political winds.

On the evening of 3 September Malan had a meeting with the prime minister and his cabinet supporters at his official residence at Groote Schuur on the next day's vote. Pirow behaved as if the last six years had never happened. To Malan's astonishment, he proclaimed himself an ardent republican.[386] Up until then the NP was convinced that Pirow would stand by Britain in a war. Earlier in the day Strijdom had written to C.R. Swart, who had lost his seat in the election, that he was certain that Pirow would convince Hertzog to declare war against Germany.[387]

English-speaking UP MPs, who respected and admired Hertzog, were baffled by his blindness to the aggressive nature of Nazi Germany. Pirow's pro-German activities after June 1940 eventually led to many of them blaming him in their post-war memoirs for the prime minister's stance. For Nicholls, he was the decisive factor to influence Hertzog to accept neutrality,[388] an opinion shared by Bertha Solomon, UP MP for Jeppe.[389] Blackwell was convinced that Pirow had manipulated Hertzog by not fully informing him of the German threat to world order as he was obsessed with the strength of Nazi Germany which could not be resisted.[390]

Writing his memoirs in the 1960s, Piet van der Byl, as a former close friend, concluded that Pirow had been misled by Hitler when he had met him in 1938.[391] Hertzog's biographers concur that there is no evidence that Pirow had influenced the prime minister to be pro-German and to opt for neutrality.[392] Hertzog, old and exhausted,

386 Van Wyk, *Vyf dae*, pp. 73, 78–79, 82, 84, 87, 89.

387 ACA, UFS, C.R. Swart collection, File 3/1/22, Strijdom – Swart, 3 September 1939.

388 Nicholls, *South Africa in my time*, p. 353.

389 B. Solomon, *Time remembered* (Cape Town, 1968), pp. 131, 135.

390 Blackwell, *Farewell to parliament*, pp. 60, 74.

391 Van der Byl, *Top hat to velskoen*, p. 76.

392 Le Roux, Coetzer, Marais, *Generaal J.B.M Hertzog: Sy strewe en stryd, Vol. II*, p. 645.

had become dependent on Pirow by the late 1930s, but he needed no prompting on the issue of neutrality. South Africa as a sovereign country was under no obligation to support Britain in any European war. The published recollections of Pirow's fellow ministers on the cabinet meetings of 2 and 3 September reflect the absence of undue influence by Pirow.

C.F. Clarkson, the pro-British leader of the Natal UP and the Minister of Posts and Telegraphs, kept Nicholls informed of what was happening in the cabinet. Nicholls recorded in his diary Clarkson's report that Pirow's neutrality stance was not influenced by his being sympathetic to Germany and that he was prepared to deal with pro-German and anti-war elements in South Africa with the outbreak of a war.[393] That Pirow was not seen as pro-German in September 1939 was evident in the response of Egeland – who had lost his Durban seat in the 1938 general election – urging him in a telegram to use his influence with Hertzog to stand by Smuts in declaring war on Germany.[394]

On 4 September, Hertzog introduced a neutrality motion in the House of Assembly. In the Westminster parliamentary system with its strict party control, it is rare for debates to sway votes. The war debate was the exception as UP MPs had a free vote, and they could be convinced on how to vote. This was evident in Hertzog having the sympathy of the House with his sincerity on the sovereignty of South Africa. He argued that based on the 1934 Status Acts, the Statute of Westminster, and in the absence of any obligations to Poland, South Africa had not the slightest interest in the war with Germany. Furthermore, he argued that if the country should enter the war it would shatter the achievements of fusion, and that it would take years to recover the good relations between Afrikaners and English speakers.

Hertzog spoke with such emotion and sincerity that it had a powerful effect on the House. But he weakened his case by defending and justifying Germany's behaviour, blaming the Treaty of Versailles for humiliating the Germans. He passionately rejected the claim that Hitler was out to secure world domination.

In the press gallery, Schalk Pienaar of *Die Burger*, a fiery Afrikan-

393 Nicholls, *South Africa in my time*, p. 338.
394 Egeland, *Bridges of understanding*, p. 134.

er nationalist, was horrified and had a sinking feeling that Hertzog by justifying Hitler's actions had fatally harmed the case for neutrality.[395] This was indeed the case as he had created the perception that he embraced neutrality because he was pro-German and anti-British.

Pirow, acknowledged as one of the leading orators in the House, did not participate in the debate. Sir Herbert Stanley concluded that his silence was the result of the possible fear that his German origins, connections and the fact that he had shortly before concluded a trade agreement with Germany, would make him a liability rather than an asset.[396]

In his recollections Pirow claimed that after the cabinet split, he knew that there was nothing more for him to say as the neutrality motion would be lost in the House of Assembly and that he realised that his political career was over.[397] This is not true as he was convinced that with the support of Malan, the neutrality motion would have a majority and that there would be a general election after the vote and a possible alliance with the NP. He wanted to avoid any statements that could prevent such unity. Any support of Hertzog's passionate pro-German speech could only alienate some of the English-speaking UP MP's who were close to him. He gambled on the assumption that many of these MPs he had cultivated over the years would follow his lead.

According to T.C. Robertson this was a genuine concern in the Smuts camp.[398] Long concluded that Pirow had overestimated his influence to persuade them to vote for neutrality.[399] While Pirow remained silent, Malan endorsed Hertzog's justifications of Hitler's behaviour which according to him was motivated by the desire to rectify the harshness of the Treaty of Versailles. The speeches in support of neutrality by E.A. Conroy (UP MP for Vredefort) and Harm Oost (UP MP for Pretoria District) were uninspiring – warnings about the consequences of the relationship between Afrikaners and English speakers if the UP should splinter – and left the House unmoved.

395 S. Pienaar, *Getuie van groot tye* (Cape Town, 1979), p. 18.

396 NA Kew, DO 35/1003/6, File W.G.3/4/1, High Commissioner's dispatch, 13 September 1939.

397 Pirow, *James Barry Munnik Hertzog*, p. 257.

398 *Dagbreek en Sondagnuus*, 6 September 1964.

399 Long, *In Smuts's camp*, p. 66.

H.A. Fagan, Minister for Native Affairs, was the only supporter for neutrality rising to the occasion. He argued that being pro-German or pro-British was irrelevant since the issue was South Africa's sovereignty and self-interest, but he could not defuse the impression that Hertzog and Malan embraced neutrality as they were sympathetic to Hitler.

Smuts made a powerful case that neutrality would be fatal because Hitler wanted world domination by force, and that he had to be stopped to protect South Africa. He argued that neutrality could only dissociate the country from the British Commonwealth, and this could be fatal in the future. If Hitler were not countered, he could at the point of the bayonet claim the return of South West Africa. With a powerful and aggressive Germany on the borders of South Africa, the country would be in danger.

Smuts proposed a motion to reject neutrality, but he was adamant that the government would not send troops overseas like in the last war against Germany. He made an impact on those doubting whether to enter the war. Nicholls, who made an extremely jingoistic speech, undermined the good done by Smuts by claiming that South Africa was obliged to support Britain. In effect, he claimed that parliament did not even have the right to discuss the issue. However, all MPs, apart from the handful of DP members, felt that South Africa was under no automatic obligation to support Britain.

Nicholls's speech fell on the House like a bomb, leaving MPs shocked and startled.[400] Piet van der Byl, a passionate pro-war MP, was so disgusted that he left the chamber to smoke a cigarette to calm himself.[401] In response to this disastrous speech, Long made an off-the-cuff intervention. In a measured tone, he concurred with Hertzog on South Africa's sovereignty and the right to be neutral, but passionately argued that the country was obliged to enter the war as the aggression and brutality of the Nazi state had to be confronted.

Hofmeyr also emphasised the totalitarian nature of the Nazi state and that a German victory would lead to the worldwide expansion of this oppressive system. The speeches of Smuts, Long and Hofmeyr were persuasive and secured votes to reject neutrality. Afrikaners

---

400 Long, *In Smuts's camp*, pp. 41–43.

401 Van der Byl, *Top hat to velskoen*, p. 157.

with no emotional attachment to Britain, for example Louw Steyler, a former South African War veteran and an NP MP, as well as Colin Steyn, the son of M.T. Steyn, the former president of the Orange Free State Republic, were convinced to reject neutrality. This led to the defeat of Hertzog's motion by a majority of 13 votes.

According to Wilson in the press gallery, Hertzog on hearing the result turned to Pirow who was sitting near him, as if to say that his calculations had been wrong.[402]

Pirow was shattered by the defeat. Nicholls observed that after the vote he had lost his jaunty air and looked completely deflated.[403] On leaving parliament some bystanders jeered him, but his supporters carried him on their shoulders to his car.

After his defeat, Hertzog requested Duncan to dissolve parliament and announce an election. Duncan refused to do so as Smuts would have a working majority in parliament if he were to form a government. Hertzog had no choice but to resign as prime minister on 5 September. When Smuts the next day indicated that he could form a government, Duncan accepted Hertzog's resignation. The same day South Africa declared war against Germany.

After ten years of being a cabinet minister and a member of Hertzog's inner circle, someone who was treated with respect by MPs and seen by the press as a future prime minister, Pirow was reduced to a humble opposition backbencher. Pirow had to plead to secure a place on an SAAF plane to return him to Pretoria, claiming that he had to rush to Johannesburg to protect his German mother-in-law against anti-German riots. This was after a pro-war mob had attacked Messrs. Piel's Cold Storage, the Johannesburg business premises of his in-laws, on the evening of 4 September, setting a delivery truck alight and smashing windows with a bombardment of stones. Only with difficulty could the police restore law and order.[404] The Smuts government allowed his request, but the UP would use it later in party propaganda to mock his humbling drop in status and to remind voters of his German background.[405]

---

402 Wilson, *Gone down the years*, p. 212.
403 Nicholls, *South Africa in my time*, p. 344.
404 *The Star*, 5 September 1939.
405 Unisa, United Party Archive, UP Division of Information, Files on People, File 303 (O. Pirow), D. Boshoff, "Mnr. Pirow se verantwoording".

Without his ministerial salary Pirow had no choice but to return to the Bar in Pretoria to make a living. His pre-1929 reputation as an outstanding King's Counsel meant that he quickly found his feet. He promptly appeared on behalf of three accused who were tried on a charge of forging a will to their own financial advantage and secured their acquittal.[406] However, his main focus was on his efforts to rebuild his political career by reunifying the Hertzog supporters with the NP.

On 9 September, approximately 75000 Afrikaners met at Monumentkoppie, the site of the eventual Voortrekker Monument outside of Pretoria. In an emotional meeting arranged by the Broederbond – a secret Afrikaner cultural organisation – those present pledged themselves to Afrikaner unity. After the bitter clashes of the past, it was difficult for Hertzog's followers to form a united party with the NP. Pirow especially was resented for the sneers and wounding jests which he had flung at the NP. His battering of opponents without fear of retribution had secured him the hatred of numerous enemies. Strijdom loathed him with a burning intensity for the contempt with which he had treated him in the House of Assembly, especially by referring to him as a "little country-side attorney".[407] The brusque way he had dealt with Verwoerd, a close friend and ally of Strijdom, on the welfare of Afrikaner workers in the SAR&H, had also made him a vindictive enemy.[408]

Pirow's gladiatorial approach could still be accepted as part of the cut and thrust of party politics in the NP, but what condemned him as beyond the pale was the perception that he was an unprincipled opportunist. The fact that, after years of rejecting republicanism, he had overnight become a passionate republican convinced Strijdom that he was a man without any principles. For him the events of September 1939 signified that either Pirow was an opportunist who had left Britain in the lurch after creating the perception for years that he would come to the support of Britain, or that he was a witless person who had allowed himself to be exploited to the benefit of the Empire.[409]

406 C. Margo, *Final postponement. Reminiscences of a crowded life* (Johannesburg, 1998), p. 115.

407 Schoeman, *My lewe in die politiek*, pp. 47, 49.

408 G.D. Scholtz, *Dr Hendrik Frensch Verwoerd, 1901–1966, vol. 1* (Johannesburg, 1974), pp. 91–92.

409 ACA UFS, C.R. Swart collection, File 3/1/22, Strijdom – Swart, 8 and 18 September, 17 October 1939.

Strijdom and Verwoerd had an axe to grind, but even the level-headed Geyer in his political notebook expressed his concerns: "Pirow, whose interest in politics is the advancement of the political interests of Oswald Pirow"(translated).[410] Feelings against Pirow were so strong that the British High Commissioner recorded it in his dispatch to London on 27 September 1939:

> Though South African born, he [Pirow] is not a true Afrikaner and it is not likely that he will find a happy home with the Nationalists who have been irritated by his balancing tricks and despise him for his lack of settled convictions.[411]

Pirow's public speeches in the weeks after the war vote fuelled suspicions that he was not a true Afrikaner. To attract as many Afrikaner UP supporters as possible who were content to be a part of the British Empire and had concerns about Nazi Germany, he declared that Duncan had acted absolutely within his rights in refusing Hertzog's request for a general election. He furthermore stated that Britain had been scrupulously fair in respecting South Africa's sovereign independent rights, and that the British government applied no pressure to force the country into the war. Such sentiments, as the British High Commissioner dryly observed, could not have been pleasing for the NP leadership.[412]

The High Commissioner was spot-on as Strijdom wanted nothing to do with Pirow, claiming that he would dilute the political purity of the NP. To Malan he made it clear that he would not allow the NP to be sacrificed by the creation of a new party to accommodate Hertzog and his followers.[413] Since he held Pirow responsible for Hertzog's truculent attitude to the NP – claiming that he was poisoning the former prime minister's mind – he refused to address public meetings with him.[414] Those members of the Transvaal NP who dared to be supportive of the Hertzogites were hounded by him and Verwoerd.

---

410 "Pirow, wie se aandeel in die politiek is die bevordering van die politieke belange van Oswald Pirow." WCPA, Cape Town, A.L. Geyer collection, Vol. 3, Political notebook, 9 September 1939.

411 NA Kew, DO 35/587/6, High Commissioner's dispatch, 27 September 1939.

412 NA Kew, DO 35/587/6, High Commissioner's dispatch, 19 October 1939.

413 University of Stellenbosch (hereafter US), D.F. Malan collection, 1/1/1519, Strijdom – Malan, 18 September 1939.

414 ACA UFS, C.R. Swart collection, File 3/1/22, Strijdom – Swart, 29 September and 30 October 1939.

The province's only other NP parliamentarian, W.C.M. du Toit of Marico, was marginalised for daring to be sympathetic to the Hertzogites.

Geyer felt that Strijdom and Verwoerd played a crucial role in straining relations between the NP and Hertzog's followers and that their enmity to Pirow was motivated by the fear that Pirow could become the party leader in the Transvaal. Ben Schoeman was convinced that the accusations of opportunism levelled at Pirow was because Strijdom viewed him as a threat to his own political ambitions.[415] The intensity of Strijdom's loathing of Pirow was evident in a letter he wrote to Swart on 18 September 1939. He poured out his anger about what he condemned as the hysterical worshipping and incensing (*bewieroking*) of Pirow by Afrikaner nationalists. He was outraged that students at the University of Pretoria, a hotbed of Afrikaner nationalism, received Pirow as a hero, going so far in their adulation as to pull his car through the streets of Pretoria.[416]

Strijdom's concerns about Pirow as a leadership rival could only have been aggravated by the fact that former UP MPs increasingly looked to Pirow for leadership as a shattered Hertzog had become so withdrawn that he did not even speak to them.[417] On 8 December 1939, Pirow and Kemp, in an effort to strengthen the position of the Transvaal Hertzogites in the negotiations with the NP, formed the Volksparty (People's Party). The party's goal was a republic based on equal rights for the two white groups which would only be implemented if approved after a referendum.

With a political base to bolster his position, Pirow started negotiating with the leadership of the NP to unify the two parties. In contrast to Strijdom and Verwoerd, he did his utmost to be conciliatory. He played a crucial role as a mediator between the increasingly cantankerous Hertzog and Malan in the dispute over the distribution of parliamentary seats.

Hertzog insisted that in the next general election his supporters had to be guaranteed their parliamentary seats. Malan was adamant that the former fusionist MPs could not retain their seats without

415 Schoeman, *My lewe in die politiek*, p. 49.

416 ACA UFS, C.R. Swart collection, File 3/1/27, Strijdom – Swart, 18 September 1939.

417 Schoeman, *My lewe in die politiek*, p. 61.

nomination contests. This dispute became a threat to the unification process. A concerned Pirow went to see Malan behind Hertzog's back and managed to secure a compromise. The NP leader undertook to protect former UP MPs from victimisation in the nomination process. After this, Malan increasingly by-passed Hertzog to deal with Pirow who played a leading role in the merger in January 1940 to form the Herenigde Nasionale Party or Volksparty (Reunited National Party or People's Party), popularly known as the HNP, with Hertzog as the leader.[418]

418 WCPA, A.L. Geyer collection, Vol. 3, Political notebook, 4 and 5 December 1939, and 19, 22 and 28 January 1940.

# 10
# Ridicule, January–August 1940

In January 1940, Pirow returned to a drastically altered parliament. His closest friends, Van der Byl and Stallard (elected in a by-election on 12 September 1939), were in the Smuts cabinet. They avoided bitterness towards their old friend, but most of his former allies in the UP felt that he made fools out of them by operating under false political colours. UP MPs treated him with icy disdain. The editors of UP-supporting newspapers, feeling embarrassed by Pirow whom they, in the words of Stallard, had treated as the "cynosure of the press for six years",[419] also turned on him. They participated in a whispering campaign that he had left the UDF in a mess. This was after Smuts had informed John Martin of the Argus press group that Pirow had left the UDF in "woeful state of unpreparedness" for any war.[420]

These rumours had a political purpose to undermine Pirow who was feared by Smuts as the government's most dangerous opponent.[421] Pirow was sensitive to these rumours. After years of praise, he had a high opinion of himself and expected recognition and respect for his genius. His response was to condemn these attacks as jingoism.

Accusing the English-medium press of hatred for the Afrikaner

419 House of Assembly Debates, 12 February 1940, Col. 1216.
420 NA Pretoria, J.C. Smuts papers, Vol. 246, Smuts – Martin, 4 October 1939.
421 F.S. Crafford, *Jan Smuts: A biography* (New York, 1968), p. 260.

could only have added to the alienation of his former UP colleagues, while it made no impact on former NP MPs such as Strijdom, Verwoerd, Van der Merwe and Sauer who continued to loathe him. Hell would also freeze over before Verwoerd would write a positive word on Pirow in *Die Transvaler*. This left Pirow feeling vulnerable in the HNP, especially as Hertzog was a shadow of his former self and there were serious concerns about his mental state. It was obvious to all that he had reached the end of the political road.

For the first time since 1915 Pirow was without a powerful backer to support and protect him. Apart from feeling isolated and insecure, Pirow struggled to come to terms with his status as backbencher. Long observed that Pirow was visibly unhappy on the opposition benches.[422] The parliamentary correspondent of the *Cape Times* noted that his usual energetic and confident demeanour was gone, replaced by a permanent "hangdog look".[423] Egeland, who had returned to parliament after a by-election in January 1940, was shocked to find him so deflated and spiritless.[424]

Pirow decided the best way to strengthen his position in the HNP was to confront Smuts and take him on in a parliamentary debate. On 23 January 1940, this opportunity arose with Hertzog's motion that the time has come that South Africa's role in the war with Germany should be ended and peace be restored. In doing so he justified Hitler's military actions in Europe as having been forced on him by Britain and France. The German leader, according to Hertzog, was not seeking world domination, but was only attempting to remove the horrors of the Treaty of Versailles.

In seconding the motion, Pirow made no attempt to explain why he had embraced neutrality and launched a bitter personal attack on Smuts. The day before the debate when an MP had asked him whether it would be a fight with the gloves off, he replied "not only with the gloves off but with knuckledusters on".[425] It was no empty threat as Pirow, who was a master of sarcasm and viciousness in order to belittle and wound his opponents in debates, attacked Smuts mercilessly. He accused him of behaving dishonourably in his support of

422 Long, *In Smuts's camp*, pp. 67–68.
423 *Cape Times*, 30 August 1940.
424 Egeland, *Bridges of understanding*, p. 104.
425 NA Kew, DO 35/588/1, High Commissioner's dispatch, 8 February 1940.

a war against Germany and did his utmost to tarnish his reputation by claiming that in April 1939 it was he himself, and not Smuts, who was responsible for sending police reinforcements to South West Africa to prevent any possible Nazi uprising amongst the territory's German population. Smuts, he alleged, did not want to send the police as he wanted things to develop into a possible bloodshed to ensure that South Africa would enter any possible future war against Germany. He also defended his period as Minister of Defence.

He ended his speech with a warning to Afrikaner UP MPs that the aim of the English-speaking jingo newspapers, who dictated policy to Smuts, was to turn every Afrikaner into a lackey of the Empire with the soul of a National Scout. (National Scouts were Afrikaners who had joined the British army to fight against fellow Afrikaners in the South African War.)

It was a poor speech, unfocused, rambling and vindictive, and created the perception that he was pursuing a personal vendetta against Smuts. In doing so he strengthened the alienation of his former English-speaking supporters in the UP who desired an explanation of why he had embraced neutrality. They also resented his sudden conversion to the purified tactic of abusing English speakers as jingoes. With the Afrikaner UP MPs his speech also backfired as they did not take kindly to his abuse of their beloved party leader, or to be categorised as National Scouts.

He also did himself no favours with the former NP MPs as he had created the impression that he was pursuing his own agenda instead of the interests of Afrikaner nationalism. For Swart the speech showed that Pirow was a fool and that it was a source of derision for friend and foe alike.[426] More ominously, he had aroused the resentment of Smuts who listened in silence to Pirow with his face turning red when he was at his most insulting.[427] Smuts was not a person to turn the other cheek, but as a shrewd politician, he was awaiting the right opportunity to strike back, but until then he left the counter-attacking to his acolytes.

Since Pirow had boasted that he would attack Smuts, the UP-party whips had requested his old enemy, Leslie Blackwell, to pre-

426 NA Pretoria, Strijdom papers, Vol. 51, Swart – Strijdom, 25 January 1940.
427 Schoeman, *My lewe in die politiek*, p. 63.

pare a counterattack. Blackwell had just returned from Kenya where the leaders of the white settler community had expressed their amazement that Pirow had opted for neutrality. During his 1936 visit he had created the expectation that the UDF would rush to Kenya's defence in a war involving Britain. Lord Francis Scott, a settler leader in the colony, provided him with a written statement that Pirow had made such a promise.[428] Blackwell read the letter in the House and then demanded Pirow's response.

After a lengthy silence, Blackwell launched a scathing attack on him for demanding neutrality after such an undertaking. Although theatrical in the extreme, he had succeeded in portraying his support of neutrality as a breach of faith and the fact that Smuts was fulfilling the promises he as the former Minister of Defence had made.

His attack bolstered the suspicions of former NP MPs about Pirow as a political trimmer, while strengthening the belief amongst UP MPs that as a member of the Hertzog government, he was not a straight dealer. The UP-supporting press took up Blackwell's accusation that his support for neutrality was a breach of faith. On 20 March, *Die Suiderstem* portrayed him as unprincipled and a scheming opportunist. In May 1939 the newspaper published notes that Pirow had provided for a UP pamphlet to explain why South Africa could not remain neutral after Germany had attacked Britain. The *Cape Times* (21 March 1940) condemned him in scathing terms:

> Mr. Pirow to-day light-heartedly throws overboard these products of his fertile mind and is now doubtless using his legal abilities to excogitate a separate set of arguments designed to prove the opposite. But democracy as South Africa knows it draws a distinction between a lawyer presenting a case and a statesman leading his people; in one, conviction can vary with the case; in the other, it is a matter of honour. Mr. Pirow is convicted in these words in his own writing of a failure to live up to the standards set by those who have ideals about the conduct of democratic life.

Reeling under the accusation of having behaved dishonourably by supporting neutrality, Pirow's reputation received another blow with an attack on 25 January by P.V. Pocock, UP MP for Pretoria Central and the chairman of a committee to investigate South Africa's de-

428 Blackwell, *Farewell to parliament*, pp. 73–74.

fence needs. What Pirow did not realise was that his defence of his administration of the Department of Defence during the neutrality motion of Hertzog provided an opportunity for Smuts and the UP to strike at him. Before 23 January 1940, there was only a whispering campaign.

Smuts could not afford a public condemnation because it would elicit the question why he did not raise any concerns about the state of the army while he was in the cabinet with Pirow. He also realised that Pirow could not be held accountable for the inability of the UDF to immediately enter a war. When Deneys Reitz, the Minister of Native Affairs and a close ally of Smuts, met with Anthony Eden in London in October 1939, he pointed out that the UDF was in a deplorable state, but that Pirow had not done it wilfully.[429]

However, Pirow's blistering attack on Smuts made it possible for the prime minister to unleash a coordinated attack on him. In the House of Assembly, Pocock claimed that he had spent none of the money budgeted for defence and that he had left the UDF in a dismal state, leaving the country defenceless. He in effect accused Pirow of misleading parliament about the true state of the UDF's military readiness and that his reputation as competent and a go-getter was a mere facade.[430]

A furious Pirow, who had already used his speaking opportunity in the debate, could only respond with an interjection, "Why don't you ask the Prime Minister?", drawing attention to the fact that as a fellow cabinet member Smuts had never criticised his stewardship of the Defence portfolio and had approved all his defence plans.[431]

This was not how the UP-supporting press saw it. In a leading article under the heading "What Pirow didn't", the *Cape Times* (26 January 1940), which only five months earlier had praised him to the skies, condemned him for giving the country an army without equipment, artillery without ammunition and an air force without modern planes. The *Rand Daily Mail* dubbed him the "Get nothing done ex-Minister of Defence".[432]

---

429 NA Kew, DO 35/1003/6, File G3/4/11, Summary of a meeting between A. Eden and D. Reitz, 23 October 1939.

430 House of Assembly Debates, 25 January 1940, Col. 141–147.

431 NA Kew, DO 35/588/1, High Commissioner's dispatch, 8 February 1940.

432 Calpin, *There are no South Africans*, p. 298.

It was a shock for Pirow to turn overnight from the blue-eyed boy of the UP-friendly press into what Pirow ruefully described as an "evil person".[433] The shock was aggravated by the lack of support in his own party. For the parliamentary correspondent of the *Cape Times*, it was obvious that the former NP MPs enjoyed Pocock's assault on Pirow.[434] This fuelled his eagerness to get at Smuts.

On 7 February, confident that he could force Smuts to concede that he had left the UDF in a good state, he launched an attack on Smuts during the War Measures Bill. Pirow's confidence was boosted by the fact that Smuts had retained the high command he had created for the UDF. The exception was Broeksma who was replaced as the Secretary of Defence. He was appointed as the Attorney General of the Cape Province and Judge Advocate General of the UDF. In addition, Collyer who had provided the theoretical base for the bush-cart approach had become Smuts's military secretary on 11 September 1939.[435] After condemning Smuts once more for breaking his pledge on neutrality, he challenged him to formulate what was wrong with the UDF when he took over as Minister of Defence. He also attempted to counter the accusation that his support of neutrality was a breach of faith by stating that as the Minister of Defence he had only promised that the UDF would rush to defend Kenya as the "protector of white civilization".

So vehement and personal was his attack that Sauer noted it was motivated by hatred.[436] The prime minister again left it to his supporters to do the counterattacking. The most damaging onslaught came from Stallard, an honoured guest at the UDF's military exercise of August 1939. In a tone of sincere sorrow he rejected the accusations that Pirow was an inferior administrator, but made the more damaging accusation that he was deceitful in claiming that the sole purpose of the UDF was to fight a "black horde" from the north. For him there was no doubt that up to September Pirow was convinced that in the near future the country would be committed to a war with a first-class power, meaning Germany. In the words of the *Cape Times*

433 *Die Suiderstem*, 16 March 1940.

434 *Cape Times*, 26 January 1940.

435 Van der Waag, "Smuts's generals", pp. 33, 45, 58.

436 University of the Free State, Archive for Contemporary Affairs, C.R. Swart collection, File 3/1/25, P. Sauer – C.R. Swart, 9 February 1940.

(13 February 1940) it was an "oration that was little short of brilliant" and "no mean or trivial attack".

The speech made such an impact on the House that Hertzog felt obliged to defend Pirow as having acted correctly in preparing the country's defence preparations for nothing but neutrality. Unfortunately, his speech was so rambling and disjointed that the House found it difficult to follow his train of thought, and it did little to restore Pirow's tarnished reputation.

The UP did not let up in its hounding of Pirow and started to target his period as the Minister of Railways and Harbours. G. Dolley (MP for Uitenhage) condemned him as a disastrous minister who had bought – without a tender process – German locomotives and 21 Junkers planes from Germany at a cost of £498 027. He was especially outraged that Germany, when war broke out, was in possession of £42 836 worth of Junker engines and equipment South Africa had already paid for.[437] Dolley's attack did Pirow no harm as it was evident to all South Africans that under his stewardship the SAR&H was an improved and more efficient department.

To Pirow's frustration it was more difficult to defend his reputation as Minister of Defence, but he did not let up in his efforts. On 19 February, at a big HNP public meeting in the Pretoria City Hall, he claimed that South Africa in September 1939 was better prepared for a war than Britain and challenged Smuts to acknowledge this.[438]

While Pirow was strutting on the public stage, Smuts was preparing a counterattack with the assistance of Collyer, a fierce Smuts loyalist, who had provided him with a detailed memorandum on the state of the UDF in September 1939. The document, compiled early in 1940, was in effect a charge sheet against Pirow as Collyer held him responsible for the fact that the UDF was unprepared to fight an immediate war. Ignoring Pirow's statement of 2 May 1939 that the UDF was in no state to participate in a major war, he accused him of exaggerating the preparedness of the UDF to parliament and that his statements were in effect "smoke and mirrors".[439] In his determination to get at Pirow, he even resorted to Sauer's claim of 2 May 1939

437 House of Assembly Debates, 14 February 1940, Col. 1566–1572.
438 *Pretoria News*, 20 February 1940.
439 Kleynhans, "'n Militêre debakel".

that South African troops were so poorly armed that to put them into a combat situation amounted to "nothing less than murder".[440] He conveniently ignored the fact that Sauer had opposed every penny budgeted for the UDF as money wasted on British imperial interests. The memorandum was a powerful weapon in the hands of Smuts who was determined to settle a score with Pirow.

On 14 March, in the Defence budget debate, a confident Pirow set out to force Smuts to concede that as a fellow member of the Hertzog government he had approved and supported his defence policy, and that he was kept fully informed of the UDF's state of readiness. He rejected the accusations thrown at him as false and unfair, challenging Smuts to provide the facts and figures of his alleged incompetence, or to appoint a parliamentary select committee to investigate his alleged neglect of duty. He threatened that if the prime minister did not formulate his charges, the country would know that false accusations had been levelled against him.[441]

Smuts protested that he was baffled by Pirow's anger about his silence, as he personally had not laid any charges against him, but in the face of his challenge he could no longer remain silent. In a measured tone he proceeded to savage Pirow's tenure as Minister of Defence as all just grandiose plans and talk. He had no criticism of his five-year plan for the UDF as it was a good plan, but accused him that he had done nothing but make beautiful speeches and had failed miserably to implement this plan.

In a mocking tone, with UP MPs encouraging him with loud cheers and laughter, he condemned as a folly the hiring of the HMS *Erebus*. (On the request of Winston Churchill, the loan had been cancelled in September 1939.) In doing so he distorted events by ignoring the intention to create an anchorage for the monitor at Robben Island claiming that with the *Erebus* moored in Cape Town harbour it was a greater threat to the city than to any enemy. The firing of its guns would cause great destruction to the docks and half of Cape Town would collapse. He then went on to compare Pirow's

440 NA, Pretoria, Smuts papers, Box 132, "Statement of local military position on 7th September, 1939 and steps taken thereafter", pp. 5, 32. (I am grateful to Evert Kleynhans for providing me with a copy of this document.)

441 House of Assembly Debates, 14 March 1940, Col. 3419–3430.

1934 vision and the real state of the UDF in 1939, listing the lack of weapons, including a shortage of 833 Bren machine guns, omitting the fact that not even he himself could convince the British government to sell them to South Africa. With a continuous stream of interjections, Pirow attempted to disrupt Smuts's onslaught, but the prime minister with contemptuous ease batted them away. Resorting to Collyer's memorandum, he quoted Sauer's "plain murder" claim if the UDF had to face a combat situation.

The most damaging blow to Pirow came with an interjection of a UP MP. This was after Smuts mocked Pirow's intention to create a mechanical battalion by pointing out that the UDF only had two obsolete tanks, two obsolete armoured cars and two armoured trains. "And bush carts" a UP MP called out.[442] In the aftermath of Germany's destruction of the Polish army with its *blitzkrieg* doctrine of dive-bombers and tanks, the bush-cart approach seemed comical. With this interjection UP MPs collapsed into mocking laughter.[443]

Smuts then pronounced that he was going to carry out the five-year plan. He concluded on a devastating note:

> … the fact of the matter is that when the hon. Member [Pirow] left the department our defence system even after his five-year plan was something on paper with which we could not go out to face any enemy, it was more of a danger than a protection to the country, and in those circumstances the hon. Member has no reason for boasting of his achievements.[444]

Within a few minutes Smuts had reduced Pirow from a respected and feared politician into a figure of ridicule. After 14 March 1940, any speech by him would be interrupted with calls of "bush cart" and mocking laughter. In responding to his speeches, UP speakers would brush it off, jeering that any comment by the creator of the bush carts was not worthy of consideration.

In contrast to the UP's hounding of Pirow, there was little support for him in the HNP's parliamentary caucus. The former NP MPs, after years of being on the receiving end of his sneering sarcasm,

442 This interjection is not recorded in the Debates of the House of Assembly, but appears in the detailed summary of the debate by *Die Burger*, as well as in the memoirs of Ben Schoeman, *My lewe in die politiek*.

443 Schoeman, *My lewe in die politiek*, p. 63.

444 House of Assembly Debates, 14 March 1940, Col. 3436–3440.

relished the fact that Smuts had humiliated him. In his recollections Pirow admitted that he found the open pleasure these MPs derived from his savaging far more painful than the attack itself.[445]

Sauer was one of those who made no attempt to hide his satisfaction. In a letter to C.R. Swart he expressed his admiration for the cool and calm way Smuts had cut Pirow down to size. For him Pirow's failure in the Defence budget debate was final proof that he was a political lightweight:

> I never knew that Pirow could be so utterly useless as I now discover ... Blackie [Swart], you must come and help. This utter superficial, frivolous bantam rooster will become a great danger for us in the future. (translated)[446]

Smuts's hatchet job on Pirow led to jubilation in the UP-supporting press. *Die Suiderstem* (15 March 1940), which until September 1939 was sycophantic in its admiration of Pirow, praised the speech as "*Pirow ontmasker*" (Pirow unmasked). The HNP-supporting newspapers were lukewarm in their support of Pirow. *Die Burger* had a tradition of reporting parliamentary debates in the most heroic light for NP MPs. The furthest the newspaper would go was to point out that Pirow was on the defensive against Smuts, and that his debating performances were improving.

The lack of support by his own party harmed Pirow as he was an effective speaker when the political tide and wind were favourable, but not so when he had to deal with a hostile House.[447] During Smuts's attack, a seething Pirow promised that he would respond during the committee stage of the Defence budget. Four days later he had his opportunity, condemning the prime minister's claims on the state of the UDF as "perfectly preposterous". But the main objective of his attack was to damage Smuts's reputation as a war leader by claiming that the cancellation of the loan of the *Erebus* had left Cape Town at the mercy of German naval raiders. Against what the *Cape Times* described as "uproarious government laughter", Smuts once

445 *Die Nuwe Orde*, 30 May 1946.

446 "Ek het nooit geweet dat Pirow heeltemal so betekenloos is as wat ek nou uitvind... Blackie, jy moet kom help. Hierdie heeltemal oppervlakkige ligsinnige kapokhaan gaan vir ons 'n groot gevaar word in die toekoms." UFS, ACA, C.R. Swart collection, File 3/1/27, Sauer – Swart, 14 March 1940.

447 Long, *In Smuts's camp*, pp. 67–68, 78.

more portrayed the hiring of the HMS *Erebus* as a costly and grandiose scheme that was more a danger to the city than to the enemy.

Smuts kept the pressure on Pirow. On 15 April, in the Committee of Supply meeting for the Department of Defence, he once more laid into him for leaving the UDF "practically speaking, in an unarmed and hopeless state". In effect, he accused him of being a liar because he had left the country with the wrong impression that "our defence was in a magnificent state".[448]

Pirow responded that it was Smuts who was misleading the country with deliberate false statements because he knew that Britain had refused to sell modern armaments such as machine guns. While he for once controlled his temper, he levelled the accusation in a tone of sorrow that a former cabinet colleague could attack him in such a way. In this he was supported by Klasie Havenga, who pointed out that Smuts as a member of the Hertzog government was jointly responsible for the state of the UDF, especially since Pirow had taken him into his confidence on military affairs.

It was an effective response. Even *Die Burger* was impressed and on 20 April published a cartoon with Pirow planting a solid punch on Smuts's jaw in a boxing ring. However, Pirow's behaviour after Havenga's speech, when Blackwell rose to address the chamber, destroyed any possible positive outcome.

Cartoon by Boonzaier in *Die Burger*, 20 April 1940.
Pirow knocks out Smuts.

448 House of Assembly Debates, 15 April 1940, Col. 5017–5021.

Pirow had a low opinion of Blackwell, viewing his attacks on him as an opportunistic ploy to secure a position in the cabinet. When Blackwell started his speech, Pirow left his seat. Blackwell, who was about to condemn his attack on Smuts, shouted that he should remain seated and Pirow snarled back, "Are you so important?", and stormed out of the chamber. An outraged Blackwell exploded: "The hon. Member is walking out like a whipped pup, frightened as usual to face the music." He then proclaimed that the dismal state of the UDF was the result of Pirow's pro-German sympathies. As proof, it was pointed out that his daughter had attended a Nazi labour camp in Bavaria. Blackwell was referring to an interview Else Pirow had with the *Daily Express* in London on 6 June 1939 stating that at home the Pirows spoke in German, thought in German, and that she thought of Germany as "home". She was on her way to Germany and admitted that it was her lifelong ambition to be a good German.[449]

Blackwell furthermore claimed that Pirow's defence policy was a deliberate attempt to sabotage the security of South Africa, and that he was the local version of Vidkun Quisling. (The debate took place against the background of the German invasion of Norway where Quisling, a former Minister of Defence, had played a leading role in collaborating with the German invaders. His name became synonymous with treason and he was executed after the war.) Blackwell demanded that instead of appointing a select committee to investigate Pirow's tenure as Minister of Defence, the House should impeach him for his neglect of duty and for playing a double game.[450] Blackwell in his 1946 memoirs ruefully conceded that it "would be wrong to put him [Pirow] down as a mere Quisling",[451] but he had effectively created the image of Pirow as a German agent.

During the parliamentary session Pirow had not made a single pro-Nazi or pro-German statement and the HNP MPs were outraged by the accusation, but he forfeited their support by not facing Blackwell, a man they viewed with contempt as a beyond-the-pale jingo.[452] His behaviour had ultimately destroyed any remaining hope of being a leading figure in the HNP.

449 NA, Kew, KV 2/908, Clipping of the *Daily Express*.

450 House of Assembly Debates, 15 April, Col. 5025–5028.

451 Blackwell, *Farewell to parliament*, p. 74.

452 Schoeman, *My lewe in die politiek*, p. 64.

Keith Hancock concedes that to place the blame for the state of the UDF on the shoulders of Pirow was "perhaps unfair" seeing as he was handicapped because neither the government nor the people of South Africa were willing to contemplate any substantial switch of economic resources to produce military weaponry.[453] He was an able administrator, and before 1940 his management of the UDF was not questioned as he had improved it.

F.S. Crafford, a Smuts's biographer of the 1940s, correctly points out that the prime minister's savaging of Pirow served the political purpose of the hour: to boost the confidence of the hard-pressed UP with its small parliamentary majority, to enhance his own reputation as a parliamentary strategist, and to weaken Pirow as a dangerous opponent. He deprived him of the electorate's confidence by stripping him of his reputation for thoroughness and administrative ability.[454]

For the rest of his life it rankled with Pirow that Smuts, who was informed of his bush-cart methods, had used it to destroy him.[455] In reality, the shattering of his reputation was a case of self-destruction. As Blackwell gleefully informed the House of Assembly:

> The hon. gentleman who conducts the campaign against the hon. member for Gezina is the hon. member for Gezina himself. He is his own worst enemy in the House.[456]

By turning his administration of the Ministry of Defence into a public issue, Pirow had created the perception that he was a thin-skinned egoist that cared more about his reputation than the state of his country, and that he was pursuing a petty vendetta against Smuts. In doing so he provided an opening for Smuts to attack him, as the prime minister reminded him while putting the boot in during the Defence budget debate:

> Yes, the hon. member does not like this accusation and I would never have made it if he had not made this challenging speech of his.[457]

453 Hancock, *Fields of force*, pp. 331, 332.
454 Crafford, *Jan Smuts*, p. 261.
455 *Die Brandwag*, 18 December 1953; Pirow, *James Barry Munnik Hertzog*, p. 219.
456 House of Assembly Debates, 15 April 1940, Col. 5026.
457 House of Assembly Debates, 14 March 1940, Col. 3438.

The attack on him was so savage that the journalist G.H. Calpin wrote: "Perhaps on no occasion has a South African minister had to undergo such a scathing indictment." Pirow buckled under the onslaught. Overnight the charming, confident and feared political gladiator collapsed into a self-pitying whinger that either stormed out of the House when under attack or "glowered in fury and blanched in anger".[458] For Egeland he cut a pathetic figure in the face of this merciless attack.[459] Most MPs would have concurred with Rudyard Kipling's memorable line in his iconic poem "If" – that if you could meet triumph and disaster and treat these imposters as the same, you would be a man. Pirow's lack of mettle to cope with disaster after years of triumph and success left him a diminished figure in parliament, and especially in the HNP.

Outside the confines of parliament, supporters of the HNP still had a high regard for Pirow. Also, the NP-supporting press, despite its dislike of Pirow, did not advertise the UP's demolition of him and party branches invited him to address public meetings and *stryddae* (battle days) where he was received with adulation. These meetings did much to restore Pirow's self-confidence. In August 1940, in the wake of the defeat of France by Nazi Germany in June 1940 and with Britain fighting for survival, parliament met for a supplementary war budget. The *Cape Times* (30 August 1940) noted that he had regained some of his old aggressiveness and that the hangdog look that distinguished him in the previous session was gone.

Hertzog used the opportunity to introduce a "termination of war motion", demanding that South Africa should immediately seek peace with Germany and Italy as there was not the slightest hope of a British victory. Pirow made a forceful speech in support of Hertzog's motion, claiming that with Smuts's war policy South Africa would be lucky not to become a German colony:

> It is no longer a question whether we are going to win or lose, but a matter of whether there will be an unconditional surrender, or whether on the other hand, more or less satisfying terms can be fought for.[460]

458 Calpin, *There are no South Africans*, p. 353.

459 Egeland, *Bridges of understanding*, p. 104.

460 House of Assembly Debate, 29 August 1940, Col. 11.

The speech secured the warm approval of *Die Burger*. Even the *Cape Times* (16 September 1940) was impressed but noted that he neutralised this initial good impression with his "desire to be known as the Opposition's principal little knuckle-duster".

His confrontational approach was evident in his opposition to the War Measures Amendment Bill that gave the government extensive powers for internal security, allowing the Governor General almost unfettered powers to make regulations by means of proclamation for the maintenance of public order. Pirow opposed the Bill, portraying himself as a defender of democracy against an increasing autocratic Smuts who acted as though he had declared war against the Afrikaner – a war conducted in a more intensive manner than the war against Germany and Italy. His attack fell flat when Colin Steyn, Minister of Justice, pointed out that the security measures were based on those Pirow as the Minister of Defence had designed for a state of emergency. Despite his best efforts, Pirow was unable to rectify the damage done to his parliamentary standing.

# 11

# The New Order, September–December 1940

By August 1940, Pirow was a marginalised figure in parliament and the HNP caucus. He was fully aware that the former purifieds who were in control of party structures did not want any former fusionists representing them in parliament. With the enmity of Strijdom and Verwoerd knowing no limits, Strijdom was for example outraged by positive references to Pirow in the headlines of *Die Burger* in April 1940.[461] The odds were against him to win a nomination contest in Gezina. His only hope was to create a powerbase for himself in the party. To do so, he resorted to his favourite political strategy, linking up with the momentum of a prevailing political winner. He hitched his ambitions to the seemingly unstoppable military might of Nazi Germany, embracing national socialism and anti-Semitism.

After the collapse of France in June 1940, the defeat of Britain and the disintegration of the British Empire seemed inevitable. The popular feeling amongst many Afrikaners was that Britain had lost the war and that in this changing world South Africa for its own safety had to cut its ties with the British Empire. For *Die Burger*, in its editorials of 29 and 31 October 1940, the collapse of France could be compared to the legacy of the French Revolution of 1789 that had destroyed the political order of the *ancien régime*.

---

461 ACA UFS, C.R. Swart collection, File 3/1/27, Strijdom – Swart, 26 April 1940.

A new political order had to be created to replace the collapsing British system of liberal-democratic capitalism. The HNP leadership, struggling to form a party and policies that would satisfy both former purifieds and fusionists, was unable to provide clear and strong guidance on a new political order.

Pirow, seeing an opportunity to exploit the situation, found the fascist and anti-Semitic New Order for South Africa (NO) as a study group within the HNP on 25 September 1940. He set out the NO's ideals in a forty-page booklet, *Nuwe Orde vir Suid-Afrika* (New Order for South Africa), claiming that the old order of imperialist-controlled, capitalist-dominated parliamentary democracy, the source of all *ellende en verdriet* (misery and sorrow) in South Africa was finished. He claimed that a new political order was needed to reject a wasteful and inefficient parliamentary democracy. Democracy had to be eradicated root and branch as it could not solve the challenges facing South Africa, namely that of dealing with black, coloured and poor white people. By purging the country from the influence of British and Jewish capitalism, a new order of society and government could be created. The Afrikaner had to follow the example of Germany, Italy, Spain and Portugal, an authoritarian political system based on *staatsgesag* (state authority) and *volksdissipline* (discipline of the people). The state would be in control of the mines and all industries while there would be strict control over the press, broadcasting films, theatres, and any possible source of propaganda that could be used for nation building. To prepare the youth for *nasiediens* (service to the nation) there would be strict military training, as well as compulsory disciplined labour service for all "non-whites". The new political order had to be based on the fundamentals of the Afrikaner character, no equality or integration between black and white, Christian and republican in character. This meant that all ties with the British Empire had to be severed. Ultimate control of South Africa was the prerogative of the Afrikaner and "anti-national, un-national and unassimilable elements" would be excluded, in other words, Jews would be forbidden to enter South Africa.[462]

Pirow's anti-Semitism eschewed crude propaganda based on blood and race, while he had no time for conspiracy theories of ritual

462 UF, ACA, Oswald Pirow collection, File 2, "Die Nuwe Orde".

murders and the Protocols of the elders of Zion. This meant that the NO distinguished between three categories of Jews: First, the small group which had assimilated with the Afrikaners and would have full citizenship rights; second, the group who came to South Africa before World War I, who would be disenfranchised but could remain in the country if they behaved; and third, those Jews who entered the country after 4 August 1914 and who were regarded as illegal immigrants with no right to residence. Jews who had anglicised their surnames would have to revert to their original ones, while such name changes would be forbidden.[463]

The founding of the NO came as a big surprise to the leadership of the HNP as Pirow had made no attempt to forward any national socialist principles in the discussions to formulate the HNP's policies earlier in the year. In his negotiations with the NP in January 1940 on what a republic should entail, there was not a single reference to national socialism.[464]

For Strijdom, Verwoerd and Geyer it was obvious that he became a convert when Germany started to win the war in May 1940. Strijdom was disgusted that Pirow overnight embraced policies that he had hounded the NP for between 1933 and 1939. He who, as a protector of capitalism, had condemned the NP's stance on the exploitative nature of capitalism, had suddenly became a harsh critic of the system, and after years of rejecting the NP's anti-Semitism, suddenly revealed himself as an anti-Semite.[465]

Geyer viewed Pirow as a pathetic person saying that the founding of the NO was an obvious gamble on a German military victory and the hope that Hitler would appoint him as South Africa's ruler after a German-dictated peace.[466] Publicly, Pirow would vehemently deny accusations that the founding of the NO was based on opportunism, but in private he conceded that he was gambling on a German victory when Ben Schoeman asked him what he would do if Germany should lose the war. He retorted with a smile: "*Dan gaan ek plaas*

463 G. Shimoni, *Jews and Zionism: The South African experience (1910–1967)*, (Cape Town, 1980), p. 131.

464 US, D.F. Malan collection, 1/1/1629, Negotiations on what a republic should entail, January 1940.

465 NA Pretoria, Strijdom papers, Vol. 52, Strijdom – Swart, 7 December 1940.

466 WCPA, A.L. Geyer collection, Vol. 3, Political notebook, 23 May 1941.

*toe"* (Then I am going to my farm). He made the same remark to a shocked Malan who viewed it as a contemptuous attitude to the cause of Afrikaner nationalism.[467]

A year before his death in 1959 Pirow ruefully conceded to Horace Flather, former editor of the *Natal Daily News*, who knew him well in the 1930s, that the NO was indeed an opportunistic gamble:

> If only I had the moral fortitude of Smuts I should have gone with him instead of with Hertzog. What a difference it would have meant to my political life. But I had seen the Nazi might, talked to Hitler and some of his leaders, and I was convinced that they were irresistible. Well, they weren't. And that's the way it is – the bounce of the ball.[468]

Malan, apart from being appalled by Pirow's cynical opportunism, was aware of Pirow's competence and energy and viewed the NO as a danger to the HNP and the Afrikaner. In a private conversation he urged him not to proceed with his plans. He pointed out that 90 per cent of the NO's programme was already HNP policy, and that his forming of a group in the party could only encourage disunity. Instead he had to work through party structures, the Federal Council and conferences, to bring new ideas into the party.[469]

Pirow ignored Malan's plea and as he did not formally prohibit the founding of the NO, he claimed that the propagating of national socialism was done with his approval.[470] An office for the NO was opened in Pretoria, while Gert Yssel, a prominent former NP supporter and an outspoken critic of Strijdom's hostile attitude to former fusionists, was appointed as a salaried organising secretary[471] and started to recruit members.

In the lead in signing up was 16 MPs. Apart from C.W.M. du Toit, they were all former fusionists who felt marginalised in the HNP. They placed their hopes on the NO and leadership of Pirow to survive in a hostile political environment. To spread the message of

---

467 Schoeman, *My lewe in die politiek*, p. 82.

468 Flather, *The way of an editor*, p. 10.

469 US, D.F. Malan collection, 1/1/1751, Geyer – Otto du Plessis, 1 March 1941.

470 US, D.F. Malan collection, File 1/1/1749, S. Bekker – P.R. Botha, 12 February 1941.

471 M. Roberts and A.E.G. Trollip, *The South African opposition 1939–1945: An essay in contemporary history* (Cape Town, 1947), p. 215.

the NO, Pirow created study circles with at least five members and they were updated with regular bulletins.

Since 1933 there were numerous movements propagating fascism in South Africa. The most prominent one was the Greyshirts of L.T. Weichardt. These movements were mere splinter groupings adhering to bizarre conspiracy theories, led by people without any credibility and they had no influence on mainstream Afrikaner politics.[472] In 1940, with the NO it was a different matter.

The war had shattered the political mould and Pirow's articulation of a new political order struck a note with many Afrikaners who dreamt of a republic and a new political and socio-economic system to replace British-dominated capitalism – who in their eyes had exploited the Afrikaner for generations. Pirow seemed the person that could bring about this change. That he attempted to do so while he was a member of the HNP gave him credibility, especially as – apart from *Die Burger* – the other HNP-supporting newspapers provided extensive publicity for the NO. *Die Vaderland* (14 October 1940) gave him the opportunity to write a lengthy article to set out the ideals of his new order. *Die Volksblad* (21 October 1940) hailed Pirow as the man pointing the way for South Africa to follow. Otto du Plessis, editor of *Die Oosterlig,* was an admirer of Hitler and national socialism, and joined the NO in January 1941. He threw his full weight behind the movement.[473]

Observing the growth of the NO, a concerned Malan at the end of October 1940 gave a formal warning at the HNP conference in Cradock that he would mercilessly resist any group formation within the party. Pirow protested that his movement was a study group that could not be seen as a threat to the party as he was only proposing ideas for consideration, and that he was loyal to Malan.

That his proclamation of loyalty was not an empty one was evident on 6 November 1940 when Hertzog walked out of the HNP. This was after the party's Orange Free State conference rejected his objections to a republican system which, according to him, would reduce English speakers to second-class citizens. Hertzog predicted

472 P.J. Furlong, *Between crown and swastika: The impact of the radical right on the Afrikaner nationalist movement in the fascist era* (Johannesburg, 1991), p. 22.

473 A. Appel, *Die Oosterlig: 'n Pershistoriese studie* (Port Elizabeth, 1985), pp. 149, 158.

that Pirow would follow him out of the party.[474] A striking aspect of this break was that all those with a personal attachment to Hertzog stayed loyal to him. Senator W.J.C. Brebner and Havenga followed Hertzog into the political wilderness by resigning from parliament on 12 December 1940.

On 30 January 1941, Havenga formed the Afrikaner Party (AP) to keep the ideals of Hertzog alive. Pirow remained in the HNP as he was too ambitious to follow his mentor. He would claim that he remained a Hertzog admirer, but that the pledge at Monumentkoppie on 9 September 1939 was so sacred to him that he would continue to work for a united Afrikaner front. He was adamant that only the HNP could save the Afrikaner from the dangers of British imperialism and urged Hertzog supporters to stay in the party. This had a significant impact since only ten of the 37 MPs that had left the UP with Hertzog would join the AP. Pirow vowed that he would follow Malan with the same loyalty as he had done with Hertzog. In January 1941 in the first HNP parliamentary caucus meeting of the new parliamentary session, he proposed Malan as the leader of the party. This left Pirow in a strong position in the party.

Pirow's declarations of loyalty did not dilute Malan's fear that he was a danger to the Afrikaner. In his personal copies of NO propaganda literature, the sections on the rejection of parliamentary democracy and the lauding of national socialism are heavily underlined with disapproving exclamation marks.[475]Addressing a public meeting in Boksburg on 20 November 1940, he warned that a new political order was not something that could be worked out on paper and forced onto the *volk* as it had to be born out of their traditions. He had the full support of Geyer who made it clear that he was not willing to replace the existing political system, despite all its flaws, with an alien one that would end in a dictatorship in which Afrikaners would lose their political rights. On 20 November 1940, under the heading "*Ons glo dit nie*" (We do not believe it), he condemned the NO in *Die Burger*.

474 *Die Transvaler*, 7 November 1940.

475 US, D.F. Malan collection, 1/1/1750, "Advokaat Pirow aan die woord voor studiekring, 27 February 1941"; 1/1/170, NO's news bulletin number 6 of 20 November 1940.

The warnings by Malan and Geyer did little to counter the public interest in Pirow's vision of a new political order. This was reflected in the *Nuwe Orde vir Suid-Afrika* having seven reprints between December 1940 and May 1941.

Pirow, with the passion of an itinerate preacher, spread his message of a new order by addressing a series of large and enthusiastic public meetings. These crowds were receptive to his message as he had a reputation as an outstanding government minister who had done much to address the economic hardship of poor whites with the railways and the SSB. Most Afrikaner nationalists would have been unaware of his shattered parliamentary reputation as it received no attention in the NP-supporting newspapers. Even if they had known about his mauling at the hands of Smuts it would not have altered their high opinion of him as the prime minister was perceived as the British Empire's handyman.

Pirow also used his rhetorical skills to present national socialism in the most utopian way as the panacea for all the ills of modern society. Many Afrikaners, not fully realising what the ideology entailed, were won over. One of these was Ben Schoeman, who was part of a committee of nine with whom Pirow discussed the founding of the NO and its ideals in September 1940. Years later, he ruefully admitted in his memoirs that he did not fully comprehend the totalitarian nature national socialism entailed as there was no debate or criticism of the ideology amongst Afrikaner nationalists to guide him. Crucially, Schoeman felt that if the HNP could be convinced to accept the NO's principles, it would place the party in a favourable position when Germany had won the war.[476] If Schoeman, who had a reputation as a crusty and independent-minded parliamentarian, could be won over with such ease, other Afrikaners such as poor and struggling farmers would not be more sceptical.

A hallmark of Pirow's public meetings was that he was received with such appreciation that it bordered on idolatry. On 28 November 1940, in Vryburg in the northern Cape, a crowd of between 2000 and 3000 people cheered his statement that the war was in effect over and that capitalism and democracy had to be replaced as it was rotten to

476 Schoeman, *My lewe in die politiek*, pp. 79–81.

the core.[477] At an OB-arranged Day of the Covenant celebration on 16 December at Coega in the Eastern Cape, a crowd of 2000 people awaited Pirow's arrival at the Port Elizabeth railway station. He was carried shoulder high out of the building to a car. At the monument for Piet Retief at Coega, approximately 15 000 people received his message of a state based on *volksdissipline* (national discipline). Another huge and emotional crowd then accompanied him back to the railway station where they bid him farewell with *volksliedere* (Afrikaner folk songs).[478]

Pirow had broken out of his political isolation in the HNP, leaving Geyer deeply concerned. On 27 December in his political notebook he condemned Pirow as one of the *selfsoekende demagoge* (self-seeking demagogues) in the party who embraced the ideals of an exclusively Afrikaner republic, alienating potential supporters for the party.[479]

477 *Die Burger*, 2 December 1940.

478 *Die Burger*, 18 December 1940.

479 NA Cape Town, A.L. Geyer collection, Vol. 3, Political notebook, 27 December 1940.

# 12

# Marginalisation, 1941

With the advent of 1941, Pirow's campaign for a new political order received a boost when Hans van Rensburg replaced the erratic and incompetent Laas as the leader of the OB. He was a close friend of Pirow since 1924 when he became Roos's private secretary. Pirow's friendship and patronage was responsible for his meteoric rise in the civil service and in the ACF. As the Minister of Justice, Pirow made him the Secretary of the Justice Department, and in 1939 he was appointed as Administrator of the Orange Free State province as well as the commanding officer of the ACF forces in that province.

With the backing of the OB, the NO seemed unstoppable. On 12 January 1941, at an OB meeting in Delareyville in the western Transvaal, Pirow was met at the neighbouring town of Sannieshof by a convoy of cars that accompanied him to the outskirts of the town. He rode into town on a horse with the old South African Republic's flag in his hand, followed by an OB horse commando.[480] In his speech to a large group of people he made it clear that he fully associated with the aims of the OB, but that he hoped that in the future there would be less culture and more purposeful activity as the OB had to be the storm troopers of Afrikanerdom.[481]

At the end of January 1941, Pirow's campaign encountered its first setback. The Transvaal synod of the Gereformeerde Kerk (Re-

480 *Die Vaderland*, 13 January 1941.
481 *Rand Daily Mail*, 14 January 1941.

formed Church), concerned about the irresponsible propaganda and enthusiastic reception of national socialism, launched an investigation into the ideology. The synod unanimously accepted a report of Dr C.J.H. de Wet and Dr J.D. du Toit of the theological seminary in Potchefstroom which condemned the principles of the NO as heathen:

> Firstly, as Bible faithful and as Calvinists we cannot accept the cardinal point of the "new order" as it deifies state power and idolises the nation. Out of this must follow the renunciation of God… The main principle of the "new order" is in essence heathen, the realisation of the state entity found in the pagan empires of antiquity. (translated)[482]

Although devastating, the criticism of the Gereformeerde Kerk did not seem to halt the momentum of Pirow's campaign. On 3 February he attended an HNP-fundraising bazaar in Douglas in the Northern Cape. He was met outside of town by a convoy of cars and horse carts and escorted to the market square where he made a short speech, enjoyed a barbeque, and was then carried on the shoulders of spectators to the platform for the main speech. After prolonged applause, he explained the NO and its aims.[483]

He received more invitations from HNP branches to address public meetings and address large crowds of up to 2000 people in urban and rural places such as Brixton in Johannesburg and Mossel Bay in the Western Cape. How crowds were swept along by his oratory was evident in mid-February at a meeting in Heidelberg when at the end of his speech he was acclaimed with a loud cry of "*Ons bring hulde*" (We pay homage).[484] Heidelberg would be the political high-water mark for Pirow as Malan decided to act against him: During the 1941 parliamentary session, the UP used the presence of the NO

482 Voorop moet staan dat ons as Bybelgelowiges en Calviniste die hoofpunt van die "nuwe orde" geensins kan aanvaar nie, want die "nuwe orde" gaan uit van die vergoddeliking van die staatsmag en vergoding van die nasie as sodanig. Hieruit moet noodsaaklik volg die verloëning van God… Hierdie hoofbeginsel van die "nuwe orde" is in sy grond heidens en as sodanig die verwerkeliking van die staatsgedagte wat ons alreeds by die heidense rykhede van die oudheid vind. (*Die Burger*, 1 February 1941).

483 *Die Burger*, 4 February 1941.

484 *Die Transvaler*, 19 February 1941.

in the HNP with great effect to portray the official opposition as a threat to democracy.

The 1941 parliamentary session opened with a rare moment of consensus when Smuts announced that Hertzog had been granted a parliamentary pension in recognition of his services to the country. Pirow expressed his appreciation while he paid tribute to Hertzog as the greatest Afrikaner of his day. Then it was back to the rough-and-tumble of party politics. In a no-confidence motion in the government, Pirow launched a scathing attack on Smuts for not being able to control UDF soldiers that had launched violent attacks on civilians who opposed South Africa's involvement in the war. He also accused Smuts of dragging South Africa into an unnecessary war to maintain a system for the parasite and the exploiter, while thousands of South Africans were starving as they had to live on the breadline because of government policies. He warned that the day of reckoning was coming as Afrikanerdom would one day secure the reins of government and would never relinquish it. An outraged Blackwell responded: "The bully and the Teuton can be found in his speech."[485]

In subsequent debates, the UP with great effect exploited the NO's support for national socialism to demand that the HNP repudiate Pirow. This onslaught fuelled the fears of Malan that the presence of the NO would harm the HNP at the ballot box. On 28 February 1941, the party's policy committee dedicated an entire meeting on how to deal with the NO. The committee concluded that the NO's rejection of democracy could only end in a serious disaster for the Afrikaner. Instead the existing political and economic system had to be reformed. The committee urged HNP-supporting newspapers to counter the NO's influence by doing more to convey the party's policies to the public.[486]

In this period, there was also a growing resentment amongst HNP supporters about the fact that Pirow was allowed to operate his own organisation within the party. M.D.C. de Wet Nel, Secretary of the Transvaal HNP, found in April 1941 after a tour of the province that Pirow's use of party structures to condemn and reject the party-political system fuelled suspicion and disunity amongst party members.[487]

485 House of Assembly Debates, 5 February 1941, Col. 2236.
486 US, D.F. Malan collection, 1/1/1751, A.L. Geyer – Otto du Plessis, 1 March 1941.
487 Furlong, *Between crown and swastika*, p. 162.

Malan's efforts to neutralise Pirow were bolstered when the highly regarded Professor H.G. Stoker, a philosophy lecturer at the Potchefstroom University, supported the stance of the Gereformeerde Kerk that the principles of the NO were incompatible with Afrikaner Calvinism, which made the individual accountable and in service to God and not to an all-powerful state.[488] Theologians of the two other Afrikaans churches followed Stoker's lead. Professor G.M. Pelliser of the Nederduits Hervormde Kerk theology faculty at the University of Pretoria emphasised the freedom of the individual and that it was the duty of the church to criticise and to protest against any organisation or system that undermined this freedom.[489] In March 1941, *Die Kerkbode*, influential mouthpiece of the DRC, condemned any political system that encouraged a totalitarian state based on an alien ideology.[490]

Verwoerd provided momentum to these condemnations by emphasising in his editorials of March and April that a national socialist dictatorship was alien to the *volksaard* (national character) of the Afrikaner. The republics of the Voortrekkers, the Orange Free State and the Transvaal were democracies as the Afrikaner's democratic tradition was rooted in the Calvinist uprising against papal autocracy. Democracy was a cornerstone of the Calvinist civilisation.

The condemnation of the Afrikaans churches was a blow to Pirow as Afrikaner church ministers had an enormous influence in their congregations. His response was to claim that the criticisms of the theologians were based on a misapprehension because NO principles were Christian in nature. Du Toit, a former Gereformeerde minister, produced a pamphlet in the form of a fictional discussion between a Karoo farmer and his local church minister on the NO and Christianity in which it was claimed that national socialism had existed in Israel.[491] Furthermore, Pirow proclaimed that Paul Kruger was a national socialist and that he was merely adapting the old Boer president's ideas to the 1940s.[492]

488 *Die Vaderland*, 5 March 1941.
489 *Die Burger*, 11 March 1941.
490 A. Olivier, *Bode op die spoor van die woord: 150 jaar met Die Kerkbode* (Cape Town, 1998), p. 134.
491 *Die Vaderland*, 26 July 1941.
492 *Die Vaderland*, 3 March 1941.

His efforts at damage control were to no avail and supporters started to drift away. Ben Schoeman turned his back on the NO when he realised what a national socialist dictatorship entailed.[493] In March 1941, P.J. Meyer, as a Broederbond official, toured the Eastern Cape where Pirow had some successful meetings to explain the HNP's proposed republican constitution. He found it relatively easy to convince fellow Broeders to reject the principles of the NO.[494]

In tandem with the propaganda campaign against national socialism, the HNP leadership started to marginalise Pirow and his followers in party structures. On 8 March 1941, at a meeting of the head committee of the party in the Transvaal, Strijdom and Kemp replaced Du Toit as the chairman. Pirow, eager to present himself as an ordinary musket bearer in the cause without any leadership aspirations, then resigned as a member of the head and executive committees. On 9 April 1941, the Federal Council of the HNP condemned the NO's rejection of democracy, while its national socialist principles were rejected as alien to Afrikaner traditions and *volksaard*.

A few weeks later, on 10 May 1941, the head committee of the Transvaal HNP affirmed the decision of the Federal Council by declaring that the party would implement a democracy based on the system of the old Boer republics. At the party's national congress in Bloemfontein on 3 June 1941, Malan attacked the NO by condemning group formation in the party. Pirow listened attentively while making notes, but he did not respond.[495] When he did address the conference, it was to demand South Africa's immediate withdrawal from the war, and to express, to loud applause, his loyalty to and confidence in Malan.

On 14 June, at an Afrikaner festival in Brits, Pirow eventually responded with a defiant speech. After protesting that he would do nothing to harm Afrikaner unity as he was a loyal supporter of Malan, he proclaimed that he would continue with national socialistic propaganda in the HNP, seeing that the conference had not prohibited it. He stated that if one rejected national socialism, it was the result of not having studied the goals of the NO.

493 Schoeman, *My lewe in die politiek*, p. 82.

494 US, D.F. Malan collection, 1/1/1755, P.J. Meyer – D.F. Malan, 15 March 1941.

495 WCPA, Cape Town, A.L. Geyer papers, Vol. 3, Political notebook, 6 June 1941.

His speech oozed confidence and a patronising attitude towards the HNP leadership. The *Cape Times* (20 June 1941) described it as an "over-weening self-assurance in the face of his party bosses". Pirow's defiance can only be attributed to the realisation that his days of using the party to spread NO propaganda were over, and that he was convinced that he had generated enough grassroots support to proceed on his own.

To maintain support amongst Afrikaners, Pirow proclaimed the NO as the Afrikanerdom's main bulwark against the threat of communism. He portrayed himself as an expert on communism based on his 1925 visit to Moscow and the horror and devastation of communism he had witnessed there. At a public meeting in Pretoria on 25 June 1941, he claimed that the Afrikaner national socialism of the NO was the most effective way to oppose the terror of communism.[496] This was a message he again emphasised in a pamphlet *Kommunisme, nasionaal-sosialisme en Suid-Afrika* (Communism, national socialism and South Africa) in July 1941:

> The New Order is the only effective weapon against Communism and we will take the lead in the struggle against this international infestation. (translated)[497]

Verwoerd viewed Pirow's self-appointed status as the protector of the Afrikaner against communism as just another opportunistic ploy to undermine the HNP's support of parliamentary democracy. He urged Malan to close the NO down.[498]

With Malan biding his time, Verwoerd took the battle to Pirow in *Die Transvaler*. On 7 and 8 August, he condemned his stance on communism as an insult to the Afrikaner because it implied that the *volk*'s religious sentiments, traditions and nationalism were so feeble that it could provide no defence against communism, and that it was therefore necessary to adopt another country's philosophy of life. He contemptuously rejected Pirow's anti-communism as nothing more

496 *Die Vaderland*, 26 June 1941.

497 Die Nuwe Orde beskik oor die enigste doeltreffende wapen teen die Kommunisme en ons gaan derhalwe in die stryd teen daardie internasionale verpesting die voortou neem. (US, D.F. Malan papers, O. Pirow, *Kommunisme, Nasionaal-sosialisme en Suid-Afrika*, July 1941).

498 US, D.F. Malan papers, 1/1/1827, Verwoerd – Malan, 28 July 1941.

than an attempt to secure a personal following. Verwoerd reiterated that national socialism was alien to the Afrikaner with its Christian republican nationalism. A defiant Pirow responded that *Die Transvaler* wanted to split the HNP and in doing so was doing the work of the Smuts government.[499]

On 8 and 9 August, at public meetings in Nylstroom and Rustenburg, Malan entered the fray by condemning national socialism as incompatible with the traditions of the Afrikaner. As a result, Yssel resigned as the NO's organiser, claiming that he did not want to contribute to any disunity amongst Afrikaners.[500]

On 12 August 1941, Malan confronted Pirow at the Transvaal congress of the HNP in Pretoria. He condemned him for group formation and disunity in the party, and that his propagating of national socialism was mere opportunism while rejecting the principles of national socialism. Pirow's sister thanked Malan for his speech, praised his stance on national socialism, and assured him of the full support of HNP women in the province.

Speaking as the provincial leader Strijdom was adamant that the party rejected any alien ideology being forced onto the Christian nationalism of the Afrikaner. He then proposed a motion that the decision of the Federal Council that party members could only propagate formal HNP policies be confirmed. Pirow protested that he was a loyal member of the party and that the right to propagate the NO's ideals was a matter of conscience. All he wanted to do was to prepare the public for a political system that the HNP with time would have to embrace. Malan responded that there was no possibility of this happening as the NO's rejection of the party-political system had a paralysing effect on the party. At the end of the debate Du Toit proposed an amendment to Strijdom's motion, namely that the NO should be allowed to continue with its propaganda in the party. Of the 600 conference delegates, only 20 voted against the Strijdom motion.

Realising that he had reached the end of the road with the HNP, Pirow did his utmost to be expelled, hoping to secure support and sympathy amongst Afrikaners, and a possible alliance with the OB.

499 *Die Vaderland*, 9 Augustus 1941.
500 *Die Oosterlig*, 11 August 1941.

On the eve of the conference Van Rensburg had publicly supported him against what he described as a witch hunt against the NO in the HNP. He also made it clear that the OB was open to national socialists.[501] To secure their expulsion, Pirow and sixteen other MPs signed a declaration that they would continue to propagate NO propaganda in the party.[502]

In *Die Transvaler* an outraged Verwoerd demanded that action be taken against Pirow as the HNP could not allow a party within a party. A shrewd Malan refused to do so because it could turn Pirow into a martyr,[503] especially as he knew that the NO leader had been marginalised.

By then *Die Oosterlig* had turned its back on the NO and Otto du Plessis resigned as a member.[504] The Afrikanereenheidskomitee (Afrikaner Unity Committee), who as its name indicated attempted to bring the various Afrikaner groupings together, also turned on Pirow. Prof. L.J. du Plessis, chairman of this committee, condemned the NO in strong terms:

> … an organisation that has been developed against party policy to propagate a system under an imported name that has been rejected by the party, condemned by the church, and is in conflict with the principles of the *volk* (translated).[505]

After the Transvaal congress, the accusation that Pirow was an opportunist exploiting the seemingly inevitable victory of Nazi Germany for his own ambitions, started to strike home. J.H. Theron, in a letter to *Die Oosterlig,* spoke for many when he pointed out that if the war had not broken out in 1939, Pirow would still have been in the cabinet with Smuts, keeping his distance from Afrikaner nationalists in the political wilderness.[506]

501 Marx, *Oxwagon sentinel*, p. 416.
502 *Die Transvaler*, 13 Augustus 1941.
503 Van Heerden, "Nasionaal-sosialisme as faktor in die Suid-Afrikaanse politiek, 1933–1948", p. 232.
504 UFS, H.O. du Plessis collection, E. Pirow – Du Plessis, 10 September 1941.
505 … 'n organisasie opgebou het teen die party-beleid en dit wel om 'n stelsel te propageer onder 'n ingevoerde naam wat deur die party verwerp is, deur die Kerk afgekeur is, en in stryd is met die grondslae van ons volkslewe. (UFS, ACA, H.F. Verwoerd collection, Minutes of the Afrikanereenheidskomitee, Bloemfontein, 1 September 1941).
506 UFS, ACA, J.H.O. du Plessis papers, J.H. Theron – Du Plessis, 13 August 1941.

Pirow did his utmost to hold on to the support he had generated by attempting to convince Afrikaners that national socialism would be to their benefit:

> The New Order is not a German system. In South Africa it will be an Afrikaner nationalism-socialism. We do not look at the majority of voters. Our plan is to disenfranchise those who are not willing to live out their Afrikanerhood. We are not going to wait for fair weather friends. In the future only one section will count, and that is the voice of the true Afrikaner. This is the direction in which we want to lead the volk and give guidance to the party… We stand for the dictatorship of the true Afrikanerdom. (translated)[507]

On 22 September 1941, Pirow received a boost when Hertzog announced his conversion to national socialism. He had remained close to a lonely and isolated Hertzog in his political retirement and was a regular visitor to his farm. On one occasion Hertzog also went to visit Pirow on his farm.[508] It can only be assumed that his desire to maintain contact with the old general was the result of a combination of guilt and sincere affection, but also of political ambition. The former premier still had some influence and his support for Pirow could be handy in the future. An embittered Hertzog, bruised by his political rejection, had become disillusioned with the weaknesses, manipulative and exploitative nature of the democratic process and capitalism with its "the devil takes the hindmost" attitude. This led to his claim that national socialism was part of the *volksaard* and the only way to avoid the mud pool of party politics.[509]

His conversion caused a sensation and acute embarrassment for Havenga and the AP. Havenga gently rebuked his beloved leader, making it clear that the AP rejected national socialism. Hertzog's announcement was of no real advantage for the NO as it fuelled the

507 Die Nuwe Orde is geen Duitse stelsel nie. In Suid-Afrika sal dit 'n Afrikaanse nasionaal-sosialisme wees. Ons kyk nie na meerderheid van kiesers nie. Ons plan is om almal te ontkieser wat nie bereid is om hul Afrikanerskap uit te leef nie. Ons gaan nie wag op mooiweersvriende nie. In die toekoms sal net een deel tel, en dit is die stem van die regte Afrikaners. Dit is in hierdie rigting wat ons die volk wil lei en aan die party 'n leidraad gee… Ons staan die diktatuur van die ware Afrikanerdom voor. (US, D.F. Malan papers, 1/11847, Speech of Pirow at a function of the HNP in Capital Park, Pretoria, 30 August 1941).

508 Pirow, *James Barry Munnik Hertzog*, p. 259.

509 Roux, Coetzer, Marais, *Generaal J.B.M. Hertzog*, Vol. 2, pp. 737–749.

perception that a sad and lonely old man had been exploited and manipulated by Pirow. For Pirow the statements by Van Rensburg that national socialists were welcome in the OB, and Hertzog's conversion to national socialism, was proof of substantial support for him. At the NO's congress at the end of September, he once more rejected the Transvaal HNP's condemnation of the NO and declared that its MPs would remain members of the party's parliamentary caucus until they were expelled.

He also took the battle to the HNP leadership, condemning Verwoerd and Malan as the disrupters of Afrikaner unity.[510] This led to Strijdom distributing a pamphlet, "*Beroep van Transvaalse H.N.P.-leiers: Moet niemand steun wat party beveg*" (Call of the Transvaal HNP leadership. Do not support anyone who is fighting the party), urging Afrikaners to reject the dictatorship of the *volksvreemde* (alien) system of national socialism. The irony was that although Pirow propagated a disciplined state, he rejected the discipline of the HNP after the Transvaal conference had condemned the principles of the NO and demanded his submission to party structures.[511]

At a public meeting in Pretoria on 8 November 1941, Pirow once more threatened that he would not cooperate with the HNP parliamentary caucus if he could not, with the party's blessing, make propaganda for national socialism. An outraged Strijdom went on a tour of public meetings with the message that Pirow, after years of enthusiastically supporting the Jewish-capitalist democracy of the British Empire, had only changed his political colours when he became convinced that Nazi Germany would win the war.

Malan continued to ignore Pirow as he did not view him as a threat. After the Transvaal conference there was no possibility of the NO MPs winning the HNP nomination in their constituencies to contest the 1943 general election. He instead focused his energy on the OB which had a membership of up to 300 000 and had become a threat to the HNP's claim as the mouthpiece of Afrikaner nationalism. In addition, he viewed the organisation as too authoritarian. He

510 UF, ACA, H.F. Verwoerd papers, File 1/1/1, Van der Reyden – Verwoerd, 3 October 1941.

511 US, D.F. Malan collection, 1/1/1897. Strydom – Malan, 1 October 1941 with the pamphlet attached.

was especially concerned about its militaristic nature and its threats to initiate an armed rebellion against the Smuts government. By then some of the OB members, the paramilitary *Stormjaers* (storm troopers), had resorted to violence and sabotage. Malan set out to destroy the movement's influence. In October 1941, he instructed HNP members to resign from the OB. They did so in large numbers.

# 13
# Implosion, 1942–1943

Pirow, frustrated by Malan's refusal to expel him, decided to create a confrontation that would secure him sympathy as a victim of the HNP's lack of concern about Afrikaner unity. On 12 January 1942, Du Toit requested Sauer as the chief whip to convene a special parliamentary caucus meeting to discuss the right of HNP MPs to be members of the OB and NO. As the regular caucus meeting was to be held in six days' time, and MPs had to prepare themselves for the parliamentary debate later in the day, Sauer refused to do so.

The next day Pirow demanded from Malan an immediate caucus meeting for the sake of party unity and *volkseenheid* (unity of the Afrikaner). Malan responded through Sauer that the issue could wait until the scheduled meeting. Pirow retaliated that seeing as Malan did not care for *volkseenheid* it forced the NO MPs to act as an independent parliamentary group, although they would remain members of the HNP.[512] Malan ignored this provocation, arguing that if Afrikaner unity was so important to Pirow, he would have waited for the next scheduled caucus meeting. He furthermore suspected that Pirow wanted to turn the NO into the parliamentary wing of the OB. On the day Pirow announced his withdrawal from the caucus he had a meeting in parliament with J.A. Smith and advocate J.D. Jerling,

512 US, D.F. Malan papers, 1/1/1940, Du Toit – Malan, 12 January 1942; 1/1/1943, Pirow – Malan, 13 January 1942; 1/1/1944, Sauer – Pirow, 13 January 1942; 1/1/1945, Pirow – Malan, 14 January 1942.

senior figures in the OB leadership. The presence of the bearded OB leaders and their numerous bodyguards caused quite a sensation in the parliamentary corridors.

Instead of confronting Pirow, Malan set out to marginalise him by not introducing the usual motion of no confidence in the government, but instead introducing one calling for a republic based on the national character and traditions of the Afrikaner. Pirow was in a no-win situation. To oppose the motion would be seen as a rejection of republicanism, while to support it would imply the rejection of national socialism. During the debate on 15 January, he failed to rise to the occasion. In a short and unimpressive speech, he supported the motion, but pointed out that it did not go far enough as the republic had to be based on Afrikaner national socialism. He denied that the ideals of the NO were based on the German model as it was inspired by the political order of Salazar to whom he paid a glowing tribute. He also used Hertzog's rejection of democracy to bolster his case,[513] but provided no clear motivation for the existence of the NO. According to the *Cape Times* (19 January 1942), "The performance of Mr. Pirow recorded a low-water mark in the deterioration of a reputation…" His speech created an opportunity for Strijdom to emphasise that the ideals of the NO meant the rejection of the Afrikaner tradition of democracy, and to condemn Pirow as an opportunist.

Another source of embarrassment for Pirow during the debate was Smuts's amendment requesting parliament to approve South Africa's declaration of war against Japan. On 7 December 1941, the Japanese empire had launched a surprise attack on the United States of America (USA) at Pearl Harbour and invaded British and Dutch colonies in the Far East. Pirow's fear about Japanese aggression had been realised. On 19 February 1940, at an HNP public meeting, he had raised the possibility of Afrikaners fighting with Britain in a war with Japan. With his embracing of national socialism, and with Japan as a German ally, he became silent on the Japanese threat. A silence the *Cape Times* (16 January 1942) mocked with relish.

On 20 January, Pirow's ambitions received a shattering blow as the OB ended any speculation of an alliance with the NO when its governing council made it clear that the movement did not want to be

513 House of Assembly Debates, 15 January 1942, Col. 130–132.

tied to any political party.[514] Various reasons were responsible for this decision. Despite their friendship, Van Rensburg did not rate Pirow as a politician. According to Heimer Anderson, his OB aide, he never took any advice from the NO leader. He told Anderson more than once that Pirow had no feeling for politics, that he was in effect a stupid one.[515] (It is striking that Van Rensburg in his memoirs only praises Pirow's abilities as a hunter.) Van Rensburg furthermore had to consider that some senior OB members did not see Pirow as a true Afrikaner. Nic Deacon, a salaried official of the NO found that they struggled to explain their perception of the NO leader, but as one put it to him:

> I cannot describe it to you. If you do not have the attunement as an Afrikaner to the differences between yourself and Pirow, then I cannot really explain it to you. But he does not have the same mindset as the average Afrikaner, or the good Afrikaner. (translated)[516]

According to the British High Commissioner, Pirow was distrusted by the OB as an opportunist who wanted to exploit the movement for his own purposes.[517] This was indeed so. For many OB members he remained unforgiven for his politics in the 1930s. According to Ray Rudman, an OB general and a virulent anti-Semite, Pirow was not to be trusted as he accepted legal briefs from Jewish clients while, according to him, Mrs Pirow had Jewish blood. He contemptuously referred to Pirow as Oswald Shapiro.[518]

To add to Pirow's woes, Malan still refused to act against the NO MPs. This left him and his followers no choice but to resign from the HNP on 26 January 1941, using as a pretext Malan's alleged weak leadership. The HNP would point out with glee that he was never

---

514 Van Heerden, "Nasionaal-sosialisme as faktor in die Suid-Afrikaanse politiek, 1933–1948", p. 278.

515 NWU archive, OB archive, Interview with H. Anderson, Tape 16–18, no date.

516 Ek kan dit nie vir jou beskryf nie. As jy nie die aanvoeling as 'n Afrikaner het wat die verskil tussen Pirow en jouself is nie, dan kan ek dit eintlik nie verduidelik nie, maar hy val nie in dieselfde geestesveld as wat die deursnee-Afrikaner of die goeie Afrikaner val nie. (NWU archive, OB archive, Interview with Nic Deacon, Tape 69, January 1975).

517 NA Kew, DO 35/588/3, High Commissioner's dispatch, 18 May 1942.

518 NWU archive, OB archive, Interview with R.K. Rudman, Tape 104, 24 October 1975.

expelled from the party. On 4 February, Pirow's loathing for Malan erupted in a venomous attack on him in the House of Assembly. This was after the leader of the HNP had condemned the OB for its growing radicalism, while he also exposed alleged criminal activities in the organisation.

He read a statement from Johannes van der Walt, a well-known professional wrestler and leading OB officer who had fallen out with the organisation. A bombshell was the claim that the OB had betrayed Robey Leibbrandt to the police. Leibbrandt, a South African boxer and Hitler admirer, was in Germany when the war broke out in 1939. He joined the German army and underwent training as a paratrooper. In 1941, he was infiltrated into South Africa to initiate acts of sabotage against the Smuts government but was captured before causing any serious harm. Van der Walt claimed that he had been instructed by advocate J.D. Jerling to murder an unnamed person, and that Jerling had committed financial fraud.

Pirow, after proclaiming himself a proud OB member, attacked Malan for making libellous statements he would not dare to make outside of parliament. In the same speech, he accused the government of using undercover agents to incite anti-war violence. He also condemned the harsh treatment that arrested OB saboteurs had to endure, as well as the government's intention to use the death penalty for those convicted for acts of sabotage.[519]

An outraged A.M. Conroy, the volatile Minister of Lands, exploded that Pirow was just another Quisling. The common perception of Conroy was that of a noisy but harmless windbag, but the counterattack of Eric Louw, HNP MP for Beaufort West and a feared debater, was another matter. After stating that Pirow's attack on Malan was motivated by personal hatred, he proceeded to demolish him as a two-faced opportunist who trim his sails to prevailing winds: That he was a man who once had rejected republicanism, the OB and national socialism, only to change after June 1940 into a super-republican, a national socialist and a supporter and protector of the OB. He continued that Pirow had only parted with the HNP to become the political leader of the OB as he viewed it as the rising political force in the country.

519 House of Assembly Debates, 4 February 1942, Col. 1462–1472.

It was a devastating attack that could only have fuelled OB suspicions that Pirow attempted to exploit their movement for political gain.

On 6 February, Malan made an even more destructive attack on Pirow when he addressed his constituents in Piketberg. In a calm and measured speech, he condemned him as an ambitious and scheming opportunist who gambled on a German victory after he had failed to secure a position in the leadership of the HNP. To explain his lack of haste to act against him, he referred to a New Testament parable: Under the cover of darkness an enemy had sown weeds in a clean wheat field, and out of fear that the crop could be damaged by a too hasty weeding process, they were left in the field until harvest time when it would be easy to distinguish between weeds and wheat. With this approach, the *volk* could clearly identify the weeds that were planted in the HNP.[520]

Pirow, after this message was spread through the country by the Afrikaans press, had no credibility left amongst HNP supporters. By the end of February, Gerard Bekker, a loyal Pirow supporter, found during a visit to the Eastern Cape that NO support was limited to OB members.[521] Pirow used parliament in an attempt to improve his political standing. On 10 February, he introduced a motion – which the HNP was eager to pass – to denounce the influence of communism in South Africa and to demand that a parliamentary select committee be appointed to inquire into communist activities. His enemies in the UP and HNP viewed the motion as opportunism, while they found it odd that he could be so passionate about the horrors of communism but remain silent on the crimes of the Nazis. Any possible positive impact his motion could have made was neutralised when he immediately left the chamber after his speech. His absence led to Blackwell's adjournment of the debate.

When the motion was debated on 13 February, the HNP proposed an amendment to insist on immediate action against the communist threat. Eric Louw argued that for the HNP it was a serious matter, and not one to be exploited for opportunist reasons. He furthermore pointed out that Pirow as the Minister of Justice had ignored warn-

520 *Die Burger*, 7 February 1942.

521 UFS, ACA, O. Pirow papers, File 1, G. Bekker – Pirow, 28 February 1942.

ings about the communist threat and had claimed that it was a mere nuisance. On 8 August 1929, after Smuts had demanded stricter legislation to deal with communist agitation amongst black people, Pirow responded that communism was merely a nuisance, but that it was potentially a great danger and that it would receive the attention of the Department of Justice when required. Louw distorted the statement Pirow had made, and in doing so succeeded in portraying him as a bungler.

The next day, during the Railways Part Appropriation Bill, Pirow suffered further embarrassment when he came to the defence of the Spoorbond after the government had cancelled its accreditation as a trade union. UP MPs gleefully reminded him of his own conflict with the union in the 1930s. On 4 March, Pirow was once more accused of hypocrisy when he demanded the appointment of a judicial commission to investigate the treatment of detainees held for acts of sabotage under emergency regulations. He was reminded that the existing guidelines were the ones that he had designed as the Minister of Justice, and that the Nazis he admired were in the habit of shooting innocent people in mass executions.

On 20 March, Pirow had some parliamentary success when he raised the conscription of Dutch citizens living in South Africa to fight in the Dutch army. While the Appeal Court was still considering the legality of their conscription in South Africa, a number of Dutch men were ordered to leave the country. On Pirow's insistence, Smuts halted all such deportations until the judgment of the Appeal Court.

Apart from this concession, the 1942 parliamentary session had been a disaster for him. In the words of the *Cape Times* (5 February 1942) he was reduced to a "foreign adventurer", determined to damage South Africa. Attacked from all sides, Pirow seemed to be shell-shocked. The result was infrequent and gloomy appearances in the House of Assembly, while he made no attempt to disguise his profound contempt for parliament.[522] On public platforms he lacked energy and enthusiasm. A public meeting on 13 April in Wynberg, Cape Town, ended in chaos because of his contemptuous and aggressive behaviour to those present.[523]

522 NA Kew, DO 35/588/3, High Commissioner's dispatch, 8 June and 28 September 1942.

523 *Die Burger*, 14 April 1942.

The NO had become a moribund. With its 17 MPs and lack of grassroots supporters, the organisation was mocked as a "collection of generals without an army".[524] The condemnation of national socialism, by Afrikaans churches especially, handicapped the efforts to revive the NO. Professor Stoker in a private letter to Pirow explained the reason for this. Although Afrikaners agreed with the NO's enmity to liberalism and communism, their culture and religion, permeated with Calvinism, made national socialism unacceptable to them.[525]

That the NO parliamentarians propagated abstract political ideas while ignoring the daily challenges of their constituents also alienated some Afrikaners. This was reflected in a letter A.A. le Roux wrote to J.M. Conradie, UP MP for Rustenburg, to express his disgust with his member of parliament, possibly Jan Grobler of Brits:

> I want to put a request to you as our member is useless. He is busy with a new order. I do not know who gave him the order, but he talks about a New Order because Pirow talks that way. (translated)[526]

The aggression and imperialistic behaviour of Nazi Germany furthermore bolstered the perception of national socialism as a threat to the freedom of the Afrikaner. A. van Tonder's statement to Otto du Plessis that Afrikaners did not want to exchange British imperialism for German imperialism and that the HNP should not play the role of a Quisling to Nazi Germany, reflected the attitude of many Afrikaners.[527] Rudolph Hiemstra, a former SAAF officer who resigned from the UDF as he had refused to fight against Germany and had become an NO official, found that he could not convince other former officers to join the movement.[528]

---

524 Roberts and Trollip, *The South African opposition 1939–1945*, p. 147.

525 H.G. Stoker – Pirow, 26 September 1942. (The letter is in possession of Prof. P. Stoker, Potchefstroom. I am grateful to Victor Correira for providing me with a copy.)

526 Ek wil graag 'n versoek aan jou rig, want ons lid is nou in daardie opsig 'n nul. Hy is besig met 'n nuwe order, en wie hom die order gegee het weet ek nie, hy praat in elkgeval van so 'n Nuwe Order, omdat Pirow so praat. (Unisa, UP archive, J.M. Conradie papers, File 9 Correspondence 1940, A.A. le Roux – Conradie, undated letter).

527 UFS, ACA, J.H.O. du Plessis collection, A. van Tonder – J.H.O. du Plessis, 13 August 1941.

528 Hiemstra, *Die wilde haf*, p. 217.

Although Pirow was effectively marginalised, the HNP took no chances and continued to hound him to prevent any possible comeback. Addressing the national congress of the party in Pretoria on 16 September 1942, Malan condemned him as an enemy of the Afrikaner as he had encouraged disunity amongst them with his support of unacceptable totalitarian ideology.[529] By then Malan was kicking a down-and-out Pirow as he had become alienated from the OB. The final straw for OB members was his condemnation of the *Stormjaers* who had resorted to acts of sabotage to hamper the war effort. Pirow denounced these acts, making it clear that the *Stormjaers* were playing at being soldiers. According to Heimer Anderson the more radical OB members viewed Pirow and the NO with disdain as salon types who could only debate, write papers, criticise and condemn while doing nothing to oppose Smuts and British imperialism. Steve Hofmeyr, leader of the *Stormjaers* and a former private secretary of Pirow while he was the Minister of Justice,[530] confronted him for his lack of support.[531]

Another prominent OB member who shared this low opinion of Pirow was John Vorster, the future prime minister, whose activities had led to his internment. He stated that the NO could not be taken seriously.[532]

Pirow's political isolation was aggravated by the death of Hertzog on 21 November 1942. Although his relationship with the former prime minister was one that he had cultivated to his own advantage, there was also genuine affection. He attended the funeral on the Hertzog farm in Witbank where Havenga delivered a passionate eulogy.

During this period there were also signs that some of Pirow's followers in parliament realised that the NO was a political dead end. Jan Grobler confessed that he had developed doubts about the rejection of parliamentary democracy. With the NO falling apart, Pirow's only remaining hope was a military victory by Nazi Germany. With an international order dominated by Hitler and national socialism,

529 US, D.F. Malan collection, 1/1/2029, D.F. Malan's speech at the national congress of the HNP, Pretoria, 16 September 1942.

530 Van Rensburg, *Their paths crossed mine*, pp. 50, 198.

531 NWU archive, OB archive, Interview with H. Anderson, Tape 16–18, no date.

532 NWU archive, OB archive, Interview with B.J. Vorster, Tape 226, 7 November 1981.

he would be in a position of strength in South Africa. This hope was shattered by the catastrophic destruction of the German Sixth Army at Stalingrad in the Soviet Union, and the growing military involvement of the United States in the war. By January 1943, Germany's defeat seemed inevitable.

Pirow arrived late in Cape Town for the 1943 parliamentary session and was not present when Smuts introduced a motion of condolence for Hertzog. That Pirow was in no hurry to get to the House of Assembly was understandable as parliament was a reminder of his political isolation and failure. On 28 January, the House debated a government motion to enable South African forces to fight in Europe. Parliamentary approval was required as Smuts's war motion of 4 September 1939 had promised not to send troops "overseas as in the last war". Pirow vehemently opposed the motion and he once more laid into the prime minister's betrayal of Hertzog in September 1939. He furthermore mocked what he termed Smuts's optimistic prophesies about Allied victories.

The UP MPs responded by mocking his bush-cart strategy. Still smarting from his mauling of March 1940, he attempted to set the record straight about the strategy. He urged his UP critics to ask the prime minister where these bush carts hail from as the strategy was based on discussions with the British Imperial General Staff after the British had used such carts in India. If he were to be held responsible for this rotten plan, it was because he accepted advice from the British.[533] Pirow's defence was to no avail as nothing could alter the perception that he had been a disastrous and disloyal Minister of Defence. The *Cape Times* (29 January 1943) condemned his speech as vicious and facetious, the act of a frustrated and disappointed Quisling.

Pirow's behaviour during the rest of the parliamentary session destroyed any possible surviving remnants of his once glittering parliamentary reputation. On 8 March, during the budget debate, he condemned the quality of government ministers as well as South Africa's alliance with the Soviet Union against Germany. In response to an interjection, he made it clear that he was not returning to parliament, as "I am fed-up with the whole affair".

533 House of Assembly Debates, 28 January 1943, Col. 555–556.

Parliament was also fed-up with him. Hofmeyr, as the Minister of Finance, responded that he had descended to the cesspool and the gutter with his attack. Forced by the Speaker to withdraw this statement, Hofmeyr made it clear that Pirow had brought the debate down to the lowest level that has ever been attained in a budget debate.

On 12 March, Pirow made his final speech in the House, warning about the dangers of the Soviet Union encouraging communism and a black revolt in South Africa. Eighteen days later he announced that the NO would not participate in the parliamentary election of 1943. This announcement did not have the full support of all his followers in parliament. J.H. Viljoen, the AP MP for Hoopstad, predicted to Havenga that some NO MPs would stand as independents in the election.[534] He was proven correct as three of them – Du Toit, C.J. van den Berg and Grobler – decided to contest the election.

At the NO's conference in Pretoria on 18 May 1943, Pirow attempted to portray the decision not to contest the election as an attempt to create a new spirit in South African politics – a willingness to make sacrifices to bring about Afrikaner unity. He urged NO supporters to vote for republican-minded and anti-communist candidates, while he vowed that he would never again attempt to enter parliament. The meeting was a melancholy affair, aggravated by the setting in the Hollandia Hall that was used as a dance venue: As it was to host a Victory Dance in support of the Allied war effort, the hall was decorated with 15 Union Jacks as well as a flag bearing the legend "God Save the King".

The *Pretoria News* (19 May 1943) observed that the audience was dull and listless, and the faces of the NO MPs were a picture of unrelieved gloom, while Pirow's speech was uninspiring. The harsh reality was that no one was convinced by his claim of a noble sacrifice for Afrikaner unity. After years of rejecting parliamentary democracy, it was impossible for the NO to contest the election, while he was seen as a joke. The British High Commissioner's dispatch to London at the end of the parliamentary session reflected how the once feared Pirow had been reduced to a pitiful figure:

> He is now an embittered and frustrated lawyer politician, whose gamble on a German victory has led him to disaster. [...] Even

534 NA Pretoria, N.C. Havenga collection, Vol. 53, J.H. Liebenberg – N.C. Havenga, 2 April 1943.

> his personal appearance has changed. Instead of the rather cocky Mr. Pirow of pre-war years an older shrunken figure, resembling a hunted fox, haunts the lobbies and dining rooms of the House of Assembly.[535]

The UP won the general election with a comfortable victory of 89 seats to the 43 of the HNP, nine of Labour and the seven of the DP. The AP had failed to win a seat. All three former NO MPs who stood as independents suffered crushing defeats. The election had turned Malan and his party into the undisputed representatives of Afrikaner nationalism. After the election, the NO existed only in name, while the OB had been reduced to a rump. As it became obvious to all that Hitler could not win the war, the support for the two movements continued to decline even further. The HNP with the enthusiastic backing of the Afrikaans press, churches, universities and cultural organisations, was going from strength to strength.

535 NA Kew, DO 35/111p, File G581/18, High Commissioner's dispatch, 4 June 1943.

# 14

# Desperation, 1944–1948

Stuck in the political wilderness, Pirow attempted to revive his legal practice. Although he lacked the edge of the advocate that had left the Pretoria Bar in 1929, he was not a burnt-out case and could rise to the occasion. After the war, Bellwood witnessed with admiration his devastating cross-examination of a state witness who had been brought from London in a big Companies Act case in which Norbert Erleigh, a well-known Johannesburg financier, was in the dock for fraud and theft.[536] It was these courtroom performances that ensured that Pirow's legal skills remained in demand.

In February1948, he was the defence counsel in the Alexander libel trial that attracted international attention. F.M. Alexander, an Australian, was the propagator of the so-called "Alexander Technique" which even his biographer, Michael Bloch, found difficult to explain. The technique was based on the notion that individuals developed bad habits in their postures that accounted for much that went wrong in their health. The "Alexander Technique" provided a practical method of identifying and overcoming these habits. This would improve mental and physical health. In 1944, Dr Ernst Jokl, Director of Physical Education in South Africa, with the support of Dr E. Cluver, Director of the South African Institute for Medical Research, published an article in a government journal, *Manpower/*

536 Bellwood, *South African backdrop*, pp. 62–63.

*Volkskragte*, in which he condemned the "Alexander Technique" as a "dangerous and irresponsible quackery". Alexander sued for libel and £5000 in damages.

In the trial Pirow appeared on behalf of the defendants and was at his aggressive best, but was unable to cross-examine Alexander who could not attend proceedings since he was recovering from a stroke. The weakness for the Jokl and Cluver defence was that they lacked any practical knowledge of the "Alexander Technique", while Alexander's witnesses could testify on the practical benefits. Despite Pirow's best efforts, the judge ruled in Alexander's favour as he concluded that the defendants, although showing that Alexander was a quack in the sense that he made ignorant pretence to medical skill, they had misrepresented and overstated the views and claims made by him. Alexander was awarded £1000 in damages with the legal costs of the trial.[537]

High-profile court appearances such as the Alexander case could not compensate for Pirow's loss of political status. After ten years of being a cabinet minister and being treated as an equal by prime ministers, kings and statesmen, he found it difficult to be a mere advocate at the Pretoria Bar. Craving respect and the trappings of power, he was determined to return to the mainstream of politics and to restore his battered reputation.

He did his utmost to reconcile with the HNP. Within months of the 1943 election he reached out to Malan by proposing a collective security pact among all opposition groups.[538] Malan ignored him. Despite this rebuff, Pirow continued his efforts to reconcile with his former party. At the NO conference in June 1944, he made it clear that although the objective of the movement was to establish national socialism in South Africa – which meant the rejection of the party system – he unconditionally supported the HNP.[539] The party's leadership once again ignored him.

*Die Volksblad* (13 September 1944) pointed out that if he continued to embrace national socialism he would be kept at arm's-length.

---

537 M. Bloch, *F.M. The life of Frederick Matthias Alexander: Founder of the Alexander Technique* (London, 2004), pp. 2, 197–228.

538 Stultz, *The Nationalists in opposition 1938–1948*, p. 99.

539 Van Heerden, "Nasionaal-sosialisme as 'n faktor in die Suid-Afrikaanse politiek, 1933–1948", pp. 340–341.

For Pirow to abandon national socialism so soon after leaving the HNP on this principle was an impossible demand. Doing so would mean a loss of face and a bolstering of his image as an opportunist. The only political lifeline available to him was the intense desire amongst Afrikaner nationalists to unify those splintered amongst the AP, NO, OB and HNP.

On 23 September 1944, he wrote an open letter to Malan and Van Rensburg to urge Afrikaner unity.[540] Malan ignored the letter. The HNP leader instead reached out to Havenga whose dignified and moderate campaign in defence of democratic politics as leader of the AP in the 1943 election had raised his already significant stature amongst South Africans. He was so respected that in both the HNP and the UP there was a desire to have him as a member. While Smuts was reluctant to reach out to him, Malan felt that Havenga could play a crucial role to secure the support of Afrikaners in the AP and UP. In April 1945, he approached Havenga for closer cooperation between the two parties, making it clear that he would keep Pirow out in the cold because of his rejection of democracy.[541] This decision meant, to quote Patrick Furlong in his study on the impact of the radical right on the Afrikaner nationalist movement, that Pirow had been "consigned to political oblivion" by Malan.[542]

To counter his isolation, Pirow started a newsletter on 1 December 1944, "*Adv. Pirow se Nuusbrief*" (Adv. Pirow's Newsletter), a weekly analysis of international and local political events in which he dished out advice to party leaders. According to N.M. Stultz in his study of the HNP in opposition, Pirow was a "shrill and increasingly isolated voice" in South African politics.[543]

On 8 May 1945, Nazi Germany surrendered unconditionally after the Red Army's capture of Berlin and Hitler's suicide. Pirow was adamant that Germany's defeat did not signify the end of his efforts to campaign for national socialist ideals. For him the Soviet Union's new status as a superpower occupying half of Europe provided an

540 NWU, OB Archive, Kommandant-Generaal, Box 2, File 5/28, Open letter by Pirow, 23 September 1944.

541 US, D.F. Malan papers, 1/1/2168, Malan – Havenga, 2 April 1945.

542 Furlong, *Between crown and swastika*, p. 216.

543 N.M. Stultz, *The Nationalists in opposition 1938–1948* (Cape Town, 1975), p. 99.

opportunity to make a political comeback as he was convinced that the ideological differences between the USA and the Soviet Union made another world war inevitable: a war in which South Africa could not be neutral and which would smash the mould of local party politics.[544]

While waiting for the outbreak of hostilities between the two superpowers, Pirow portrayed the NO as a defender of white civilisation in Africa against the threat of communism. His activities were observed with some concern in the office of the British High Commissioner in Pretoria. The fear was that the large number of Afrikaner mineworkers on the Witwatersrand who could not relate to the Labour Party, HNP or UP could be attracted to the NO.[545] This was indeed Pirow's hope as he felt the HNP could not win the 1948 election, and that tens of thousands of Afrikaners, disillusioned with party politics, would look to him for leadership.[546]

To achieve this objective, he had to raise his profile. There were only two options available: public meetings and media exposure. In July 1945 he addressed an anti-communist *stryddag* (struggle rally) in Lichtenburg, but he lacked the organisational structure and funds to arrange a succession of such meetings. More crucially, he had no newspaper support. All the Afrikaans newspapers, apart from the AP-supporting *Die Vaderland*, were propaganda tools for the HNP. This left him with no choice but to create his own newssheet.

On 4 October 1945, he started *Die Nuwe Orde*, a weekly newssheet which incorporated his newsletter. To put the management of *Die Nuwe Orde* on a professional footing, he created a company in February 1946 to carry the publication costs. This company was called Die Nuwe Staat Uitgewers- en Publisiteitsmaatskappy with Dr H.O. Monnig, an agricultural expert and businessman, as the chairman of the directors.[547] In reality, *Die Nuwe Orde* was a one-man show, as Pirow paid the printing costs and during lunch times – while eating a sandwich at his desk in the Tudor Chambers – he did most of the writing.[548]

544 *Die Nuwe Orde*, 7 February 1946.
545 NA Kew, DO 35/1119, File G581/88, High Commisioner – Sir Eric Machtig, 9 October 1946.
546 *Die Nuwe Orde*, 10 January 1947.
547 *Die Nuwe Orde*, 16 May 1946.
548 Meiring, *Tien politieke leiers*, p. 93.

The main task of *Die Nuwe Orde* was to create an image of Pirow as a political sage that the HNP needed in its fold. From the first issue flowed, in the words of Stultz, "a continuous stream of gratuitous advice especially on Afrikaner unity to all opposition leaders".[549] He used the newssheet to defend and justify his past political actions by publishing between November 1945 and November 1946 his self-deluding political recollections. Pirow's recollections reached a wider audience when *Dagbreek en Sondagnuus*, an Afrikaans Sunday newspaper edited by Willem van Heerden – a close political ally in the 1930s – published parts of it in 1948.

He made every effort to portray himself as a political giant. His European visit in 1938 was covered in fine detail as a noble quest to prevent a world war. He condemned Smuts as a person who wanted a war on behalf of the British Empire at the cost of the Afrikaner, and in doing so he destroyed Pirow's career. He used E.S. Crafford's statement in his biography, *Jan Smuts* (published in 1945), that Smuts's 1940 hatchet job was unfair but a party-political necessity to destroy him as a political threat.[550]

A striking aspect of *Die Nuwe Orde* was Pirow's anti-Semitism. In the first issue Pirow declared "that if every Jew could vanish from the earth, the world as a whole would be a much better place".[551] At a glance, five months after the end of the war and the exposure of the Holocaust in which six million Jews had perished at the hands of the Nazis, this stance seems baffling. It could only have caused revulsion amongst many Afrikaners. And yet, for Pirow it made political sense to portray himself as an unrepentant anti-Semite. To ride the wave of desire for Afrikaner unity back into the HNP, he had to represent a significant group of Afrikaners. To maintain the loyalty of his small group of followers in the NO and to attract new members, especially amongst the pro-Nazi former members of the OB who were struggling to find a political home after the collapse of their movement, he had to maintain his credentials as South Africas's leading anti-Semite. In August 1946 he condemned Jews as a source of trouble over the centuries and the war crimes trial of Nazi leaders

549 N.M. Stultz, *The Nationalists in opposition, 1934–1948*, p. 99.
550 *Die Nuwe Orde*, 30 May 1946.
551 Shain, *A perfect storm*, p. 270.

at Nuremberg as a potential case of mass murder to satisfy revengeful Jews.[552]

In *Die Nuwe Orde* of 26 September 1946, he defended Erich Holm, a South African who was convicted of high treason for broadcasting Nazi propaganda to South Africa from Germany during the war. With the conviction and execution of leading Nazi war criminals at Nuremberg in 1946 – in his eyes judicial murders – he published on 18 October 1946 a full-page front spread of the names of the executed war criminals surrounded by a black border and the heading, "In memory of the martyrs of Nuremberg".

These statements brought him no support from former OB members who remained suspicious of him as an opportunist and felt that he was not a true Afrikaner, while it left the HNP determined to keep him at arm's-length. His marginalisation was emphasised when Havenga and Malan in March 1947 formed an alliance to contest the coming general election. Pirow had no choice but to declare his support for the HNP and AP alliance, and to order NO supporters to join either party. In doing so he effectively conceded that the NO had no reason for its continued existence. The HNP's leadership once more ignored his offer of unconditional support.

In September 1947, Pirow was charged under the Riotous Assemblies Act for inciting public violence. On 9 May 1946, *Die Nuwe Orde* had published an article under the heading "*Neem die wet in eie hande*" (Take the law into your own hands) after black students attended a student "rag" event of the University of the Witwatersrand. In an article, not written by Pirow, but approved by him as the editor, physical attacks on black students fraternising with white students, were encouraged:

> Although it is an offence to incite people to violence today we offer this advice: where non-Europeans intrude among Europeans throw them out on their necks… There are many occasions when a blow of the fist is a sign of vitality and not a sign of lack of refinement.[553]

In court Pirow testified that *Die Nuwe Orde* was aimed at stimulating intellectual debate on political issues and that only intelligent persons,

552 *Die Nuwe Orde*, 1 August and 29 August 1946.

553 NA Kew, KV 2/908, Untitled newspaper clipping, 6 September 1947.

who would not resort to violence, read the newssheet. The aim of the article was not to encourage violence but to warn white people – lulled into a sense of false security – into a full awareness of the colour question. The policy of the newssheet was a "peaceful solution of the native problem". His defence left the court unconvinced and he was found guilty and sentenced to a fine of 40 pounds, or two months hard labour.

Already seen as beyond the pale by many Afrikaners, his conviction destroyed any fragment of hope to play a role in bringing about Afrikaner unity. By September 1947, *Die Nuwe Orde*, struggling to find subscribers and running at a financial loss – at its height the newssheet had a print run of only 2250 copies – had to be reduced from a weekly to a monthly sheet.[554]

With the failure of Pirow's role as a self-appointed champion of Afrikaner unity, the only way to find his way out of the political wilderness was to establish a reputation as an original political thinker providing solutions to the challenges facing white South Africans in an evolving world. World War II had broken down the old social order that had made white supremacy acceptable. At the newly established United Nations in New York, racism, colonialism and oppression were being challenged by Third World countries.

In South Africa the combination of grinding poverty in the overpopulated and eroded native reserves in rural areas, and labour shortages in the increasingly industrialising urban areas, led to the migration of the black population to towns and cities. The result was that existing infrastructures were unable to deal with the influx. By 1946, towns and cities were encircled by large crime-ridden shanty towns in which black people lived in squalor. These dismal living conditions, combined with the harsh and exploitative treatment in the mines and factories, fuelled a growing black militancy culminating in boycotts, protest marches and strikes.

In August 1946, a strike by black mineworkers was suppressed with great brutality. The once moribund African National Congress (ANC) under the dynamic leadership of Dr A.B. Xuma, representing the black majority, demanded equal political rights. The suppression of the miner strike led to the Natives Representative Council – whose criticism, advice and recommendations had been ignored over

554 *Pretoria News*, 5 and 19 September 1947.

the years by the Hertzog and Smuts governments – to adjourn until discriminatory legislation had been appealed. The same year South Africa's racial policies were vehemently criticised at the United Nations.

These developments led to concern amongst white people about their hegemony. It convinced the UP and the HNP that the old system of segregation was no longer tenable and had to be replaced with a new one taking black aspirations into account. In August 1946, Smuts appointed a commission under the chairmanship of Judge H.A. Fagan to find a solution to the challenges of governing a growing black urban population. In response, Malan appointed Sauer in July 1947 to lead a commission to formalise a racial policy for the HNP.

For Pirow this growing angst amongst white people provided an opportunity to push forward his own proposals and to secure a possible return to the HNP. His political blueprint was segregation on a pan-African basis: that apart from areas such as North (Zambia) and South Rhodesia (Zimbabwe), Kenya and South Africa, the rest of Africa should be given its independence; and that sovereign black states in South Africa based on the "native reserves" should be established. White people had to provide the money to create these states.[555] For Indian people – the fifth columnists of pan-Asianism according to Pirow – the solution was simple: They had to be repatriated to India.[556] Coloured people had to be provided with land to govern themselves in a territory stretching from Vanrhynsdorp in the Northern Cape to Keetmanshoop and Rehoboth in South West Africa, and from Upington to the sea. They would be obliged to live in this area and he advocated forced removals if they should refuse to go. White people already living in this area had to be removed as a sacrifice for white survival.[557]

Just like the HNP studiously ignored him, the proposal of pan-African segregation was ignored. For a hurt Pirow it was a case of the Afrikaner leaders feeling that they had all the wisdom in the world, and that the audacity of anyone disagreeing with them meant that you were not a good Afrikaner.[558]

555 *Die Nuwe Orde*, 3 January 1947.

556 *Die Nuwe Orde*, 24 January 1947.

557 *Die Nuwe Orde*, 7 February 1947.

558 *Dagbreek en Sondagnuus*, 15 February 1948.

For Pirow the lack of a political platform to disseminate his political views was a source of deep frustration, especially as both the Sauer and Fagan reports were published by March 1948. Fagan concluded that total segregation was impractical and that as urbanisation was a natural process, it should not be halted. The focus had to be on the controlling of urbanisation and the future of South Africa had to be based on the mutual dependence of black and white. Pirow rejected the report for ignoring cultural differences between black and white, and said that Fagan's recommendations would encourage racial integration. According to him this meant that the black worker would be absorbed as a proletarian in South Africa's economic structure, and that this would lead to a class struggle, intensified by racial differences.[559]

On the other hand, the Sauer report promised stricter segregation measures at all levels of society with influx control. Politically, black people had to develop in their own territories according to their own national character. For Pirow the Sauer report was flawed as it ignored the aspirations of the black man to be sovereignly independent.[560] To convey his own pan-African segregation proposals to the wider public, he needed a political platform that would attract attention.

This led to Pirow's gamble to seek an alliance with Sir Oswald Mosley, the former leader of the British Union of Fascists (BUF), to form an international anti-communist movement. After 1945, Mosley, just like Pirow, was determined to exploit anti-communist fears to secure a political comeback. His book, *The alternative* (published in October 1947), was an attempt to readjust national socialism to the post-war world, and to relaunch his political career. In the book he envisioned his task as a defender of Europe against the barbarism of the Soviet Union. His main strategy was the ideal of a unified Europe – "Europe a Nation" – which would preserve European independence in a world of superpowers. This unified Europe would be protected by tariffs and secure its wealth from an Africa ruled by white people. Africa would provide Europe with raw materials,

559 J.P. Brits, *Op die vooraand van apartheid: Die rassevraagstuk en die blanke politiek in Suid-Afrika, 1939–1948* (Pretoria, 1994), pp. 42–43.

560 University of Birmingham (hereafter UB), Sir Oswald Mosley papers, OMD7/1/1, "Statement by Mr. Pirow, 12 April 1948".

making it self-sufficient and independent of American financial support. In the process Africa would benefit, as Europe would play a crucial role in developing the continent. Mosley formed the Union Movement in February 1948 to encourage European unity, prevent Europe from falling to communism, and to oppose Europe's pauper existence on the American dole.[561]

Pirow initiated the possibility of a meeting with Mosley after an ex-BUF man in South Africa had given him a copy of *The alternative*. According to Stephen Dorril, Mosley's best biographer, *The alternative* was a pretentious book, ignored by the British press.[562] Pirow in *Die Nuwe Orde* of December 1947 praised it as "one of the most important products of one of the clearest political thinkers today".[563]

On 29 December 1947, he wrote to Mosley to express his admiration and suggested a meeting between them to form an international league against communism with its headquarters in London, and with Mosley as its president. He also expressed his wish to visit the USA to attract American support for such an organisation, and to recruit Charles Lindberg – the famous aviator who before the Japanese attack on Pearl Harbour on 7 December 1941 was an isolationist and seen as sympathetic to fascism – to their cause.[564]

Pirow and Mosley had much in common. Both were highly intelligent, confident and charismatic, and were regarded as good sportsmen. Mosley was a skilful amateur boxer and an outstanding fencer who had represented Britain. Both were former aviators – Mosley participated in World War I as a pilot in the Royal Flying Corps. Both had public images as embracers of modernity and with reputations as men of action, energy and as original political thinkers. However, the difference was that the bald and rather dumpy Pirow, married to the daughter of a cold-storage company owner, lacked the glamour of Mosley. The Union Movement leader was tall, broad-shouldered and a baronet from a wealthy family. He was married to Cynthia Curzon, daughter of Lord Curzon, a former viceroy of India. Both were

561 R. Skidelsky, Oswald Mosley (London, 1990), pp. 485–486.

562 S. Dorril, *Black shirt: Sir Oswald Mosley and British fascism* (London, 2006), pp. 564–565.

563 NA Kew, KV 2/908, Extract from the *Daily Worker*, 31 December 1947.

564 NA Kew, KV 2/908, Pirow – Mosley, 29 December 1947 and 21 January 1948.

ambitious with the ability to trim their sails to prevailing political winds and to exploit political parties and their leaders as vehicles for their ambitions.

Mosley was elected to parliament in 1918 as a member of the Conservative Party but abandoned the seemingly declining Conservatives for the rising Labour Party in 1924. By then he was such a political star that 70 Labour-held constituencies vied with one another to secure him as a candidate. Mosley used his considerable charm on Ramsay MacDonald, leader of the Labour Party, to advance his career. In 1929, he became a government minister, although not in the cabinet, but resigned in 1930 to form his own political grouping, the New Party. This was after his recommendations on how to counter the economic hardships of the Great Depression had been rejected. Mosley, after his party was decimated in the 1931 general election, visited Benito Mussolini's fascist Italy. Viewing fascism as the coming political force, he formed the BUF in 1932. Anti-Semitism was the backbone of BUF policy and from 1936 he had close ties with Nazi Germany. That year he married his second wife, Diana Guinness, in Berlin with Hitler present.

Mosley's unscrupulous use of crude anti-Semitism, the thuggery and unprovoked violence of BUF members dressed in black uniforms, and his stance after 1938 that war with Germany had to be avoided as the calls to oppose Nazi aggression was part of a Jewish conspiracy, made him an isolated and despised figure in Britain. The BUF was never able to attract more than a handful of supporters. In May 1940, he was arrested as a threat to state security and kept in prison until 1943. His release on health grounds led to a public outcry. The war had destroyed what had remained of his political reputation. Like Pirow he craved respect. *The alternative* was the product of his desperation for a political comeback.

British intelligence informers in Mosley's inner circle, at least three of them, provided crucial information on the interaction between Pirow and the former BUF leader. Mosley, according to informant B.1.c./2487, welcomed Pirow's visit as he felt that the NO leader had a good chance of coming to power in South Africa within two years when the Smuts regime would be smashed.[565] The fact that

565 NA Kew, KV 2/908, Report of informant B.1.c./2487, 9 January 1948.

Mosley thought that Pirow could come to power was an indication of his notorious lack of judgement and reflected an important difference between them. Mosley had an enormous ego, bad judgement and no capacity for introspection. He was the architect of his own downfall by leaving the Labour Party.

Pirow, although vain and arrogant, could be brutally honest about his own flaws, and had a career based on cold, rational decisions for political survival. This meant that he was politically far more successful than Mosley. The prime ministership of South Africa had been within his grasp and it was historical events beyond his control in September 1939 that led to his expulsion from the cabinet. He only broke with mainstream politics, and parliamentary democracy, to gamble with fascism and a German military victory when he felt that he had no choice but to do so.

Pirow's decision to reach out to such a discredited politician as Mosley was a gamble, but a calculated one. As he felt that a war between the USA and the Soviet Union was inevitable, he was without doubt that a fervent anti-communist stance was the ticket to secure a political comeback. While in London, he informed J.A. Gray, an acquaintance of his 1938 visit, that with the outbreak of hostilities, South Africa would need a new fusion government and that he was determined to participate in this war.[566] He felt that London, and Mosley, would provide the much-needed publicity to remind South Africans of his strong political views on communism as well as his statesmanlike abilities: that he was the person who at the end of 1938 had predicted that a war with Germany was inevitable. In addition, with London as the capital of a vast empire in Africa, his proposed blueprint of racial segregation on a pan-African basis would secure extensive publicity.

Pirow left South Africa on an SAA flight on 7 April at 02:00 and arrived in London on 8 April at 15:15. Mosley and Lady Mosley met him at the airport. The contrast to his arrival in 1938 could not have been starker. Ten years earlier Europe's attention was focused on him. On his arrival in London back then, he was welcomed by a Secretary of State, leading establishment figures, police protection and a large crowd of spectators and journalists. In 1948, the only

566 Wits, J.H. Hofmeyr papers, Aa 1905, J.A. Gray – Hofmeyr, 23 April 1948.

Desperation – Pirow, Sir Oswald Mosley and Lady Mosley, 8 April 1948.
*From: National Portrait Gallery, London.*

state representation was the Metropolitan Police's Special Branch who noted that 20 people awaited his arrival, and that Mosley had pulled out all the stops to welcome him with a hired Daimler car, and a van with an amplifier for a speech by his guest.

Pirow refused to make any public statement, and on Mosley's prompting only said that he was happy to be in Britain, and that he had a fairly comfortable flight.[567] He then went to spend a weekend at Mosley's country home in Wiltshire. British intelligence with its informants, and the interception of mail, was fully informed of the discussions between Mosley and Pirow who hoped to use each other for a political comeback. This was evident from an intercepted letter by G.F. Green to Arnold Leese in which it was noted that the two got on very well: "The two 'O's are most friendly and impressed – and each willing to use the other as a mounting-block."[568]

567 NA Kew, KV 2/908, Metropolitan Police (Special Branch), 9 April 1948.
568 NA Kew, KV 2/908, Extract from int. letter from G.F. Green, to Arnold Leese, mentioning Pirow, 17 April 1948.

According to informant B.1.c/2628 who found Pirow to be well mannered, arrogant, ruthless and enormously energetic, the NO leader was of the opinion that Smuts would win the next election with the barest majority and that in the coming war with the Soviet Union the government would ask him and his friends to form a coalition. He would refuse the offer as time was on his side. In the meantime, his main object was to infiltrate 100 per cent pro-British sections of society in South Africa. The last section must have struck British intelligence as far-fetched as the report was filed with the instruction to be used with caution.[569]

British intelligence concluded that Pirow's chief motive to visit Mosley had nothing to do with fascism, but an attempt to revive his own career:

> Of the two men, Oswald Pirow is probably the more astute and there are indications that his projected political link with MOSLEY is envisaged by PIROW primarily as affording means for building up his own future plans. As evidence of this he has shown no very marked interests in the activities of the Union Movement…[570]

Pirow's high hopes of reviving his career with much needed publicity came to nothing, as the British press was determined to keep Mosley isolated. It was the official policy of the British Broadcasting Corporation to ignore him. A press conference at Mosley's London home on 12 April to hear Pirow propagating his ideal of racial equality coupled with segregation, self-governance and eventual independence for the black man in his own areas in Africa was poorly attended. He forcefully stated his case that the African as a race had not received even a small part of what is due to him. His plan would give the black man an ultimate national ideal, the same ideal as that of any European nation.

He also claimed that his visit was to determine how close the world was to a third world war. In doing so he reminded those present of his visit to Europe in 1938 and his prediction that a war with Germany was imminent, and prophesised that a third world war with the Soviet Union was inevitable.[571] He also made it clear that fas-

569 NA Kew, KV 2/908, Report of 19 April 1948.

570 NA Kew, KV 2/908, Extract from a report on fascist activities (March–April 1948), 27 April 1948.

571 NA Kew, KV 2/908, Press statement by Pirow, 12 April 1948.

cism was as much outdated as democracy but was vague on what would replace democracy. Pressed on the point by journalists, he argued that a new system had to evolve out of the various political beliefs that would provide a government that would be approved by all. Parliament would not be disregarded but had to be turned into a working place instead of a talking shop. This would not be based on Mussolini's types of corporation, but on occupational representation. Farmers would for example argue what is good for farming, and in an election a farmer would vote for the good farmer.

A journalist confronted him on his stance to the "Jewish question". His answer was that an ample national home should be provided for them, and that except for those who had been living for generations in a certain country, they should all be sent to that national home. Pirow's confident performance at the news conference impressed British intelligence:

> It is difficult to assess precisely what Pirow's real influence in South African politics is today. There is little doubt however that he is an able man, biding his time, and confident that events will yet throw him up into a position of leadership. An eminent KC, he is a forceful personality, and must certainly be considered as being influential in Nationalist circles.[572]

Before leaving Britain on 24 April, Mosley and Pirow announced their intention to launch an organisation, the "Enemies of the Soviet Union", to expose Soviet aggression and to counter the activities of the many pro-Soviet organisations.[573] On his departure from London the Special Branch noted that only Mosley and his family, as well as four other men, came to the airport to bid him farewell.[574] This was a sure indication that his visit had failed to secure much-needed publicity.

A bigger disappointment awaited his high hopes to meet Franco and Salazar in Spain and Portugal. The Spanish embassy arranged a seat on an aircraft from Britain to Spain reserved for Spanish diplomats, but he failed to meet Franco.[575] In Portugal nothing came of

572 NA Kew, KV 2/908, "Oswald Pirow and the Union Movement. Statements at conference report, 16 April 1948".

573 NA Kew, KV 2/908, Newspaper clipping of *Union*, 1 May 1948.

574 NA Kew, KV 2/908, Metropolitan Police (Special Branch), 24 April 1948.

575 NA Kew, KV 2/908, Extract from a report on fascist activities (March–April 1948), 27 April 1948.

his wish to meet Salazar, but he did have a meeting with Dr Marcelo Caetano, chairman of Portugal's only political party, the União Nacional.[576] Nothing would come of his plans to visit the USA – he had difficulties to secure a visa because of his fascist views.[577]

An even bigger disappointment awaited Pirow back in Pretoria as the South African press, obsessed with the coming general election, gave his London visit hardly any attention. *Die Burger* and *Die Transvaler* simply ignored him, while the UP-supporting English-medium press just mentioned it in passing. The *Cape Times* referred on page three to the announcement on the "Enemies of the Soviet Union" in a few lines.

Cartoon in *Cape Times*, 10 April 1948. Mosley wants to know why Pirow does not have a moustache.

576 NA Pretoria, PM 22/3/2 vol. 1, P.R. Botha – J.C. Smuts, 4 May 1948. (I am grateful to Frik Nothling for this document.)

577 NA Kew, KV2/908, R. Thistlethwaite – Director General of the Security Service, 15 June 1948.

The visit instead bolstered the perception of Pirow as a figure of ridicule. The *Cape Times* (10 April 1948) published a cartoon with an outraged Mosley demanding to know why Pirow did not have a moustache like Hitler.

*The Natal Mercury* (15 April 1948), correctly concluding that the meeting was a stunt to recapture the glamour he formerly enjoyed as Minister of Defence, mocked his belligerent talk of a crusade against communism by publishing a cartoon of him wielding a sword on one of his bush carts with a mangy horse harnessed back to front.

Pirow's gamble to use the publicity surrounding his meeting with Mosley to enhance his own position in South Africa had failed. On 26 May, his political isolation was intensified with the HNP's shock victory over the UP. With the fiercely anti-communistic HNP in power, he found it difficult to portray himself as the country's leading anti-communist crusader. In power, the HNP brutally bolstered white supremacy, while it ended diplomatic relations with the Soviet Union, banned the South African Communist Party, and sent a squadron of fighter planes to the United Nations forces in Korea to join the battle against communist aggression.

The HNP's victory meant that nothing came of the grandiose scheme to create the "Enemies of the Soviet Union". As Pirow's intention was to use such an organisation to bolster his position in a UP-governed South Africa, it was promptly dropped and never again mentioned.[578]

578 NA Kew, KV 2/908, "Contact between Oswald Pirow (Chairman of the New Order Party, South Africa, formerly Minister of Defence in the Hertzog cabinet) and Sir Oswald Mosley (Leader of the Union Movement, London)".

# 15

# Rehabilitation, 1948–1956

The HNP's surprise victory was such a debilitating blow to Pirow that it impacted on his legal practice. It became obvious to his fellow advocates that he was merely going through the motions. Isie Maisels, a leading member of the Johannesburg Bar, concluded that he was trading on his pre-1929 reputation. In 1949, they were opposing counsels in the Appeal Court in a case dealing with the granting of a liquor licence, and it was obvious to him that Pirow had not consulted his brief. The opposing team's junior counsel, who told him that Pirow had ignored the "Heads of Argument" he had prepared for him, confirmed this.[579]

His established reputation meant that clients, unaware of his increasingly poor court performances, demanded his services. The Cape provincial administration insisted that Pirow join their legal team in an appeal in the Appeal Court to set aside a decision of the Cape Supreme Court dealing with a property development case. According to Marius Diemont, the Cape administrator's legal advisors informed him that his team "needed a little muscle" and that Pirow would lead the assault in the Appeal Court. He discovered in Bloemfontein that Pirow had not read the brief properly. He suspected that he had not read it at all. During court proceedings, Pirow, claiming

579 I. Maisels, *A life at law: The memoirs of IA Maisels, QC* (Johannesburg, 1998), pp. 78, 134.

a sore throat, left the talking to Diemont. When he did intervene, he jeopardised their case as he made a concession that was incorrect. Despite the handicap of having Pirow on the team, Diemont eventually won the case. Pirow then claimed that the fee was inadequate and demanded a larger one from the instructing attorney.[580]

Gustaf Pienaar tells an anecdote of a junior counsel who was unhappy with Pirow's lack of preparation for a court appearance. Pirow pointed to the judge and told him to stop worrying since he had appointed the judge when he was the Minister of Justice.[581] It was not an empty boast as his seniority and background meant that judges were far more respectful and tolerant towards him than they were to other advocates.

Pirow's eccentricity, charm and ability as a great conversationalist also ensured that he remained a popular member of the Bar, securing a comfortable income, and making it possible to maintain his dream of a political comeback. In the prime of his life at the age of 58, he was unable to submit to his political isolation, especially as Strijdom, Verwoerd, Sauer and Swart – people he viewed as political pygmies – were running the country. Behind a carefully constructed facade of self-imposed isolation, he did his utmost to restore his battered reputation, secure acknowledgement and respect of his abilities and talents, and possibly a senior role in the running of the country.

The difficulty with Pirow's dream was that he no longer had a political platform. The NO existed in name only as it had no membership list, or subscriptions.[582] A mere 100 people attended the movement's conference on 7 August 1948. The lack of funds, combined with the low circulation figures of *Die Nuwe Orde*, led to the decision that its publication had to be halted.[583] *Adv. Pirow se Nuusbrief* was started again on 16 August 1948. To revive his political career, he did his utmost to show that the founding of the NO was not an

---

580 E. Kahn, *Law, life & laughter encore: Legal anecdotes & portraits from southern Africa* (Cape Town, 1999), pp. 218–219; M.A. Diemont, *Brushes with the law* (Cape Town, 1995), pp. 83–84.

581 G. Pienaar, "Advokaat Oswald Pirow" http://www.litnet.co.za/advokaat-oswald-pirow/ (Accessed 31 March 2017).

582 NA Kew, KV 2/908, "Oswald Pirow and the Union Movement Statements at conference report, 16 April 1948".

583 *Adv. Pirow se Nuusbrief*, 16 August 1948.

attempt to trim his sails to Nazi Germany winning the war, but that the idea of such a movement had started before Hitler had come to power. Also, that he had started to implement his ideas for a new order when he became a government minister in 1929. His support for national socialism was part of his desire to fight communism, as Germany was the main bulwark against the Soviet threat.[584]

Pirow was speaking to himself as *Adv. Pirow se Nuusbrief* had hardly any subscribers. He continuously had to urge – or rather beg – his few readers to pay their subscription fees, pointing out on one occasion that 80 per cent of them had not paid to receive his letter. The reason for this was that Afrikaners had rejected national socialism, and after the destruction of Nazi Germany there was no future for this toxic ideology. A growing number of former NO and OB members repented their past and found their way back into the NP, and even into parliament. Pirow became more critical to the wartime actions of Germany and he conceded that awful things had happened in Nazi concentration camps.[585] However, he was unable to reject national socialism as it would have been an acknowledgement that the founding of the NO was an opportunistic gamble.

As the publicity value of linking up with Mosley brought about no rewards, Pirow maintained irregular contact with him. His letters, apart from thanking Mosley for hosting his daughter Henry-Li over the Christmas of 1949,[586] were motivated by a desire to impress him. That he went out of his way to create a good impression with someone as discredited as Mosley was an indication of how the ridicule and isolation he had endured since 1940 had undermined his once supreme self-confidence. He even resorted to lies to impress the British fascist.

Mosley, according to informant B.L.c./2762, had received a letter from Pirow in June 1948 in which he claimed that he had been offered – but had refused – two posts in the South African cabinet.[587] This was fiction as there was not the remotest possibility that Malan, Strijdom, Verwoerd, Louw, Swart and Sauer, who all viewed him as a pariah, would allow him into the government. In January 1950, he

584 *Adv. Pirow se Nuusbrief*, 16 August 1948, 3 May 1949.

585 *Adv. Pirow se Nuusbrief*, 16 November 1948.

586 UB, Sir Oswald Mosley papers, OMN/B/2/3, Pirow – Mosley, 15 January 1950.

587 NA Kew, KV 2/908, Summary of the informant's report, 24 June 1948.

informed Mosely that the NO has made more progress than any other time since 1945.[588] This was a lie as the movement existed in name only, but then Pirow's desire to attract Mosley's admiration was an irrational one.

It is possible that his desire to impress Mosley was a reason why he took up fencing in 1950. Mosley was a skilful fencer while Pirow did not have any such talent. He approached fencing contests like a boxing match, beating opponents purple and blue with his foil.[589] He was so desperate for Mosley's good opinion that he informed him in March 1950 that in one week he was offered both a judgeship and a seat in the cabinet.[590] This was fantasy since there was no offer of a judgeship, while a post in the cabinet was a pipedream, seeing as the government was packed with ministers who loathed him. What his lie to Mosley did reflect was that despite his cultivated image of self-imposed isolation, he doggedly and unrealistically retained the dream that the NP would reach out to him, welcoming him back into the fold with a post in the government. And yet, by July 1950, he informed his old friend Arthur Barlow that in politics his attitude to the UP and NP was "a plague on both your houses".[591]

It can only be assumed that in the space of a few months he had eventually accepted the fact that the HNP would never make its peace with him, and that his political writings were ignored. In February 1951, John Sweeny of the United States of America's embassy reported to Washington that Pirow's following was "a very small one" and that he was unable to exert any significant influence.[592] All that was left for Pirow was to continue plugging his vision of pan-African apartheid, and the idea that white people had to be seen as protectors of the interests of the black majority.

In the *Boikot-Nuus/Boycott News* of 30 October 1950, official mouthpiece of the Suid-Afrikaanse Beskermingsbeweging (South

588 UB, Oswald Mosley papers, File OMN/B/2/3, Pirow – Mosley, 15 January 1950.

589 Meiring, *Tien politieke leiers*, p. 93.

590 NA Kew, KV 2/908, Pirow – Mosley, 6 March 1950.

591 Unisa, UP Archive, Arthur Barlow papers, File 1, Pirow – Barlow, 23 June 1950.

592 United States State Department Confidential Files. South Africa Internal Affairs and Foreign Affairs, 1950–1954, FI 23646 reel, J. Sweeney – Department of State, 5 February 1951. (I am grateful to Frik Nothling for this document.)

African Protection Movement), an organisation focused on at Indian shopkeepers in "white areas", he pointed out that if white people took their guardianship of the black majority seriously they had to demand the permanent removal of Indians from the country as they were parasites exploiting black people.

In 1951, the AP and HNP merged and adapted the unified party's name to the NP. The party remained determined to keep Pirow out in the cold. And yet, 1951 was a turning point in Pirow's efforts to restore his reputation. At the end of that year, the translated official German minutes of his meetings with Hitler and Von Ribbentrop were made public. Count Ciano's unflattering opinion of Pirow was also released.[593] What these documents conveyed was that Pirow did not go to Berlin and Rome as a fascist sympathiser, and that he had confronted Von Ribbentrop on the Nazis' treatment of Jews. Pirow, with his shrewd political antenna, promptly started to adapt his politics. The national socialism propaganda and his anti-Semitism disappeared from his newsletter and the NO faded away.

Seen as a figure of historical importance, *Die Vaderland* in February 1952 under the heading "*Pirow vertel*" (Pirow tells) published his 1946 recollections – purged of its anti-Semitism – about his meetings with Chamberlain, Hitler, King Carol and Mussolini. He was commissioned by *Die Huisgenoot* (5 December 1952), Afrikanerdom's leading family magazine, to write an article on the events leading to coalition in 1933. On 18 December 1953, *Die Brandwag* magazine published a long and friendly interview with him on his political career. The release of the captured German documents also started the rehabilitation of Pirow amongst English-speaking journalists and businessmen who were close to him up until September 1939.

Ironically, the process of rehabilitation had started with his old enemy Leslie Blackwell who had been appointed as a judge in 1943. In his 1946 memoirs, he conceded that Pirow was not a Quisling and that it was his ostracisation after 1939 that had pushed him further and further into a fascist direction.[594] It is possible that Blackwell as a judge was aware that the Smuts government would find no evidence of any collaboration between Germany and Pirow. At the end

593 *The Argus*, 22 December 1951.
594 Blackwell, *Farewell to parliament*, p. 74.

of the hostilities, Brigadier R.J. Palmer, Commissioner of the South African Police, contacted British military intelligence to determine if any evidence of contact between Pirow and Nazi Germany had been found in German documentation captured. British intelligence found no incriminating documentation.[595]

The political marginalisation of English speakers after 1948 also encouraged a changed attitude towards Pirow. They increasingly feared that the NP was turning South Africa into an Afrikaner state in which there was no place for them. Their concerns were fuelled by the government's attempts to remove coloured people from the common voters' roll in the Cape Province. Constitutionally, the NP had to secure a two-thirds majority in a joint parliamentary sitting of the House of Assembly and the Senate. However, when the NP introduced a Bill on 8 March 1951 to place coloured people on a separate voters' roll in order to elect four white parliamentary representatives, this constitutional clause was ignored. It was claimed that the constitutional developments giving South Africa independence from Britain in the 1930s signified that the entrenched clauses were no longer binding.

On 14 May 1951, parliament passed the Separate Representation of Voters Bill, but in March 1952 the Appeal Court nullified the Act for ignoring the entrenched clauses. The NP, arguing that the court decision invalidated parliamentary sovereignty, promptly passed the High Court of Parliament Bill that turned parliament into a High Court to repeal the decision of the Appeal Court. On 27 August 1952, parliament constituted itself into a High Court and declared the Separate Representation of Voters Act valid. Two days later the Cape Supreme Court declared the High Court of Parliament Act invalid.

For most English speakers the attempt of the NP to remove the coloured franchise raised fears for the status of English as an official language. If the NP could be allowed to circumvent the two-thirds principle in the constitution on the franchise, it could also do so on the protection of English as an official language. This meant that many in the English-speaking community, remembering Pirow as a prominent fusion minister and champion of reconciliation between

595 NA Kew, KV 2/908, Brigadier Sir David Petrie – Brigadier R.J. Palmer, 5 September 1945.

the two language groups, viewed him as someone that could be used against the NP.

The role of the courts in frustrating the plans of the NP also altered the attitude of the government towards Pirow. In May 1952, the Minister of Justice, his old enemy C.R. Swart, who was transforming the judicial bench as it was dominated by English speakers, offered him a position on the bench of the Transvaal Supreme Court. Pirow declined the offer, claiming that he could do more for the country as an independent supporter of the government.[596]

His dream of being welcomed back into the political mainstream as a champion for the English-speaking community was the reason for this decision. He became increasingly critical in his newsletter of the NP's attempts to circumvent the constitution. He bluntly stated that the High Court of Parliament Act was a monstrosity and to compare such a court with the British Privy Council was sheer nonsense. Also, to give a court of laymen a say about the judgments of the Appellate division was sheer folly as some of the MPs scarcely qualified as halfwits. He increasingly became more critical of the NP's leadership in his newsletter that received publicity from the English-medium press. In December 1953, he insisted that Malan had to retire as soon as possible as he was too old to deal with the challenges facing the country. Sauer was once again condemned as not having the necessary ability to be the Minister of Railways.

Pirow's criticism of the government and the way it implemented apartheid convinced a number of English-speaking businessmen that his considerable talents were wasted in the political wilderness. By September 1952, leading figures in the mining industry toyed with the idea of using Pirow to create a new centre party to include moderate elements of the UP and NP. Pirow made it clear that he was not interested in such a proposal as he was not willing to return to electoral politics. But as the UP had no race policy, while the NP's version was bound to fail as it did not go far enough, he was prepared to take part in a non-party movement to encourage his vision of pan-African apartheid.[597]

In a leading article on 20 September 1952, Rayner Ellis, editor of the *Rand Daily Mail,* poured scorn on these businessmen's support

596 *Die Transvaler*, 27 May 1952.
597 *Rand Daily Mail*, 17 September 1952.

of his plan. He mockingly expressed the hope that the mining men are better at mining than politics or else the mines would have closed down long ago.[598] Ellis's mockery did not halt their determination to use Pirow. A meeting was announced for 25 September 1952 in the Darragh Hall in Johannesburg to discuss his proposed pan-African plan. A group of 200 people was individually invited while it was announced that if the meeting was a success, Pirow would address a succession of them.

At the meeting, about 150 people and a large group of pressmen were present. Pirow had a sympathetic audience, although there was an atmosphere of scepticism. *The Star* (26 September 1952) pointed out that although those present at the meeting viewed his plan as impractical, he was doing a public service to encourage a debate on the future of apartheid by putting pressure on the NP to clearly state what its policies entailed.

There would be no further public meetings by Pirow, but between 20 and 22 October 1952 *The Star* published his pan-African apartheid plan under the subsequent headings of "Can the white man in Africa survive?", "Divide Africa between white and black" and "Give black man his share of Africa" to explain his vision of black independent states. Pirow argued that the colour of a man's skin was no real criteria for a civilisation test, while it was futile to imagine that equal rights could indefinitely be withheld from people of colour, but that equal rights in the same state would inevitably lead to a coffee-coloured race and the disappearance of Western civilisation. He argued that unless a just and overgenerous solution was found, the stay of the white man in Africa would be limited. The solution was not to suppress the black man, but to establish separate white and autonomous black states free from all control by white people.

His plan had two development phases. The first one was urgent urban relief. He described the provision of housing, schools, hospitals and transport of black people in South African towns and cities as "positively disgraceful". The solution was to grant them their own municipal boards and councils to administer pass laws, transport, trading and other aspects of urban life. The next phase was to create independent black states in southern and central Africa. Swaziland

598 J. Mervis, *The fourth estate: A newspaper story* (Johannesburg, 1989), p. 309.

and Zululand could be consolidated, while Basutoland (Lesotho) and Transkei could be similarly treated. A homeland for coloured people stretching from the Northern Cape to Rehoboth in South West Africa (Namibia) was also proposed. White people would only be allowed in these independent black states if their presence was necessary for the development of such areas, while black people could only be migrant labourers in the white states.

The English-medium press gave extensive publicity to Pirow's proposals. The Bloemfontein-based *The Friend* (29 September 1952) reflected the opinion of the anti-NP press that although his plan was impractical, the government would do well to heed his view that the security of the white man was based on a generous justice to the black man:

> What is important is that Mr Pirow, unlike the Nationalist extremists, has had the courage to recognise and face the great moral issues involved in the problems of our multi-racial society. Until the people as a whole recognise them we will never find a way of living amicably together in this country – and until we do that we will never be a nation in the full sense of the word.

The *Cape Times* in a lead article asked whether his plans could not break the political deadlock in South Africa and become the basis of an accepted plan. Amongst Afrikaners his plan fell on deaf ears. For the NP leadership, especially with Verwoerd as the Minister of Native Affairs, Pirow remained unforgiven for his actions in the 1940s. *Die Transvaler* (26 September 1952), Verwoerd's old newspaper, merely mentioned Pirow's meeting on his pan-African plan in a short paragraph, without any effort to report his proposals. Geyer, by then South Africa's High Commissioner in London, and Phil Weber, his successor as editor of *Die Burger*, took note of *The Star* articles, but concurred that his proposal contained nothing new, and were disappointing and superficial.[599]

As the interest in Pirow's proposals faded, he forwarded *The Star* articles to Mosley who published them as "An African solution: The Pirow proposals" in the August 1953 edition of his journal, *The European*. (In 1974, Mosley would claim credit for him and Pirow

599 US, P.A. Weber papers, 296.K.Ge (110/2), P.A. Weber – A.L. Geyer, 2 November 1952.

as the proposers of the NP's Bantustan policy).[600] Pirow published a more detailed version of his plan in a booklet, *Die witman se weg na selfbehoud* (The white man's road to self-preservation).

Although Pirow's proposals fell on deaf ears in the NP, the English-medium press went a long way to further his rehabilitation. Publicly, Pirow was adamant that he had no intentions of returning to party politics,[601] but privately the attention given to him fed his dream that he would be recalled to mainstream politics by public demand. This was evident in the introduction to his "An African solution" in *The European*:

> At present he stands aside from current politics and in the future should be in the best position to unite all sections of South African opinion in a constructive policy. His practical proposals have, therefore, a particular interest.[602]

That his dream of returning to public life without being involved in electoral politics was not an irrational one would be proven by the political comeback of H.A. Fagan, his old classmate and fellow cabinet minister. In 1960, Fagan, who had retired from the bench, published *Our responsibility: A discussion of South Africa's racial problem* in which he expressed his deep concern about the racial situation in the country, the shortcomings of the apartheid system and his recommendations to remedy the situation. He also became involved in the National Union, a small party formed by Japie Basson who was expelled from the NP for daring to oppose Verwoerd's move to abolish the system of white native representation in 1959. It was his book, *Our responsibility,* that contributed to Sir De Villiers Graaff's decision to offer him a UP senate seat. He felt the party would benefit from Fagan's wisdom and expertise.[603]

That Pirow was convinced that he would be called upon for a leadership role amongst English speakers is reflected in a letter that the British intelligence services intercepted from A. Victor Heipner to Robert Row in 1953. Heipner mentioned that the Republikeinse Bond (Republican League), a splinter organisation and the last re-

600 O. Mosley, "African solutions", *Books and Bookmen*, January 1974, p. 31.
601 *Die Vaderland*, 19 September 1952; *Die Volksblad*, 26 September 1952.
602 UB, Oswald Mosley papers, OMD 7/4/9.
603 Schoeman, *My lewe in die politiek*, p. 416.

maining remnant of the OB with the mission to encourage South Africa to become a republic, approached Pirow to be its leader. Pirow, according to Heipner, refused the offer as the British element in South Africa was flustered and without a leader, and he felt that he could unite all Europeans in Africa. Becoming the leader of a small extreme nationalist Afrikaner group would endanger his ambitions.[604]

Pirow's dream of becoming the leader of English-speaking South Africans was not without basis as a significant section of this community in Natal and the Eastern Cape felt alienated from the NP with its intentions to turn South Africa into an Afrikaner state. They also found it difficult to relate to the UP with its small but vocal liberal wing that would eventually form the Progressive Party in 1959. Already in 1948 Pirow had noted that conservative English speakers were prepared to cooperate with Afrikaners but felt that they were treated as second-class citizens by the HNP.[605]

The seemingly unstoppable expansion of communism, combined with the anti-colonial movement in Africa and Britain's decline as a world power, fuelled the anxiety and conservatism of English speakers in southern Africa. The ultra-conservatism of a significant number of them was reflected in 1959 with Mosley's visit to South Africa. Ivor Benson, the acting editor of the *Rand Daily Mail*, expressed his support for Mosley's ideas of white supremacy. This led to his immediate dismissal.[606] It was also evident in the declaration of unilateral independence from Britain by the conservative English settler community in Rhodesia (Zimbabwe) under the leadership of Ian Smith in 1965. Pirow believed that he could provide leadership to the numerous conservative English speakers who had no political home. This meant that he did his utmost to extend a hand of friendship to them.

Addressing the Afrikaans Club at the University of the Witwatersrand in August 1956, he urged Afrikaners not to abuse their power, and to reach out to English speakers.[607] He personally did so

604 NA Kew, KV 2/908, Extract from copy of intercepted letter from A. Victor Heipner, 10 December 1953.

605 *Adv. Pirow se Nuusbrief*, 16 August 1948.

606 A. Sparks, *The sword and the pen: Six decades on the political frontier* (Johannesburg & Cape Town, 2016), p. 118.

607 *Cape Times*, 17 August 1956.

by reconciling with Harry Lawrence, his former cabinet colleague and a senior UP MP. Lawrence was appreciative that they could be friends again as he confessed a deep respect and affection for him.[608]

However, the odds were stacked against Pirow to become the leader of the English-speaking community. Although very conservative in their politics, they still cherished the constitutional link with Britain and revered Churchill for his role in the war against Nazi Germany, while viewing Pirow's war position with distaste. It was the norm for English-speaking politicians in the 1950s to have served in World War II. In addition, the UP was perceived as the only realistic alternative to the NP, while the party would become increasingly conservative to hold on to its support in Natal and the Eastern Cape. Lastly, a third world war between the USA and the Soviet Union, which Pirow had hoped would shatter the political mould, never happened. Nothing would come of Pirow's ambition to become the leader of conservative English speakers.

Politically isolated and with time on his hands, Pirow started to write novels. His first book, *Piet Potlood* (1948), was an adventure story for children based on the South African War. His increasingly longer stays on his farm, Valhalla, profoundly influenced his writings. He loved the natural beauty of the Graskop area. By 1948, he had stopped hunting and would sit for hours to observe the behaviour of animals in a hide he had created in a tree at a waterhole on his farm.

He also became obsessed with Graskop's turbulent early nineteenth-century history: Slave raiders and adventurers from the Portuguese settlement in Lourenço Marques, the Voortrekkers, local black communities, the Shangaan and Zulu exiles under the leadership of Soshangane who was responsible for a reign of terror, had clashed with much bloodshed in the area surrounding his farm. This resulted in him writing fictional folklore about the Shangaan whose language he could speak.[609] A striking aspect of his writing was that – apart from two stories – white people are absent in them, and they were filled with admiration for the Shangaan. He saw himself, in a patriarchal mould, as a defender of their traditional culture.

608 *The Star*, 22 November 1957.
609 Meiring, *Tien politieke leiers*, pp. 93, 95–96.

This was evident in *Mlungo Mungoma (Die blanke waarsêer)* [Mlungo Mungoma (The white soothsayer)], published in 1949, and *Sjangani,* published in 1950. *Mlungo Mungoma* is the fictional tale of Orn Olen, a young Scandinavian, who was raised in the Transvaal and fought with the Boers in the South African War. During the guerrilla phase, he ended up alone in the Bushveld. Here he fell under the influence of Humo, a Shangaan witch doctor, and became part of the Shangaan community. Named Mungoma, the highest Shangaan grade for a witch doctor, he became revered as a soothsayer and prophet. *Sjangani* is the heroic adventure story of a Shangaan child. Zulu raiders had slaughtered his family and he had to protect himself against enemies and wild animals while lost in the bush for many months. The book was translated into English as *Shangani,* and after Pirow's death into German. Bram Fischer, a leading communist, later read it to his son Paul as part of his daily routine to read him adventure stories of southern Africa.[610]

*Sikoro (Avonture in die spookland van die Bantu)* [Sikore (Adventures in the ghostland of the Bantu)] was published in 1952. In the introduction he claimed that until he was nine years old, most of his playmates were black children and that he grew up with their myths, legends and stories of the supernatural. He said that *Sikoro* was an attempt to tell these stories to white people in a sympathetic way as knowledge of and respect for the culture of the black majority was essential for white trusteeship.[611] It was also the message he conveyed in September 1953 to the Afrikaanse Skrywerskring (Afrikaans Writers' Circle) in a lecture on black people in Afrikaans literature. He urged Afrikaner authors to write more sympathetic about the lives of black people in order to encourage good relations between the two races.[612]

In 1955, he published in English *Ashambeni,* the adventures of a Bushveld dog and his master Maskakatsi, a young Maluleke chief. It was set in the same period of turmoil and violence as *Sjangani*.[613]

---

610 S. Clingman, *Bram Fischer: Afrikaner revolutionary* (Cape Town, 1998), p. 217.

611 O. Pirow, *Sikoro* (*Avonture in die spookland van die Bantu*) (Johannesburg, 1952), pp. 1–5.

612 *Die Transvaler*, 12 September 1953.

613 J. Barendse, "Oswald Pirow's Ashambeni (1955): a 'history' of dogs, humans, werewolves", *Tydskrif vir Letterkunde*, 55, 3, 2018, pp. 96–107.

The book was in effect a history of all Pirow's dogs, but especially that of Bismarck, his favourite dog for lion hunting. According to Pirow they understood each other so well that Bismarck could read his thoughts, and that he knew what the dog would do before it made any movement.

It is doubtful whether Pirow succeeded in changing the attitude of ignorant and racist white people about the spiritual world of the Shangaan, but his books reflect his gradual evolution from a poisonous racist into a more tolerant paternalist. But he failed in his hope to make his mark as a writer, as his books had limited sales and were quickly forgotten. In studies on Afrikaans literature, he is only mentioned in passing as a folklorist.[614]

614 N. Bosman, "Brongebruik in die populêre historiese roman, met spesiale verwysing na Engela van Rooyen en Oswald Pirow", *Suid-Afrikaanse Tydskrif vir Kultuurgeskiedenis*, 23 (10 June 2009).

# 16

# Biographer and prosecutor, 1957–1959

There is no evidence in any of the private archival collections of prominent HNP leaders that those in power took any notice of Pirow's newsletter. Hell would freeze over before Strijdom, who had succeeded Malan as prime minister in November 1954, would take note of him. This irked Pirow and in September 1955 he condemned the NP's intolerance towards well-disposed critics.[615] For Bresler it was obvious that he was deeply disappointed that the NP ignored his plan for pan-African apartheid.[616] By the end of 1956, it was obvious to him that there would not be any return to public life. All that remained was to defend his reputation and secure a place in South African history.

To do so he decided to write a biography of Hertzog with the intent to settle a score with the NP leadership, especially Malan. To Hans van Rensburg, the former OB leader with whom he was rekindling his old friendship, he made it clear that his intention was to emulate Émile Zola's famous polemic *J'accuse* in which he had exposed the corruption of the French establishment during the Dreyfus scandal.[617] In his introduction he claimed that he was motivated to write the book as most Afrikaners did not want to hear the name

615 *Cape Times*, 13 September 1955.

616 Bresler, *Tilt the sack*, p. 201.

617 NWU, OB Archive, Hans van Rensburg collection, Box 2, File 2/16, Pirow – Van Rensburg, 19 June 1957.

Hertzog because they were "too busy worshipping at the shrine of those who cast him out and hastened him to a premature grave".[618]

Pirow became a full-time writer in January 1957. He had suffered a stroke and although he made a full recovery, he thought it best to retire from his legal practice. He used his free time to complete the Hertzog biography. The book was written in English to secure a wider audience, while he also argued that it had to be in this medium as English-speaking South Africans should know more about the man who had entrenched their language and cultural rights in South Africa.

The British publisher George Allen & Unwin published *James Barry Munnik Hertzog* in late 1957. Although highly readable, the book fails as a biography as it is too hagiographical, polemical, marred by factual errors and personally digressive. Large sections do not even refer to Hertzog as Pirow extensively recycled his own recollections to defend his tenure as Minister of Defence – especially his bush carts – and to portray his visit to Europe in 1938 as a heroic attempt to prevent a world war. He described with pride his protest to Von Ribbentrop on the treatment of Jews.

The most striking aspect of *James Barry Munnik Hertzog* was Pirow's skill to justify Hertzog's actions and legacy, as well as his own. He condemned the existing NP leadership as political pygmies, petty-minded, vindictive and disappointed place seekers who for opportunistic reasons had destroyed Hertzog, a political giant. By describing the fall of Hertzog, he created the impression that the NP leadership had done the same to him. In the process he distorted events, claiming that he had resigned from the HNP as Malan had handed over affidavits on young OB-supporting Afrikaners – in which he accused them of sabotage – to the Smuts government for their prosecution. This was a lie and had played no role in his decision to leave the HNP. The main weakness of the book is that it is not based on any original research but on anecdotes, lengthy quotes from speeches, newspapers and extracts from existing Hertzog biographies.

A biography on Hertzog by Pirow created interest, and between 14 and 25 October 1957 the *Cape Argus* serialised a significant sec-

618 Pirow, *James Barry Munnik Hertzog*, p. 11.

tion of the book. Pirow's former cabinet colleague Harry Lawrence in a lengthy review in *The Star* (21 and 22 November) described it as "a valuable though controversial addition to the history of our young and politically storm-tossed country", and that Pirow "has a story to tell, and he tells it with characteristic vigour and forthrightness". Reviews in NP-supporting newspapers were scathing. E.A. Malgas, the retired political correspondent of *Die Burger*, in his review for the newspaper on 23 October 1957, reproduced in *Die Volksblad* on 26 October, concluded that *James Barry Munnik Hertzog* lacked intellectual rigour, and was no contribution to South African historiography as it was used to settle old political scores. "C.J.E.", the reviewer of *Die Transvaler* (6 November 1957), condemned the lack of originality and the cheap shots at Malan. It was clear that both reviewers felt that Malan had made the right decision to keep Pirow out of the NP. *Die Burger*'s columnist "Dawie", the collective penname of the editor and his deputies, shared this view. In the column *Uit my politieke pen* (Out of my political pen) of 2 November 1957, "Dawie" pointed out that the book was motivated by the NP's marginalisation of Pirow, and that the former NO leader behaved like an old and expelled buffalo – occasionally storming his former herd. There was no need to take the book, or Pirow, seriously.

The exception amongst Afrikaans newspapers was the review of Willem van Heerden in the *Dagbreek en Sondagnuus* (23 February 1958). As a passionate admirer of Hertzog, he proclaimed it an outstanding study.

*James Barry Munnik Hertzog* failed to rehabilitate Pirow's reputation, but it was in this period that the long-awaited call from the government for his services eventually came. Not for his political expertise but for his legal skills.

He was approached by Swart to lead the prosecution of a group of anti-apartheid leaders charged with high treason. This protracted court case, dubbed the Treason Trial, was a consequence of the ANC's resistance to apartheid. The early 1950s was a period in which the movement's leaders moved closer to communists and their ideas of mass action. This led to the Defiance Campaign of June to December 1952 in which the ANC in alliance with the South African Indian Congress (SAIC) contravened apartheid laws with a massive display of passive resistance. Black people were urged to ignore the use of passbooks and to use public amenities reserved for white people. Unrelenting repression by the government led to the campaign being called off, but the Defiance Campaign brought the ANC publicity that increased its membership and started a culture of mass confrontation against the apartheid state.

In October 1953, the alliance of the ANC and the SAIC was extended with the founding of the Congress of Democrats (COD), a radical white left-wing organisation that campaigned for equality and justice for all South Africans. Although the COD was a small movement, it played an influential role in the Congress Alliance, especially in drawing up the Freedom Charter. The Charter was accepted by the Congress of the People, a mass meeting of anti-apartheid organisations at Kliptown, near Johannesburg in 1955, and committed the ANC to a multiracial and social democratic future South Africa.

For the NP, the confrontational stance of the ANC was part of a conspiracy inspired by the international communist movement to overthrow the state by violence. In December 1956, the government arrested and charged 156 anti-apartheid activists of plotting to violently overthrow the government and to replace it with a Soviet-style state. The result was a lengthy legal process that dragged on for years. The first phase that lasted from December 1956 to January 1958 was the preparatory examination in a magistrates' court. (The Drill Hall in Johannesburg was converted into a court because of the large number of accused.) The purpose of this examination was to determine whether there was enough evidence to put the defendants on trial.

The defence team used this opportunity to make a mockery of the state's evidence, and ruthlessly exposed the shortcomings of the police and expert witnesses. In doing so they exposed the real objective of the trial – that it was politically motivated to silence dissent. The defence team succeeded in getting the charges dropped against 65 of the accused because of lack of evidence.

With the prosecution struggling to press its case for treason and desperate to secure convictions, Swart turned to Pirow with his reputation as a fearsome court advocate to become the lead prosecutor. Because of his stroke, Pirow hesitated to accept the appointment,[619]

619 NWU, OB Archive, Hans van Rensburg papers, Box 2, File 2/16, Pirow – Van Rensburg, 19 June 1957.

but after years of portraying himself as a leading expert on the threat of a communist revolution he felt obliged to do so.

There were also other factors: his sense of isolation and desire for recognition and respect. Piet Meiring, a former journalist who had become a senior civil servant, told how he had found Pirow in parliament awaiting a meeting with Swart, sitting alone in a passageway used only by parliamentarians and civil servants. They conversed for an hour and not a single passing MP seemed to recognise the former minister.[620] For Pirow the call to lead the prosecution team provided an opportunity to escape his loneliness, to be useful again after his stroke, but most importantly, it was a final opportunity to show himself as a true and good Afrikaner. His appointment was not the complete rehabilitation he had desired within the Afrikaner establishment, but it went some way to satisfy his craving for respect.

In January 1958, just before the conclusion of the preparatory phase, Pirow took over as the state's lead prosecutor.[621] On 28 January, Vernon Berrangé, leader of the defence team, announced that since the state had not offered efficient evidence against the accused, he would apply for the discharge of the remaining 92 defendants. Pirow opposed the motion in a dramatic speech. He argued that the accused owed their allegiance to the state and that they had committed high treason by conspiring for its subversion. For him there was a great deal of camouflage in the real objects of the Freedom Charter. He viewed the Charter as a communist document with the aim to ferment trouble and undermine the authority of the government, and that all those before the court were either communists or communist sympathisers. He furthermore rejected the Congress Alliance's claims of non-violence, stating that its activists made the most violent and inflammatory speeches, bringing the audience to the pitch of hysteria, and only then they urged those present not to resort to violence. If speakers thought the police were not present, they did not hesitate to urge violence. He quoted from a secretly recorded speech in which the speaker told the audience that they had to be violent in their resistance to apartheid, even resorting to murder.[622]

---

620 Meiring, *Tien politieke leiers*, pp. 93, 95, 97.

621 Clingman, *Bram Fischer*, pp. 235–239.

622 *The Cape Argus*, 30 January 1958.

For Nelson Mandela, one of the leading defendants, it was obvious that Pirow's presence had changed the atmosphere of the trial as many of the defendants up until then had not taken the charges against themselves seriously.[623] After the closing of the legal arguments, the presiding magistrate found that there was enough evidence to put the defendants on trial for treason.

The Treason Trial formally started on 1 August 1958 in Pretoria before a special criminal court – the Old Synagogue had been converted into a court – and a panel of three judges. The presiding judge was F. Rumpff, who had defended Pirow in 1947 when he was tried on the charge of incitement to commit public violence. The defendants were represented by South Africa's leading advocates: Bram Fischer QC, Vernon Berrangé QC, Tony O'Dowd, H.C. Nicholas, R. Welsh, Sydney Kentridge, C. Plewman and D. Osborn with Isie Maisels QC as the leader of the team. Pirow's prosecution team also consisted of legal heavyweights, and two of them, G. Hoexter and J. Trengove, would become highly regarded judges.

To focus on his duties as prosecutor, Pirow brought his last newsletter out at the end of August 1958. He took a final swipe at the NP:

> We could have taken leave of our readers with a far lighter heart if we could say that the future of South Africa was in good hands. Unluckily we cannot say this, with all due respect to the intentions of some and the unquestioned ability of more than one of the members of government.[624]

His blast at the NP leadership went unnoticed. Strijdom passed away on 24 August and the press focused on his death and the election of Verwoerd as his successor. They took no notice of Pirow's last political hurrah.

In court the Treason Trial became an ordeal for Pirow. The defence team ran circles around him, turning the once feared courtroom gladiator into a bumbling figure with whom even the judges became impatient. Ultimately, he was the wrong person to lead the prosecution in a case based on shaky legal grounds and flimsy evidence. Although he had made a full recovery from his stroke, he was old and

623 N. Mandela, *Long walk to freedom: The autobiography of Nelson Mandela* (Johannesburg, 1994), p. 198.

624 *Cape Times*, 3 September 1958.

tired with a bad habit of not exerting himself in preparing for court cases. With his high intelligence and skills as an orator, he could in smaller cases get away with a lack of preparation, but with the vastness and complexity of a charge of high treason, his tendency to take short cuts came to haunt him as he produced a shoddy indictment.

The defendants were accused of being guilty of high treason as they had conspired and acted in concert, and with common purpose, to overthrow the state with violence. They were furthermore charged with two alternative charges of contravening the Suppression of Communism Act. The judges, after the defence team's challenge, demanded a more specific charge sheet. This led to the prosecution dropping the charge under the Suppression of Communism Act and reducing the treason charge to an allegation of conspiracy. This did not satisfy the judges who concurred with Maisels that the planning of violence was necessary for treason, and that the state had to prove that the accused intended to act violently.

On 13 October, Pirow withdrew the indictment and served a new one in January 1959. This time it was specifically claimed that between 1952 and 1956 the accused intended to overthrow the state with violence. In the process, the number of defendants had been reduced to 30.[625]

At the end of January 1959, while Pirow was struggling to assemble an indictment, Mosley visited South Africa for eight days. In a world in which the British Empire was being dismantled, in which communism seemed unstoppable, and in which Britain was changing with new arrivals from the colonies, he viewed South Africa as "the final redoubt when the great collapse came" and became an outspoken defender of apartheid. He remained a marginalised figure in Britain as all his political comebacks had failed dismally, while his exploitation of concerns about the arrival of black workers from the West Indies bolstered the view of him as a figure beyond the pale. By then his Union Movement consisted mainly of violent thugs that relished assaulting black people.

Mosley claimed that his visit was purely for business reasons to look after his significant investments. In addition, apart from investing in South African shares which paid rich dividends, he was

625 Maisels, *A life at law*, pp. 146–151.

eager to distribute the Union Movement's newssheet, *Action*, in the country to secure the support of conservative English-speaking white people as a possible source of financial support for his struggling movement.[626]

It is impossible to determine whether Pirow played any role in arranging the visit. His last letter to Mosley in his British intelligence file was dated October 1954, and this letter reflects that they had not been in contact for some years. It is doubtful that he was involved in any way. The pragmatic Pirow could not reap any benefits from such a visit, while all his energy in any case was focused on the Treason Trial. More importantly, the visit could only harm his new image of respectability. The publicity surrounding Mosley's visit, especially a 1948 photo of him broadly grinning and looking extremely self-satisfied with Mosley on the front page of the *Rand Daily Mail* (28 January 1959), could only have been a source of acute embarrassment. The press took great interest in Mosley spending the day with Pirow at his home in Pretoria on Sunday, 1 February. It was nothing more than a social call, but it was a reminder to South Africans, and international observers of the Treason Trial, of his support for Nazi Germany. Fortunately for an embarrassed government, the Mosley visit was pushed out of the newspapers by the Treason Trial defence team's challenge to Pirow's new indictment.

For Maisels the charges of violence that the 30 accused had to answer for were too vague. It was simply a case of "Let's throw in everything the police have been able to find and see what comes out at the end".[627] As treason was a crime distinguished by the means used rather than the ends sought, the prosecution was obliged to provide evidence of the alleged acts of violence committed by the accused, or were alleged to have advocated. The vagueness of the indictment meant that the accused were denied the right to a proper opportunity to defend themselves. As the indictment was insufficient as a matter of law, Maisels set out to squash it.[628]

His request for more detailed particulars on the charge of violence eventually ended up in the Appeal Court in Bloemfontein but

626 Dorrill, *Black shirt*, pp. 612, 616, 627.

627 Maisels, *A life at law*, p. 134.

628 *Rand Daily Mail*, 5 February 1959; *The Star*, 5 February 1959.

failed to halt the indictment. The appeal delayed the commencement of the trial until 4 August 1959. Pirow opened proceedings by arguing that the essence of high treason was hostile intent. Such intent was evident in the demands of the accused for full equality with white people as the accused knew that to achieve the demands of the Freedom Charter meant the overthrowing of the apartheid state by violence. The hostile intent of the accused was in the adherence to a conspiracy, namely that the Congress Alliance was the vanguard of the so-called National Liberatory Movement in South Africa. This alliance was part of an international-inspired communist conspiracy to overthrow with violence all governments in non-communist countries.

Pirow claimed that the prosecution would prove the existence of this conspiracy by inference from the history of the worldwide communist movement, and the history of the extraparliamentary movement in South Africa. He emphasised that the case would be an intricate one as the prosecution would provide all kinds of evidence from thousands of documents consisting of bulletins, newspapers, minutes of meetings and other publications, as well as what had been said in hundreds of speeches. The unifying element was that the liberation movement was inspired by communist fanaticism, black nationalism and a racist hatred of white people. By acting in concert, the accused intended the violent overthrow of the state.[629] To substantiate its case, the state called 150 witnesses who testified to more than 4000 documents.

The result was a painfully slow and boring process in which over time the judges, advocates for the prosecution and defence, as well as the accused, developed a unique relationship. This led to Nelson Mandela viewing Pirow, despite his noxious political views, with some affection as a humane man without the personal racism of the government he was acting for. He especially was struck by his polite reference to the accused which contrasted with his supremacist political leanings, as well as his generosity. Pirow had donated to the defendants free of charge more than a hundred volumes of the pre-

629 H. Joseph, *If this be treason: Helen Joseph's dramatic diary of the treason trial 1956–1961* (Johannesburg, 1998), pp. 280–283; Maisels, *A life at law*, pp. 135, 150, 152–154, 187.

paratory charge. It was an act of kindness that had saved the defence team a great deal of money.[630] Maisels, who viewed Pirow as a "fair opponent", shared Mandela's opinion.[631] After his opening address, Pirow would play no part in the leading of evidence, apart from the occasional comment on the argument of the defence.

According to Helen Joseph, one of the accused, he was so slumped in a special chair – seemingly because of a poor back – that he almost disappeared from sight.[632] He eventually disappeared from the court case when he became ill with pneumonia. It was while at home on sick leave on the evening of Sunday, 11 October 1959, after retiring to bed, that Pirow died of cardiac failure.[633]

Pirow's death caused hardly a ripple in South Africa. Apart from being a long-forgotten figure, he died three days before the provincial elections. The NP, concerned about the lethargic attitude of its supporters as the UP was not seen as a threat after its crushing defeat in the 1958 general election, expected its supporting newspapers to whip up enthusiasm for the election. With Verwoerd as prime minister, Pirow remained unforgiven for his opportunism.

*Die Transvaler* merely mentioned his death in passing. *Die Volksblad* was the only Afrikaans newspaper to discuss his career in an editorial. On 21 October, *Die Burger* published a long and laudatory obituary by Hans van Rensburg. In contrast to the cool and distant attitude of the Afrikaans press, the English-medium newspapers in leading articles reflected with some warmth and sympathy on Pirow's controversial career. For the *Cape Times* (13 October 1959) and *The Star* (12 October 1959) his life was a sad tale of wasted talent and opportunity, and these newspapers reported that it was a tragedy for South Africa which could not afford to lose the talents of a man like Pirow.

On Monday, 12 October, the national flag was flown at half-mast at the Old Synagogue and tributes were paid to him. Judge Rumpff emotionally praised him as a fearless, bold, trenchant and indomitable advocate, who in his heyday was one of the country's most outstanding advocates. Ironically, Fischer as a leading communist, paid

630 N. Mandela, *Long walk to freedom*, p. 220.

631 Maisels, *A life at law*, p. 134.

632 Joseph, *If this be treason*, p. 43.

633 *Cape Times*, 12 October 1959.

tribute to Pirow on behalf of the defence team. After the tributes, the court was adjourned for fifteen minutes as a mark of respect.[634] According to Mandela, the defendants did not rejoice at his death, and his successor, J. de Vos QC, lacked the eloquence and acuity of Pirow.[635]

The trail dragged on for a few more years. As the prosecution had led no direct evidence of the existence of an international liberatory movement and had failed to prove a conspiracy to overthrow the state by violence, the accused were acquitted on 20 March 1961.

Pirow was cremated after a Lutheran Church service at the Dutch Reformed Church in Bosman Street, Pretoria, on 15 October. In Pretoria the national flag was flown at half-mast at all government buildings in a show of respect. Reverend O. Papke referred to Pirow as a person blessed by God with numerous talents and that he had served his country in many different ways, making him a gemstone in the great building that was South Africa.

The reality was that his political contemporaries did not view him as a "gemstone". This was reflected in the people attending the church service. They were mainly members of the Pretoria Bar. The Treason Trial was adjourned early to make it possible for his fellow prosecutors to attend the service, but not a single Afrikaner political or cultural leader was present. Their absence emphasised that he remained beyond the pale as an opportunist for the Afrikaner establishment.

Pirow's ashes were interred on his beloved farm. With time his family erected a cairn to commemorate him on a hill overlooking the valleys and mountains he had loved.

634 *Pretoria News*, 12 October 1959.

635 Mandela, *Long walk to freedom*, p. 220.

# Epilogue

Pirow in his introduction to *James Barry Munnik Hertzog* stated that the "book should have been called 'The Hertzog Tragedy' as his rise and fall were as complete and inescapable as if Shakespeare had written the story", and that the former prime minister had died a broken and frustrated man.[636] In writing about Hertzog's end he had composed his own epitaph. In the 1930s he was the most brilliant star in the South African political constellation: ambitious, highly intelligent, charismatic, competent, energetic, and a brilliant debater. Pirow was a man of many qualities, but they were all marred by his lack of deeply held principles. Winning, and the advancing of his career, was the primary goal of his politics.

Geyer as a shrewd political observer was spot-on when he described him as a person consumed with ambition, that he was in politics to advance his own interests. For him political parties, and people such as Roos and Hertzog, were mere vehicles for his ambitions. Ultimately, the essence of his political belief was not fascism, but his ambition on a grand scale to become prime minister.

Noel Garson in an outstanding essay on Pirow concludes that his career was destroyed by "a streak of undisciplined opportunism in his own character".[637] In reality, his career was one of calculated

636 Pirow, *James Barry Munnik Hertzog*, pp. 11–12.

637 H.C.G. Matthew and B. Harrison (eds), *Oxford dictionary of national biography, Vol. 44* (Oxford, 2004), pp. 412.

opportunism, but he was willing to take risks to satisfy his political ambitions. This was evident when in 1940, with his parliamentary career at a dead end, he gambled on a military victory by Nazi Germany with the founding of the NO. This was a gamble that went for broke and failed.

It was said of President Lyndon B. Johnson of the USA that he "was a man whose ambition could overcome almost any obstacle, save the course of history. History was moving simply too fast."[638] The same principle applies to Pirow's political career.

638 J. Darman, *Landslide. LBJ and Ronald Reagan at the dawn of a new America* (New York, 2015), p. 355.

# Bibliography


## Archival sources

*Zuid-Afrikahuis, Stichting Zuid-Afrikahuis Nederland, Amsterdam*
NZAV 1, File 1494.

*National Archives, Kew*
Avia 2/1879 File 29827/Part II
Avia 2/1879, File 29827/Part II
Avia 2/1879, File 29827/Part III
Avia 2/1879, File 29827/Part IV
DO 35/133/1
DO 35/335/1
DO 35/334/3
DO 35/333/3
DO 35/334/2
DO35/186B/11
DO 35/587/6
DO 35/588/1
DO 35/588/3
DO 35/1003/6
DO 35/1119
DO119/1052
FO 371/21682
FO 371/21791
FO 371/23964
KV 2/908
CAB 63/69

*Department of Defence Documentation Centre, Pretoria*
Personnel archives: Personnel card of Oswald Pirow
CGS 944/2

*University of the Witwatersrand, William Cullen Library*
D. Friedmann papers
J.H. Hofmeyr papers
S.G. Millin papers

*Royal Archives, Windsor*
PS/GVI/C 051

*University of South Africa Archives and Special Collections*
Arthur Barlow papers
Louis Esselen papers
C.F. Stallard papers
United Party collection
United States State Department Confidential Files. South Africa Internal Affairs and Foreign Affairs, 1950–1954, FI 23646 reel

*National Archives, Pretoria*
J.B.M. Hertzog papers
J.C.G. Kemp papers
N.C. Havenga papers
J.C. Smuts papers
J.G. Strijdom papers
PM 4/2/12 Vol. 1

*Archive for Contemporary Affairs, University of the Free State, Bloemfontein*
J.H.O. du Plessis papers
Oswald Pirow papers
C.R. Swart papers
H.F. Verwoerd papers

*Western Cape Provincial Archives and Records Service*
A.L. Geyer papers

*University of Stellenbosch, Documentation centre, J.S. Gericke Library*
D.F. Malan papers
P.A. Weber papers

*University of Birmingham*
Sir Oswald Mosley papers

*North West University, Potchefstroom, Ossewa-Brandwag Archives*
OB Archive, Kommandant-Generaal papers
Hans van Rensburg papers
Transcripts of interviews

H. Anderson, Tape 16–18, no date
R.K. Rudman, Tape 104, 24 October 1975
B.J. Vorster, Tape 226, 7 November 1981

*In private possession*
H.G. Stoker – Pirow, 26 September 1942. (The letter is in possession of Prof. P. Stoker, Potchefstroom.)

## Printed primary sources

Joubert, D., *Die Kaapse stemreg: Verteenwoordiging vir swart en bruin in 1936* (Cape Town, 1973).
Lavin (ed.), D., *Friendship and Union: The South African letters of Patrick Duncan and Maud Selborne 1907–1943* (Cape Town, 2010).
Van der Poel, J. (ed.), *Selections from the Smuts papers, Vol. 4, September 1919–November 1934* (Cambridge, 1973).
Van der Poel, J., (ed.), *Selections from the Smuts papers, Vol. 5, December 1934–August 1945* (Cambridge, 1973).

## Official publications

House of Assembly debates, 1929–1943

## Books

Anonymous, *The nation on guard: An exposition of South Africa's defence policy* (Cape Town, 1937).
Appel, A., *Die Oosterlig: 'n Pershistoriese studie* (Port Elizabeth, 1985).
Barlow, A., *Almost in confidence* (Cape Town, 1952).
Basson, J.L., *JG Strijdom: Sy politieke loopbaan van 1929 tot 1948* (Pretoria, 1980).
Beckett, F., *Fascist in the family: The tragedy of John Beckett MP* (London, 2017).
Bekker, A., *Eben Dönges: Balansstaat: Historiese perspektief* (Stellenbosch, 2005).
Bellwood, W.A., *South African backdrop* (Cape Town, 1969).
Birkby, C., *Uncle George: The Boer boyhood, letters and battles of Lieutenant-General George Edwin Brink* (Johannesburg, 1987).
Blackwell, L., *African occasions: Reminiscences of thirty years of bar, bench, and politics in South Africa* (London, 1938).
Blackwell, L., *Farewell to parliament: More reminiscences of bench, bar, parliament and travel* (Pietermaritzburg, 1946).
Bloch, M., *F.M. The life of Frederick Matthias Alexander: Founder of the Alexander Technique* (London, 2004).

Bourne, K., and Watt, D.C., (eds), *Studies in international history* (London, 1967).
Bouverie, T., *Appeasing Hitler: Chamberlain, Churchill and the road to war* (London, 2019).
Bozzoli, B., (ed.*), Townships and protest: Studies in the social history of the Witwatersrand* (Johannesburg, 1979).
Bresler, C.P., *Lineage of conflict: A South African miscellany* (Cape Town, 1952).
Bresler, C.P., *Tilt the sack* (Pretoria, 1965).
Brits, J.P., *Tielman Roos – political prophet or opportunist?* (Pretoria, 1987).
Brits, J.P., *Op die vooraand van apartheid: Die rassevraagstuk en die blanke politiek in Suid-Afrika, 1939–1948* (Pretoria, 1994).
Broome, F.N., *Not the whole truth* (Pietermaritzburg, 1962).
Calpin, G.H., *There are no South Africans* (London, 1941).
Clingman, S., *Bram Fischer: Afrikaner revolutionary* (Cape Town, 1998).
Coetzer, P.W., Le Roux, J.H., *Die Nasionale Party, Vol. IV, Die "Gesuiwerde" Nasionale Party 1934–1940* (Bloemfontein, 1986).
Coetzer, P.W., *Die Nasionale Party, Vol. V, Van oorlog tot oorwinning, 1940–1948* (Bloemfontein, 1994).
Crafford, F.S., *Jan Smuts: A biography* (New York, 1968).
Darman, J., *Landslide: LBJ and Ronald Reagan at the dawn of a new America* (New York, 2015).
De Villiers, D. and J., *Paul Sauer* (Cape Town, 1977).
Diemont, M., *Brushes with the law* (Cape Town, 1995).
Dorril, S., *Black shirt: Sir Oswald Mosley and British fascism* (London, 2006).
Du Plessis, W., *Die goue draad: Op die trekpad van 'n nasie* (Johannesburg, 1970).
Egeland, L., *Bridges of understanding: A personal record in teaching, law, politics and diplomacy* (Cape Town, 1977).
Evans, R.J., *The Third Reich in history and memory* (London, 2015).
Fagan, Q., *Henry Allan Fagan 1889–1963* (Cape Town, 1975).
Flather, H., *The way of an editor* (Cape Town, 1977).
Furlong, P.J., *Between crown and swastika: The impact of the radical right on the Afrikaner nationalist movement in the fascist era* (Johannesburg, 1991).
Giliomee, H., *The Afrikaners: Biography of a people* (Cape Town, 2003).
Haigh, S., *Strangers may be present* (Cape Town, 1951).
Hancock, W.K., *Smuts: The fields of force 1919–1950* (Cambridge, 1968).
Hiemstra, R.C., *Die wilde haf* (Cape Town, 2001).
Jacobs, G.F., *Beckoning horizons* (Johannesburg, 1985).
Joseph, H., *If this be treason: Helen Joseph's dramatic diary of the treason trial 1956–1961* (Johannesburg, 1998).

Kahn, E., *Law, life & laughter encore: Legal anecdotes & portraits from southern Africa* (Cape Town, 1999).

Kentridge, M., *I recall: Memoirs of Morris Kentridge* (Johannesburg, 1959).

Krikler, J., *The Rand Revolt: The 1922 insurrection and racial killing in South Africa* (Johannesburg, 2005).

Langer, D.J., and Raath, A.W.G. (eds), *Die Afrikanerrebellie 1914–1915* (Pretoria, 2014).

Lawrence, L., *Harry Lawrence* (Cape Town, 1978).

Le Roux, J.H., Coetzer, P.W., *Die Nasionale Party. Vol. II, Die eerste bewindsjare 1924–1934* (Cape Town, 1980).

Le Roux, J.H., Coetzer, P.W., *Die Nasionale Party, Vol. III, Die Eerste Bewindsjare 1924–1934* (Bloemfontein, 1982).

Le Roux, J.H., Coetzer, P.W., Marais, A.H., *Generaal J.B.M. Hertzog: Sy strewe en stryd, Vol. II* (Johannesburg, 1987).

Lodge, T., *Black politics in South Africa since 1945* (Johannesburg, 1983).

Long, B.K., *In Smuts's camp* (London, 1945).

Macmillan, W.M., *My South African years: An autobiography* (Cape Town, 1975).

Maisels, I. *A life at law: The memoirs of IA Maisels, QC* (Johannesburg, 1998).

Malan, D.F., *Afrikaner-volkseenheid en my ervarings op die pad daarheen* (Cape Town, 1959).

Mandela, N., *Long walk to freedom: The autobiography of Nelson Mandela* (Johannesburg, 1994).

Margo, C., *Final postponement: Reminiscences of a crowded life* (Johannesburg, 1998).

Marx, C., *Oxwagon sentinel: Radical Afrikaner nationalism and the history of the Ossewabrandwag* (Pretoria, 2008).

Matthew, H.C.G., and Harrison, B., (eds) *Oxford Dictionary of national biography*, Vol. 39 and 44, (Oxford, 2004).

May, H.J., *Red wine of youth* (Cape Town, 1946).

Meiring, P., *Tien politieke leiers: Manne na aan ons premiers* (Cape Town, 1973).

Mervis, J., *The fourth estate: A newspaper story* (Johannesburg, 1989).

Morris, H.H., *The first forty years: Memoirs of H.H. Morris K.C.* (Cape Town, 1948).

Mosley, N., *Rules of the game: Sir Oswald Mosley and Lady Cynthia Mosley 1896–1933* (London, 1982).

Muller, C.F.J., *Sonop in die suide: Geboorte en groei van die Nasionale Pers 1915–1948* (Cape Town, 1990).

Nathan, M., *Not heaven itself: An autobiography* (Durban, 1944).

Nicholls, C.H., *South Africa in my time* (London, 1961).

Olivier, A., *Bode op die spoor van die woord: 150 jaar met Die Kerkbode* (Cape Town, 1998).
Ovendale, R., *"Appeasement" and the English-speaking world. Britain, the United States, the Dominions, and the policy of 'appeasement'*, (Cardiff, 1975).
Paton, A., *Hofmeyr* (London, 1964).
Pienaar, S., *Getuie van groot tye* (Cape Town, 1979).
Pirow, O., *Sjangani* (Johannesburg, 1950).
Pirow, O., *Sikoro (Avonture in die spookland van die Bantu)* (Johannesburg, 1952).
Pirow, O., *Ashambani* (Johannesburg, 1955).
Pirow, O., *James Barry Munnik Hertzog* (London, 1957).
Pound, R., *Evans of the Broke: A biography of Admiral Lord Mountevans K.C.B., D.S.O., LL.D.* (London, 1963).
Pugh, M., *Hurrah for the blackshirts! Fascists and fascism between the wars* (London, 2006).
Reitz, H., *The conversion of a South African nationalist* (Cape Town, 1946).
Richard, D., *Moedswillig die uwe. Perspersoonlikhede in die noorde* (Johannesburg, 1985).
Roberts, M. and Trollip, A.E.G., *The South African opposition 1939–1945: An essay in contemporary history* (Cape Town, 1947).
Saker, H., *The South African flag controversy 1925–1928* (Cape Town, 1980).
Schoeman, B., *My lewe in die politiek* (Johannesburg, 1978).
Scholtz, G.D., *Dr. Nicolaas Johannes van der Merwe 1888–1940* (Johannesburg, 1944).
Scholtz, G.D., *Dr. Hendrik Frensch Verwoerd, 1901–1966* (Johannesburg, 1974).
Shain, M., *A perfect storm: Antisemitism in South Africa, 1930–1948* (Johannesburg, 2015).
Shimoni, G., *Jews and Zionism: The South African experience (1910–1967)*, (Cape Town, 1980).
Skidelsky, R., *Oswald Mosley* (London, 1990).
Smuts, J.C., *Jan Christian Smuts* (Cape Town, 1952).
Solomon, B., *Time remembered* (Cape Town, 1968).
Sparks, A., *The sword and the pen: Six decades on the political frontier* (Johannesburg & Cape Town, 2016).
Stultz, N.M., *The Nationalists in opposition 1938–1948* (Cape Town, 1975).
Thompson, L., *The unification of South Africa 1902–1910* (Oxford, 1960).
Van den Heever, C.M., *Generaal J.B.M. Hertzog* (Johannesburg, 1943).
Van den Heever, C.M., *General J.B.M. Hertzog* (Johannesburg, 1946).
Van der Byl, P., *Top hat to velskoen* (Cape Town, 1973).

Van der Waag, I., *A military history of modern South Africa* (Jeppestown, 2015).

Van Rensburg, H., *Their paths crossed mine: Memoirs of the Commandant-General of the Ossewa-Brandwag* (Johannesburg, 1956).

Van Wyk, A., *Die Keeromstraat-kliek: Die Burger en die politiek van koalisie en samesmelting, 1932–34* (Cape Town, 1983).

Van Wyk, A., *Vyf dae: Oorlogskrisis in 1939 – 'n spanningsverhaal uit SA se geskiedenis* (Cape Town, 1985).

Viljoen, J.M.H., *'n Joernalis vertel* (Cape Town, 1953).

Wilson, G.H., *Gone down the* years (London, n.d.).

## Articles

Barendse, J., "Oswald Pirow's Ashambeni (1955): a 'history' of dogs, humans, werewolves", *Tydskrif vir Letterkunde*, 55, 3, 2018.

Bosman, N., "Brongebruik in die populêre historiese roman, met spesiale verwysing na Engela van Rooyen en Oswald Pirow", *Suid-Afrikaanse Tydskrif vir Kultuurgeskiedenis*, 23 (10 June 2009).

Dedering, T., "South Africa and the Italo-Ethiopian war, 1935–6", *The International History Review*, 35, 5, 2013.

Dedering, T., "Air power in South Africa, 1914–1939", *Journal of Southern African Studies*, 41, 2, 2015.

Ellis, J., "Oswald Pirow's five-year plan for the reorganisation of the Union Defence Force, 1933–1939", *Scientia Militaria, South African Journal of Military Studies*, Vol. 30, No. 2, 2000.

Kahn, E., "A trimestrial potpourri", *The South African Law Journal*, Vol. 105, No. 4, 1988.

McCormack, R.L., "Man with a mission: Oswald Pirow and South African Airways, 1933–1939", *Journal of African History*, 20 (1979).

Mosley, O., "African solutions", *Books and Bookmen*, January 1974,

Mouton, F.A., "Die slag van Durban: Die massiewe polisie-optrede van November 1929 in Durban", *Kleio,* XXI, 1989.

"Oswald Pirow", *South African Law Journal*, (47), 1930.

Pienaar, G., "Advokaat Oswald Pirow" http://www.litnet.co.za/advokaat-oswald-pirow/ (Accessed 31 March 2017).

Pirow, O., "Drie manne uit die dae van samesmelting: Hertzog, Smuts en Tielman Roos", *Die Huisgenoot*, 5 December 1952.

Schellack, W., "The Afrikaners' Nazi links revisited", *South African Historical Journal*, 27, 1992.

Smith, J., "Oswald Pirow", *Die Brandwag*, 18 December 1953.

"The Minister of Justice", *The South African Law Times*, Vol. 1, No. 1, January 1932.

Tothil, F.D., "Why General Smuts won on 4 September 1939", *Kleio*, XIX, 1987.

Van der Merwe, W., "Suid-Afrika en 'appeasement': Oswald Pirow se 'vredesending' na Nazi-Duitsland in November 1938", *Kleio*, 20, 1988.

Van der Waag, I., "The Union Defence Force between the two world wars, 1919–1940", *Scientia Militaria. South African Journal of Military Studies*, Vol. 30, No. 2, 2000.

Van der Waag, I., "The thin edge of the wedge: Anglo-South African relations, dominion nationalism and the formation of the Seaward Defence Force in 1939–1940", *Contemporary British History*, Vol. 24, No. 4, 2010.

Van der Waag, I., "Smuts's generals: Towards a first portrait of the South African high command, 1912–1948", *War in History*, 18(1), 2011, pp. 45–46.

Van der Waag, I., "South African defence in the age of total war, 1900–1940", *Historia*, Vol. 60, No. 1, 2015.

Visser, D., "Anglo-South African relations and the Erebus scheme, 1936–1939", *Scientia Militaria. South African Journal of Military Studies*, Vol. 35, No. 1, 2007.

## Unpublished sources

Brits, J.P., "Tielman Roos se rol in die Suid-Afrikaanse politiek, 1907–1935" (D. Phil, Unisa, 1977).

Davenport, T.R.H., "The Smuts government and the Africans, 1939–48", (University of London, Institute of Commonwealth Studies. Collected seminar papers, Vol. V, 1974.

Fick, A.J., "Die Dominiumparty van Suid-Afrika, 1934–1938", (D. Litt et Phil, University of South Africa, 1979).

Illsley, J.W., "Aerial symbiosis: The interrelationship between military and civil aviation in the Union of South Africa, 1912–1940" (MA, University of Pretoria, 2018).

Kienzle, W.R., "German policy towards the Union of South Africa, 1933–1934", (Ph.D., Pennsylvania State University, 1974).

Kleynhans, E., "Armoured warfare: The South African experience in East Africa, 1940–1941" (M.Mil, Stellenbosch University, 2014).

Kleynhans, E., "Bush fighting? The Union Defence Force, interwar defence schemes and the evolving South African threat perception" (Paper delivered at the "The aftermath of the First World War in southern Africa: Repercussions and transformations", Unisa, 12–13 November 2018.)

Kleynhans, E., "'n Militêre debakel: Die Unieverdedigingsmag, die tussenoorlogse jare, en lesse van die Eerste Wêreldoorlog", Unpublished paper, Geskiedenissimposium, Suid-Afrikaanse Akademie vir Wetenskap en Kuns, 25 Januarie 2019.

Korf, L., "D.F. Malan: A Political Biography" (D. Phil, University of Stellenbosch, 2010).

Otto, W., "Die geskiedenis van die Spesiale Diensbataljon 1939 tot 1939", (MA, University of Pretoria, 1972).
Reeves, L., "The war issue and the demise of the Fusion government in 1939" (MA, University of Natal, Durban, 1984).
Van Breda, P., "Die politieke loopbaan van N.C. Havenga, 1910–1954" (D. Phil, University of Stellenbosch, 1992).

## Newspapers and periodicals

*Cape Argus*
*Cape Times*
*Dagbreek en Sondagnuus*
*Die Burger*
*Die Nuwe Orde*
*Die Oosterlig*
*Die Suiderstem*
*Die Transvaler*
*Die Vaderland*
*Die Volksblad*
*Leadership*
*Pretoria News*
*Rand Daily Mail*
*Sunday Express*
*Sunday Times*
*Sunday Tribune*
*The Friend*
*The Natal Mercury*
*The Natal Witness*
*The Star*

# Index

Subjects in photographs in ***bold.***